POSTCOMMUNIST EASTERN EUROPE

POSTCOMMUNIST EASTERN EUROPE

Crisis and Reform

Edited by Andrew A. Michta and Ilya Prizel

St. Martin's Press
New York

In association with the Johns Hopkins
Foreign Policy Institute

© The Johns Hopkins Foreign Policy Institute 1992

Scholarly & Reference Division,
St. Martin's Press, 175 Fifth Avenue,
New York, N.Y. 10010

26546302

First published in the United States of America 1992

Printed in the United States of America

ISBN 0-312-07564-2

Library of Congress Cataloging-in-Publication Data
Postcommunist Eastern Europe : crisis and reform / edited by Andrew
    A. Michta and Ilya Prizel.
        p. cm.
    "In association with the Johns Hopkins Foreign Policy Institute."
    Includes index.
    ISBN 0-312-07564-2
    1. Europe, Eastern—History—1989-   I. Michta, Andrew A.
    II. Prizel, Ilya.
DJK51.P68   1992
947.085'4—dc20   92-31868
                                                                CIP

Contents

To Cristina and Kate

Notes on the Contributors

Christopher Jones is Associate Professor of Political Science, the University of Washington Henry Jackson School of International Studies. He is author of *The Warsaw Pact: The Question of Cohesion* (in three volumes), and *Soviet Influence in Eastern Europe: Political Autonomy and the Warsaw Pact*.

Mark N. Katz is Associate Professor, George Mason University. He is author of *The Third World in Soviet Military Thought, Russia and Arabia, Gorbachev's Military Policy in the Third World*, as well as other articles and monographs.

Vojtech Mastny is Professor of European Studies at the Johns Hopkins University School of Advanced International Studies in Bologna, Italy. He is author of *Russia's Road to the Cold War: Diplomacy, Warfare, and the Politics of Communism 1941-45, Helsinki, Human Rights and European Security*, and editor of *Soviet/East European Survey*, as well as numerous other books and articles on European history.

Andrew A. Michta is Associate Professor and holder of the Mertie W. Buckman Chair in International Studies at Rhodes College, Memphis, Tennessee. He is author of *Red Eagle: The Army in Polish Politics, 1944-88* and *East Central Europe after the Warsaw Pact: Security Dilemmas in the 1990s*, as well as numerous articles on European security.

Daniel N. Nelson is Director of the Graduate Institute of International Studies at Old Dominion University. He is author of *Security After Hegemony, Romania After Tyranny,* and *The Balkan Imbroglio,* as well as numerous other articles on European security and the Balkans.

Katherine W. Owen is Instructor at Rhodes College, Memphis, Tennessee, and a specialist in West European politics.

Ilya Prizel is Associate Professor, the Johns Hopkins University Paul H. Nitze School of Advanced International Studies and East European Studies Coordinator. He is author of *Latin America Through Soviet Eyes: The Evaluation of Soviet Policy toward Latin America in the Brezhnev Years,* and of a variety of articles on Russia and Eastern Europe.

Acknowledgements

The editors would like to express their profound gratitude to Stephen Szabo of the Nitze School of Advanced International Studies (SAIS) at The Johns Hopkins University and Acting Director of the Foreign Policy Institute who supported this project from its inception. Special thanks also go to Florence Rotz, the Program Assistant of the Department of Russian Area and East European Studies at Johns Hopkins SAIS who managed endless administrative complications with grace and humor; and to Nancy McCoy, whose expert copyediting improved the typescripts immeasurably. The editors would like to thank Steven Brigham of the Foreign Policy Institute for his diligent and patient performance of the technical aspects of producing this volume. Finally, special thanks are extended to Simon Winder of St. Martin's Press, who continued to support the undertaking despite the inevitable delays.

Andrew Michta would like to thank his wife, Cristina, for her support throughout this project, and his daughter, Chelsea, for being a welcome distraction from the work. A word of sincere appreciation goes to Mertie W. Buckman and her son, Robert Buckman, of Memphis, Tennessee, for their commitment to research in International Studies. Special thanks are also owed to Rhodes College Administration for its help in this work; and to Dr. Charles Lemond, Director of Rhodes College Computer Center, for his expert advice; and deep gratitude to student assistants at Rhodes College, Caroline Lenac and Allison LaRocca.

Ilya Prizel would like to express heartfelt thanks to his colleagues at SAIS and to his research assistants, Sarita Jha and Gabrielle Haasen, for long hours of hard work and helpful research and critique. Finally, special thanks go to his wife, Kate Rothko, and his children, Peter, Natalie, and Lauren, for their sense of humor.

Andrew A. Michta, Memphis, Tennessee
Ilya Prizel, Washington, D.C.

1

The Historical East Central Europe After Communism

Vojtech Mastny

Nowhere have the reports of history's alleged death been more premature than in east central Europe. There the supposed dead body has been much alive, though not necessarily well, ever since communism and the Soviet empire collapsed in 1989. Yet what emerged from the ruins has been not so much the remnants of that which communism and the Cold War had but imperfectly superseded as vestiges of still earlier times. The return of history has been mainly that of the nineteenth and even more distant centuries. The recent upsurge of nationalism in east central Europe has entailed there a revision of the outcome of World War I and restitution of much that had preceded it. As a result, doubt has been cast on the permanence of the region's territorial arrangements—the one part of the otherwise obsolete peace settlement of 1919 that, despite its faults, could long be regarded as lasting. Yet the incipient undoing of this remaining legacy of the Great War has not been the only reason for the reassertion of the conditions that used to be considered normal before that singular calamity interrupted the continuity of Europe's development.

The demise of the Soviet and waning of the U.S. superpower have already restored the Continent's traditional international order, where there is room for merely great, as well as for medium and small powers. The bankruptcy of ideologies and evanescence of the obscene stability resting on the threat of mutual annihilation has led to the more rational preoccupation with the proper business of diplomacy: the management of conflicts arising from such normal development as the formation and liquidation of states, the drawing and redrawing of boundaries, and the plight of the people caught in all these changes.

What does the return to historical normalcy presage for the future? Does the apparent relapse into the conditions that previously failed to prevent the disaster of 1914, with all the misfortunes that followed, suggest a repetition? Certainly the end of Europe's cold war division, during which its Western part prospered as never before while its Eastern one declined by comparison, has brought unaccustomed instability to both. Yet history's propensity for repeating itself ought to be measured not only by what has survived from World War I but also by the impact of what has happened since.

Europe's New Fault Line

No sooner did the cold war division of Europe fade away than it was superseded by a new fault line. This line, rather than defining territory with any precision, pertains to the problems of transition largely determined by history. In the formerly communist countries, at issue is their dual transition from one-party rule to democracy and from command to market economy. The line divides the lands where the end of the process is at least in sight from those where it is still not.

Blurred rather than clear, the line starts in the Adriatic and continues across what used to be Yugoslavia. There it separates—to the extent that this is possible—its historically Western and Eastern-oriented peoples, now in the agony of creating new states. The division is clearer farther north, along the border between Hungary and Romania—respectively, the country most and least advanced in the dual transition. Then the line gets diffuse again in the Polish-Russian borderlands, where peoples of the former Soviet Union have been striving for new national identities. In that part of Europe, besides the Poles, only the Balts are unequivocally west of the divide.

There is yet another segment of the line, distinguishing those countries of western Europe that have been directly affected by the upheaval in the East from those influenced by it only indirectly. In this regard, the former boundary between the two German states highlights the travails of their unification. Farther south, the now open German-Czechoslovak border marks the reappearance there of mainly local mental barriers, rooted in ancient enmities. The German-Austrian border separates two nations whose historical sense of mission in the region has changed because of its recent transformation. This has given a new sense of mission to Italy, though much more to its northern than its southern part, thus making their historical division the final section of the fault line.

The Turkish Europe

Much as in the nineteenth century, the post-1989 Balkans have lived up to their reputation as the powder keg of Europe. The geography of its troubles relates to the Ottoman times. The longest-lasting remnant of the Turkish empire—the predominantly Muslim Albania—has been the most prone to export trouble. By exposing the West's vulnerability to the demographic challenge of less developed countries, the assault of impoverished Albanian migrants on the promised land of Italy in 1991 reenacted in its own way the Ottoman attack on Christian Europe centuries before.

In addition, the breakup of Yugoslavia revived the ancient Macedonian question—the epitome of an all but insoluble imbroglio of overlapping ethnic claims. There is also the same old contrast between Romania—with its Ottoman dichotomy between brutalized masses and a manipulative ruling class—and the more modern-minded, politically conscious, and egalitarian Bulgaria. Of the ex-communist Balkan nations, Bulgaria has been moving fastest on the road to democracy and—more surprising, in view of its dismal record before—to ethnic tolerance as well. Its progressing accommodation of its Turkish minority since the communist grip was broken and its recognition of the independence of neighboring Macedonia without raising any territorial claims are cases in point.

Such a readiness to learn the lessons of the past has contrasted with their neglect, evidenced in the resurgence of the fanaticism and cruelty that used to be the by-products of the Balkan people's struggle against Ottoman oppression. They have come to permeate the warfare between Serbs and Croats, into which other groups in the ethnically mixed-up peninsula have been inexorably drawn. Among these, the surviving Muslim minorities in their quest for political rights have tended to take the side of democracy against the remnants of totalitarianism in nationalist guise. This has been true of Turks in Bulgaria, Albanians in Kosovo, and Muslims of Slav origin in Bosnia-Herzegovina—all secularized communities closer to pro-Western Turkey than to the anti-Western, fundamentalist Islamic regimes of the Middle East or North Africa.

Turkey, excluded from all but a small portion of Europe in the early twentieth century, has attained growing prominence in Balkan affairs. The Turkey that arose from its successful defiance of the peace imposed on it after World War I has been very different from its predecessor. With rather than against Europe, it has sought to become a bridge between the West and the Muslim republics of the former Soviet Union. The acceptance of Turkey as a key member of the Atlantic alliance has superseded the spurious Europeanness of the former Ottoman empire, adding weight to Ankara's bid for admission to the European Community as well.

That bid has been strenuously opposed by its formal ally but historical foe, Greece, the Community's sole Balkan member and, as such, best positioned to promote higher standards of international tolerance in the area. Instead, the Athens government has been a prisoner of the past. Beating the dead horse of the megali idea of a Greater Greece, it has been the only one to stir up the Macedonian question by claiming that the area is Greek. It has become closer to the ex-communist regime in Romania than the democratic one in Bulgaria. For narrow economic reasons, in the Serb-Croat conflict it has also taken the side of the Belgrade regime, dominated by former Communists.

The Enduring "Military Frontier"

Serb-Croat warfare has centered on the area once known as the "Military Frontier," the buffer zone that the Austrian Habsburgs originally created to help defend central Europe from the Turks by settling it with Slav peasant-soldiers of both Catholic and Orthodox faiths—Croats and Serbs. This historical war zone has always differed from the less exposed lands farther west, inhabited by the Slovenes, distinct from both Croats and Serbs by language and greater readiness for accommodation. The Croats, proud of being the West's outpost in the East, have tended to look down on Serbs as semi-barbarians. Yet the same historical stereotype applied to themselves in the West, where Croat soldiers used to be repudiated for their ferocity. On both sides, belief in stereotypes has tended to invite reactions that confirmed them.

Within the Habsburg empire, the Croats and Serbs nevertheless managed to live together until it fell apart in World War I. Only then did the southern Slavs have to find an alternative—a task made urgent by their need to protect themselves against Italian expansionism. They found the alternative in creating a unified Yugoslavia as a new multi-ethnic state. The idea had been of Croat origin, and in its emphasis on partnership it differed both from that of a Greater Serbia and from that of its counterpart, a Greater Croatia. It had not gained majority support before World War I, during which Croats had fought valiantly for the Habsburgs against the Italians and the Serbs alike.

Interwar Yugoslavia resembled more an extended Serbia than a federation of equals. As such, it was increasingly resented by Croats, though not so much by Slovenes, who were in a greater need of protection against their Italian neighbors. The Croat terrorist Ustaše received support from fascist Italy. Once Yugoslavia fell victim to nazi aggression in World War II amid the widespread indifference of its non-Serb population, the substantial Serb minority in Croatia became the target of Ustaše genocide, outrageous even by the depraved standards of the time.

This slaughter was followed by lesser killings of "class enemies," regardless of nationality, at the hands of the communists, who controlled the second Yugoslav state. Yet the memory of all these excesses was eventually submerged during the long rule of Josif Broz Tito—a remarkable feat of this Croat-born revolutionary, who held the state together as long as he lived, and for several more years out of his grave, by the sheer force of his personality. Once that artificial edifice fell apart in its turn, however, the ascendant pluralism brought back the bitter memories. By the end of the nineteen-eighties, the mutual disposition of the Serbs and Croats to neither forget nor forgive had prevailed again, thus making their coexistence in a single state impossible.

The Serbs could fall back on their nineteenth-century idea of a Greater Serbia, and they began to implement it by invading Croatia, whose government's insensitivity to the need to protect Serbian minority rights provided the welcome pretext. For the Croats and Slovenes, however, there could be no return to the Habsburg empire, which could not be so easily resurrected. But neither did they have to look for protection any more against Italy, no longer threatening. So the creation of independent

Slovenia and Croatia, though as much a historical anomaly as was Yugoslavia, became inevitable. At least the new republics could face the future with greater confidence than before, for now they had friendly neighbors not only to their west but also to their north, particularly in Hungary.

A Reformed Hungary

In no part of east central Europe outside Hungary has the sense of national identity been linked so closely with the continuity of statehood, symbolized by the thousand-year-old royal crown of Saint Stephen. The Magyars, despite their proverbial pessimism, have successfully upheld their nationhood amid perceived encirclement by ethnically alien peoples. The uninterrupted existence of the Hungarian state, regardless of the comings and goings of its various lands, has contrasted with the lack of such a record among its neighbors, in turn increasing a sense of insecurity on their part. A conspicuous example has been the Romanians' insistence on tracing the continuity of their nationhood to Roman times. They and the Magyars have habitually regarded each other as intruders.

Before World War I and after it, Hungary was a prominent trouble-maker. In 1848–49, its liberal revolution posed the greatest threat to the integrity of the Habsburg realm. In 1867, the empire's transformation into the Austro-Hungarian dual monarchy, designed to placate the Magyars at the expense of all its other nationalities, encouraged the Magyars to build the country as a national state in scant regard of its ethnic minorities, which together actually were a majority. Hungary's assimilationist policy was a European anachronism in the age of rising national consciousness.

In order to maintain the state against nationalist agitation emanating from the neighboring Balkan countries, Magyar politicians had a lion's share of responsibility for the dual monarchy's foreign policies that led to World War I. Still, the price Hungary eventually had to pay for its defeat in the war was disproportionate to its follies and sins: all things considered, nationality oppression there had been benign compared with social oppression, let alone with the practices of twentieth-century totalitarianism.

The 1920 Treaty of Trianon, which cost the historical kingdom of Hungary more than two thirds of its territory and left a third of all Magyars second-class citizens of other states, inflamed the Magyars with a burning desire, second only to that of the Germans, to overturn the post-World War I peace settlement. Although the Hungarian revisionism consumed an inordinate amount of the national energy, it was only thanks to the collusion of the country's leaders with Adolf Hitler that Hungary regained some of its territories—which it was to lose again when it lost in World War II. Afterward, as long as Moscow enforced in the region its kind of "fraternal" international order, Magyar revisionism remained dormant. Accordingly, no sooner did the Soviet Union disappear as the self-appointed regional policeman than the verdict of Trianon was thrown open, putting history back on the agenda.

Yet Hungary has emerged from its twentieth-century ordeals more profoundly changed than any country in the region, except Germany. Not only has its territory diminished most drastically, but also its economy, society, and politics have been transformed beyond recognition. Nowhere in the region is there a contrast sharper than the one between the old Hungary's semifeudal economy, kept backward by an antiquated social structure, and postcommunist Hungary's fledgling market economy, propelled by the rising new middle class and making the country the most attractive of all in the former Soviet bloc to foreign investors. Nor is there a greater political contrast than that between interwar Hungary's shaky authoritarianism and its post-1989 democracy. Its political system, despite all its shortcomings, is the most stable in the region.

The crucial turning point, more lasting in its consequences than even the Soviet-imposed communist revolution from above, was Hungary's authentic national revolution in 1956. Although defeated at the time, this so unnerved the communists that they saw it necessary to introduce economic and political reforms earlier than such a course was undertaken elsewhere. In the end, they even collaborated in their own demise, thus further facilitating the emergence of a radically reformed Hungary.

The change is particularly pertinent to the question of minorities. Hungary's national hero, Lájos Kossuth, given to soul-searching after the revolution the Magyars had lost in 1849 largely because of their chauvinism, envisioned his country as a multiethnic state where different nationality groups could serve as links to their compatriots in the neighboring countries. In the old Hungary this never happened, and since then the reversed situation has instead put Magyars in those countries in the position of minorities, subject to discrimination. Now democratic Hungary has been demanding, rather than a revision of its Trianon borders, political autonomy for the Magyars beyond them. It has become Europe's leading advocate of the collective rights of minorities—the most advanced concept of their protection, eminently applicable also to the diverse ethnic remnants of the collapsed Soviet state.

Russia's New Borderlands

The breakup of the Soviet Union undid three-hundred years of Russia's westward expansion. None of the newly independent states in the area—Belarus, Moldova, Ukraine, the three Baltic republics of Estonia, Latvia, and Lithuania—had even been a separate entity before merging into the now extinct Russian empire. Instead they had belonged until then to territorial units that can no longer be reconstituted—the Commonwealth of Poland-Lithuania, Greater Sweden, Prussia, the Ottoman or Habsburg empires. This leaves them little from the distant past to build upon.

Ironically, it has rather been the Soviet experience, which they have so decisively repudiated, that has provided the newborn republics with two important preconditions of independent statehood. The first is their Soviet-drawn boundaries, which neither they nor their neighbors have so far found in their interest to question seriously; the Ukrainian-Russian dispute about Crimea—where one Soviet-made boundary against another is·at issue—has been an exception that proves the rule. The second has been the Russians' willingness to part with their empire.

Not only did the majority of Russians—quite unlike the Serbs—acquiesce in the loss of the state they had dominated, but also the bulk of the Russian minorities in its successor states preferred to support the formation of these states rather than live in Russia. Conceivably, the communists did succeed in instilling the rank and file of the former imperial nationality with enough true internationalism to ensure on its part the necessary minimum of tolerance of other peoples' self-determination. Whether the result of political maturity or simply of exhaustion, such behavior by an ex-imperial people has been extraordinary.

The armed defiance by the Russian population in Moldova of its sovereignty, however long this resistance may last, can also qualify as an exception that proves the rule. Alone in the former Soviet western borderlands, the non-Romanian inhabitants of the self-proclaimed and unrecognized "Dniestrian Republic" fear subjection to a people whom Russians have historically regarded as their inferiors. In fact, the prospect of Moldova's unification with Romania has been viewed ambivalently even by its ethnically Romanian population. Not only does it bring back memories of Bucharest's misrule between the wars, but it also envisages merger with a country even worse off economically.

In the key republic of Ukraine, Europe's fifth most populous state, Soviet rule has left the disturbing mixture of exalted nationalism and political and economic conservatism. Yet it also set to this nationalism limits that had not existed before. As a result of Joseph Stalin's shuffling of peoples and boundaries, there are no more Polish landlords and their Ukrainian peasants or widely interspersed communities of the two peoples there to hate each other. The historical conflict between the pro-Polish Uniate and pro-Russian Orthodox church now persists within a single state rather than between states. Poland was the first foreign country to recognize independent Ukraine, and their mutual relations have so far been free from serious problems.

This has not been the case with Belarus, where Polish minorities have survived. Belarus was a Polish land before becoming not only Russian but, by now, the most extensively Russified of the former Soviet Union's Slavic lands. Its borders, until arbitrarily drawn by Moscow, had been vague. To add to its identity problems, Belarus was the heartland of east European Jewry, most of which disappeared in the nazi holocaust. Less populous than Ukraine but even more exposed to the aftereffects of the Chernobyl nuclear disaster, Belarus has precious little in its past to point to a bright future as an independent state. It would seem to be a model candidate for autonomy within Russia—the only one in Europe.

The Resurgent Baltic Rim

The Baltic peoples can derive from their history more reassurance than can other inhabitants of the former Soviet state. Not only had their countries been distinct entities even before they became privileged parts of the tsarist empire, but also subsequent developments served only to reconfirm their distinctiveness. Interwar Lithuania, Latvia, and Estonia, though far from impeccable democracies, had been viable states until Stalin chose to destroy them. Even afterward, they remained the Soviet Union's most advanced and livable parts—which is why so many Russians have been eager to settle there. In addition, although almost as tainted as Ukrainians by their complicity in nazi atrocities during World

War II, the Baltic peoples have survived their totalitarian experiences with more credible democratic credentials.

These have been shaped more by the three Baltic countries' deeper historical links with the West than by anything that happened in the twentieth century. The Lithuanians, who used to be partners in the Polish Commonwealth, were the last Europeans to adopt Christianity, and they have ever since been particularly proud of their Catholicism. The mainly Protestant Latvia and Estonia have been closer to Germany and Scandinavia. Latvia's capital, Riga, and Estonia's capital Tallinn, once members of the Hanseatic League, served for centuries as the West's gateways to Russia. Estonia, where the eastern-most German university at Dorpat was probably the best in the Russian empire, has also been the closest to Finland both linguistically and culturally.

The differing characteristics of the Baltic states have proved more complementary than divisive—a rare situation in east central Europe, although similar to that in Scandinavia. Already the three republics have formed a structure of economic cooperation among themselves and have joined the larger Baltic Council as well. In addition, although they continue to be economically dependent on other parts of the former Soviet Union and must deal with the menacing presence of ex-Soviet military on their territory, their manageable size allows them to make better use of the available Western goodwill and material assistance.

All the goodwill and assistance may be needed to cope with the inherited problems of the Baltic trouble spot: East Prussia. More precisely, the area in question is the portion of it that Stalin annexed and made an administrative part of Russia while giving the rest to Poland. Because of Lithuania's independence, the territory has now become physically separated from Russia, as it had been, previously, from Germany. A return to its past is possible only sentimentally, a direction already evidenced by the growth of its Russian inhabitants' respect for its vanished German culture. Under Soviet rule the area was not only depopulated and physically devastated but also turned into a vast military and naval base—a garrison province without its like in Europe.

It is difficult to imagine that East Prussia's by now obsolete military establishment could be liquidated without something else replacing it. But any replacement is bound to be artificial, though not necessarily as artificial a solution as the proposed resettlement there of the Volga

Germans, who were themselves uprooted from their homeland by Stalin. The prospect, full of allusions to both of Poland's historical enemies—the Germans and the Russians—brings back nightmares of the time after World War I when East Prussia was but one of the area's several hotbeds of ethnic conflict, most of which have by now disappeared.

A Poland that Works

The simplification of the ethnic map of Poland has been the signal, albeit unintended, result of Hitler's and Stalin's atrocities. The two dictators' genocidal policies disposed of the country's Jewish and German minorities, while the westward shifts of its borders and populations by Stalin completed the radical transformation of the Poland that had been formed in 1918. This undoing of its post-World War I predicament as a precarious multiethnic state has not cast doubt on the legitimacy of Polish statehood; however, Poland's viability has become an issue for other reasons, rooted in earlier history.

Ever since the ungovernable Polish Commonwealth fell victim to predatory neighbors in the eighteenth century, the nation has prospered more in adversity than at times when it was able to take charge of its own affairs. The cultural achievement of the nineteenth-century Great Emigration, the vigor of the Polish underground during nazi occupation, and the later success of the Solidarity opposition are cases in point. So is, conversely, the sorry fate of the interwar Polish republic, whose democracy perished—to the extent that it had been born in the first place—even before the destruction by Hitler of what he dismissively called a "seasonal state."

Much as in the old Commonwealth, the multiplicity of political parties in postcommunist Poland—Europe's most fragmented polity—has been testing the old adage that Poland is maintained through anarchy. There again is the historical cleavage between the large minority of the nation's elite—previously more social, now more intellectual—and the bulk of its common people. Indeed, the division has grown since the people were mobilized for unprecedented political exertion in the Solidarity movement. As after the so many failed Polish uprisings of the past, fatigue set in.

Romanticism and realism have been perennial Polish themes. Periods of frustrating struggle against hopeless odds have alternated with equally unsatisfactory accommodation to superior power. This pattern, however, seems finally to have been broken by the Warsaw uprising of 1944. Ever since that self-destructive last stand against both of Poland's historical enemies, the nation's politics have been the art of the possible in ways they had not been before, bringing unprecedented results. In the nineteen-fifties Poland avoided the excesses of Stalinism that scarred other communist countries. It subsequently challenged Soviet power indirectly but effectively without using force. Solidarity used the sophisticated strategy of calibrated pressure—an amazing accomplishment for the spontaneous, grass-roots movement it was—to make the oppressive regime more respectful of the people's wishes rather than to bring it down. The pressure ultimately brought it down anyway, earning Poland the distinction of being the first in the region to break the communist monopoly of power in 1989.

Because of all that has changed since 1918—and despite all that has remained the same from the times before—the prospects for the third Polish republic have been markedly more promising than the prospects had been for its predecessors. The country has been strengthened by its becoming ethnically homogeneous for the first time. With Germany having become democratic and Russia having turned inward, it is now, also for the first time, on good terms with all of its neighbors. In contrast with the Poland of 1918, the new Polish state is the product not only of a struggle for liberation against foreign enemies but also of extensive domestic housecleaning. Further, and perhaps most pertinent for its economic viability, a rough-and-ready entrepreneurial spirit has emerged, filling the void left by the missing Jews. This spirit, much resented abroad wherever Polish petty traders have been plying their goods, may be the true harbinger of a Poland that works.

The "Sick Heart" of Middle Europe

In his 1975 diagnosis of the "Danubian lands" as the "sick heart" of modern Europe, British historian Hugh Seton-Watson singled out the Czech lands as the heart of the heart.[1] He alluded to the particular malaise resulting from exalted nationalism and, true enough, not only the Czechs but also the Slovaks have been prone to excesses of that kind. Unlike the Poles or the Magyars, they both have had the sad experience of having faced in modern history the threat of national extinction. The Czechs almost succumbed to Germanization after the Thirty Years' War; the

Slovaks narrowly escaped Magyarization as late as the early twentieth century. Neither people sought full independence before World War I. Yet after it, in forming the new state of Czechoslovakia, their leaders were outstandingly successful in satisfying nearly all of their territorial goals.

The success was more apparent than real. Czechoslovakia was almost as artificial a state as Yugoslavia. It brought together as nominal ruling nationalities two peoples that had never lived together in one state before; Slovakia, for a thousand years part of Hungary, had not even been a geographical entity until 1918. At that time, the Czechs incorporated on historical grounds a huge German minority and the Slovaks, on alleged economic and security grounds, a large Magyar minority. Although a model democracy compared with any of its neighbors between the wars, Czechoslovakia collapsed ignominiously under German pressure on the eve of World War II.

The subsequent experiences of the Czechs and Slovaks were demoralizing. There was less resistance to the hated German rule in the occupied Czech lands than almost anywhere but Austria; moreover, Czech resistance was unique in Europe in its declining rather than growing as the war progressed toward its end. Nor was the Slovaks' experience with their wartime state by Hitler's grace—the most dependent of his satellites—more edifying, despite the lingering nationalist nostalgia for it as the only Slovak state there has been.

As a victim of aggression, Czechoslovakia nevertheless qualified as a victor after World War II. It summarily expelled its German minority, judged guilty by association with the Nazis, and tried, though it did not succeed, to do the same with its Magyar minority. Not only did injustices inflicted on innocents create lasting resentments, but they also sapped the vitality of the country's democracy, helping to make it an easy prey to the communists. The excesses of Stalinism in Czechoslovakia and the durability of its communist regime were symptoms of a continued sickness of its body politic. Unlike in Poland or in Hungary, the challenge posed to the regime in 1968 by the abortive attempt at communism with a "human face" did not reverse the pattern of subservience to Moscow.

In view of such a dismal record, Czechoslovakia's "velvet revolution" in 1989 was a genuine watershed not so much by drawing inspiration from the past as by repudiating it. Bringing about a swifter and more thorough transfer of power than in other parts of the crumbling Soviet bloc, it made the Czechs and Slovaks true masters of their destinies for the first time in modern history, and under more favorable conditions than their Polish and Hungarian neighbors. Previously, the Czechs and Slovaks had paid greater price for their accommodation to oppressors than the Poles and Hungarians had paid for their readiness to resist. In a Europe free of military danger, however, martial virtues have been of diminishing value, if not a liability, compared with other assets. And Czechoslovakia has inherited from the communists a less ruined economy than elsewhere, thus gaining more time for its necessary transformation.

Much of that time has been wasted, however. The downfall of communism has opened up the latent Czech-Slovak rift, putting the very survival of the country as a unitary state in doubt. The resulting instability has hampered the otherwise promising program of economic reform. And the necessary constitutional reform—even under the best of circumstances a formidable task because of the difficulty of integrating twice as many Czechs than Slovaks in a two-member federation—has been stymied by parliamentarian squabbles, uncomfortably reminiscent of the declining years of the Habsburg monarchy. But then, the Czechs and Slovaks may be that monarchy's most authentic heirs in their ability to circumvent problems rather than confront them head on. In the absence of the kind of outside threats that proved fatal to the nation's integrity in the past, such an uninspiring approach may yet pave a way to the management, if not a solution, of problems in a prosperous, even though not necessarily happy, union Belgian-style.

The Uniting Germany

Union proved unexpectedly difficult to achieve even for eastern and western Germany, certainly during the initial years of their reunification. The new state, a result of "the first successful self-made revolution on German soil,"[2] has borne scant resemblance to the moribund Weimar Republic, which was marked by military defeat, failed revolution, and punitive peace after World War I. But neither has it resembled the preceding Second Reich, the semi-authoritarian quasi-federation, afflicted by militarism. An extension of West Germany, the unifying Germany, despite all the debilitating effects of its having to absorb what used to be communist Europe's most totalitarian state, has remained an exemplary democracy and model federation, particularly allergic to any hints of militarism.

The second unification has brought forth affinities with the times that preceded the first, when nationalism inspired poets and philosophers before it took hold of statesmen and soldiers. This was the time when German thought exerted its formative influence on the peoples of east central Europe and when German achievement set for them the European standards to be emulated. Thus, Germans made a more beneficial and lasting impact on the region when their country was still divided than after it became united.

Germany has had more experience with federalism than other parts of Europe except Switzerland. Most of the experience, however, was not happy; this applied to the Holy Roman Empire, the Germanic Confederation, and the Bismarckian Reich. Only the post-1949 Federal Republic managed to balance and integrate national and particularist interests with remarkable success. But the latter interests have recently been reasserting themselves at the expense of the former, with a momentum added by the unification.

Increasingly, the differences between parts of Germany, rather than its unity, have been shaping its new problems, including its relations with east central Europe. Apart from exacerbating tensions, some of ancient vintage, between the old and the new Länder, local interest groups have individually sought to impress their interests on national policy. This has been the case, for example, in Bavaria's catering to the pressure of its population of expellees from Czechoslovakia, thus complicating relations between the two countries for their governments.

Germany's looming superiority—economic if no longer cultural—has reawakened fears of its political domination among its historical foes—Poles, Czechs, Serbs—though not so much its historical friends—Hungarians, Bulgarians, Romanians, Croats, Slovenes. Yet economic and political preponderance need not go together. In 1916 the Mitteleuropa proposed by leading German liberal Friedrich Naumann envisaged the region organized under German economic leadership, along democratic principles, in a manner respectful of each partner's national interests. The idea lacked credibility for the restless, nationalistic Germany of his time; it fits better today's satiated one, firmly integrated in the European Community, where everyone wants to belong.

The Model Austria

The German idea of Mitteleuropa has alternated with the Austrian one. This has been lately invoked by admirers from the former Habsburg lands as a model suitable to repair the damage their forefathers had done by helping to push the old monarchy over the brink at the end of World War I. Yet that venerable structure, so civilized compared with all those that succeeded it, was not designed to mitigate conflicts, and during its long existence it proved quite prolific in generating them.

The Habsburg state was, first and foremost, an assemblage of lands gathered together to enhance dynastic power. Having accomplished its historical mission of defending Europe against the Turks, it continued by inertia rather than by any ability to adapt itself to the changing times. Its propensity for disposing of problems by ignoring or sidetracking them helped to keep old institutions usable in sluggish times, but not to create the needed new ones. This is not a prescription to be recommended to the postcommunist countries striving to join a dynamic Western Europe after their own obsolete institutions have collapsed.

More relevant to their predicament has been the success of the post-Habsburg Austria in overcoming the burdens of its difficult birth. The unhappy "first" Austrian republic, made independent against its will in 1919, succumbed willingly to Hitler less than twenty years later, and eventually went down with him in ruins during World War II. Given by the victors the godsent opportunity to be treated separately from Germany as its victim, the post-1945 "second" republic became another European success story. Although it never repudiated its nazi vestiges as decisively as western Germany, it nevertheless evolved into a genuine democracy, where the vestiges proved merely embarrassing rather than threatening. Most important, it found the national identity and international security its predecessor had so badly lacked.

As a result, Austria became, more than any other country, the envy of east central Europeans and their model. Its attractiveness has stemmed not so much from its ambivalent Habsburg heritage—which intrigued mainly intellectuals—but from its more recent economic and political accomplishments, important to the common man. Closest by its geography, size, and resources, it came to epitomize for its less fortunate neighbors what they could have been without communism.

As long as the cold war lasted, Austria's ability to thrive as a neutral state astride the East-West ideological divide was a particular source of envy. It inspired the country's sense of mission as the one supposedly best equipped to help bring the East closer to the West. To some of its admirers, the Austrian example even seemed to hold the enticing prospect of possible military disengagement in Europe. Yet Austrian neutrality—a product in 1955 of an exceptional international situation that was unlikely to be repeated—did not lend itself to imitation. The end of the Soviet threat finally deprived it of most of its relevance.

Although Austria has remained more committed economically and politically in formerly communist Europe than any other nation except Germany, its special role there has inevitably declined. While building on stronger historic links to support Croatia's and Slovenia's bids for independence, it still played a secondary role to Germany. In trying to serve as a bridge between the divided Eastern and united Western Europe, it has been hampered by its being itself an applicant for admission to the European Community. Accordingly, that role fell more naturally to Italy.

The New Role of Italy

In east central Europe, Italy has had at least as important legacies as Germany to claim and to repudiate—but more easily. It has always been a special place—the motherland of Western Christianity, the country from where the Renaissance came, and now again the nation that east central Europeans have been inclined to see as setting for them the standards of European culture. There is a timely message for them in the nine-teenth-century Italian thinkers' preoccupation with such topical issues as federalism, local rights, democracy, the self-fulfillment of nations, and the status of the minorities within them. The prophet of the Risorgimento, Giuseppe Mazzini, tried ahead of his time to reconcile nationalism with Europeanism—east central Europe's key problem today.

But such a quest was subsequently abandoned by those Italian nationalists who sought not only to "redeem" the Austrian lands inhabited by their compatriots but to grab as much more as they could. During World War I, Italian politicians spearheaded the efforts to subvert and dissolve the Habsburg empire and, once the empire was gone, bore most of the responsibility for the inequities of the peace settlement in east central Europe. Italy's annexation of the German-speaking South Tirol and territories inhabited by southern Slavs was then made worse by Benito Mussolini's meddling in Austria and the Balkans between the wars.

The fascist dictator was Hitler's partner in such infamous territorial deals as the 1938 Munich agreement and the subsequent Vienna Awards, all of which left a bitter taste among Czechs, Slovaks, Hungarians, and Romanians. In its own way, under Mussolini Italy imitated nazi aggression by annexing Albania and parts of Yugoslavia during World War II. Its subsequent defeat made it lose all these territories, suffer in turn Yugoslav aggression against its own territory, and abandon an active policy in east central Europe as a result.

Yet Italy's later recovery as a major Western democracy and its growing economic power created the necessary preconditions for its return. Not only did it earn respect as a stalwart NATO ally and a pillar of the European Community, but also the Italian communists did their share, earning respect for their country in the Soviet-controlled part of Europe by siding there with the forces of reform rather than of reaction. By 1989 Italy could consequently position itself as both a model and a mediator in the region.

Under the different circumstances, the long-simmering problem of South Tirol has turned from a local liability into a potentially larger asset by providing an example of a successful minority settlement, germane to the problems of similarly troubled areas farther east, such as the status of the Magyars in Romania. Also Italy's Slovene minority has now been contributing to rather than obstructing the development of good neighborly relations with the newly independent Slovenia. And the postcommunist Albania has even welcomed the stationing of Italian soldiers to help keep order and distribute emergency supplies in the destitute country.

Having been already before the initiators of the Alpe-Adria project for nonpolitical regional cooperation across ideological boundaries among parts of Yugoslavia, Hungary, and Austria, the Italians launched in the 1980s the more ambitious "Central European Initiative," involving political consultation and cooperation as well. The project has been handicapped, however, by Italy's own persisting weaknesses, notably its intractable North-South problem. This has assumed a new dimension because of the rise—in the very parts of the North that used to be the strongholds of fascist expansionism—of xenophobic, right-wing movements congenial to nationalist extremists in Austria, as well as in Croatia.

Thus, Italy has come closer to east central Europe in a variety of ways, including some common burdens of the past yet to be disposed of.

The Unburdening of History

In the Europe defined by its new fault line, the three Western nations—Germany, Austria, and Italy—have in different ways overcome most effectively their respective legacies left by World War I: they all became strong, prosperous democracies, committed to integrated Europe. In the Continent's eastern part, the process has been more equivocal. There the drastic reshaping against its will of the post-World War I Poland proved nonetheless beneficial for both Poles and their neighbors. Nor is the reformed Hungary a threat to its neighbors, regardless of the form the impending review of the Trianon peace settlement may take. The two creations of the 1919 settlement, Czechoslovakia and Yugoslavia, have fared less well. The former's integrity as a unitary state remains in doubt, while the latter has already disintegrated, its successor states groping for the place of their own that had eluded them earlier. So have the successor states of the ex-Soviet Union been groping.

For three reasons, however, the region's prospects for coming to grips with the burdens left to them by World War I have much improved because of what has happened since. First, there has been a radical change of opinion about the acceptability of war as a normal way of settling disputes between states, though—as Yugoslavia has shown—not within states. The change, prompted by the experience of the first world war, was reinforced by that of the second, and made seemingly irreversible by the cold war—or the nuclear "peace" it brought about. Moreover, this unprecedented change of mind has affected both peoples and governments—in Europe, not in the Third World, where the same sobering experiences have been missing.

The irreversibility of the change hinges largely on the permanence of functioning international and supranational organizations that have been established as Europe's other novelty. Unlike the recurrently destabilizing military alliances of old, these diverse groupings of mainly nonmilitary character are those that states want to join rather than wishing to form rival ones against. The disrepute that the cold war brought on "bloc" thinking has been another of its unintended benefits. Belonging to the new type of international organization entails surrendering ever more substantive elements of sovereignty, thus weakening the unaccountability of states to higher authority. The very notion that sovereignty could be surrendered voluntarily implies the compatibility of national interests with both the national interests of others and common interests. Such fresh thinking has already taken root in western Europe and has been gaining ground in east central Europe as well, though not nearly so much in areas still farther east and elsewhere in the world.

The third important difference from those millennia when want was endemic and the Great Depression became possible even in the twentieth century has been the invention of modernized capitalism. This seems at last to have found a way to ensure abundance along with elementary social justice—even if not necessarily the will to employ the requisite tools toward that end. The historic discovery evolved in response to the successive challenges that socialism posed to laissez-faire, and then both fascist and communist totalitarianism to democracy. While the challengers all managed to discredit themselves in their turn, the revitalized economic and social foundations of democracy remained firm. And, as has been noted, democratic states have been inhibited by their constitution from going to war against one another.

It is uncertain how long the transitional period of instability will last in east central Europe. Yet enough of the past has been overcome to conclude that the return of historical normalcy need not bear the seeds of another catastrophe. Neither does it herald the end of history, much less the beginning of a paradise on earth. It merely closes the door behind the dreadful deviations that have been the disgrace of the century—and this is enough of an accomplishment.

Notes

1. Hugh Seton-Watson, *The "Sick Heart" of Modern Europe: The Problem of the Danubian Lands* (Seattle: University of Washington Press, 1975), 3.

2. This is a phrase of Antje Vollmer, the deputy of the Greens in the federal parliament.

2

Russia and Germany: The Case For A Special Relationship

Ilya Prizel

I cannot conceive of concert life in Boston or New York or Chicago or Los Angeles without Tchaikovsky, Mussorgsky, Rimsky-Korsakov, Shostakovich or Prokofiev. I cannot imagine any of us, anywhere in the world, living in the world of culture of the nineteenth century without feeling at home with people like Dostoyevsky, Tolstoy, Lermontov, Pushkin, Turgenev, Gogol, and nowadays Pasternak or Solzhenitsyn.

Helmut Schmidt[1]

Wherever you see a machine, there must be a German nearby.
Russian Proverb

No relationship in Europe is more important to its stability than that of its two landed giants, Russia and Germany. A case can be made that it is the shape of this relationship that historically determined the political configuration of Europe. No two large groups of European peoples have a longer and closer history of mutual political, economic, and cultural cross-pollination than the Russians and the Germans— closeness that has engendered intense mutual admiration as well as disdain.[2] Thus, when Russo-German relations were close and harmonious between 1815 and 1887, the rest of the European system, including second-tier land powers such as France and sea powers such as the United Kingdom, could do little else but accommodate themselves to the existing order. Conversely, when Russo-German relations deteriorated, the entire existing European order was shaken, enabling France and the maritime power of the day to attempt to reshape that order.

Because the relationship between Russia and Germany throughout much of the eighteenth and nineteenth centuries was the single most important aspect of both countries' foreign policies, the policies of each toward the other acquired a certain institutional character, despite the personalistic nature of both regimes. Consequently, during the last two centuries, the relationship between Russia and Germany has operated in a rather predictable pattern. On the German side, statesmen, from Frederick the Great on, have referred to Russia as the power that would ultimately define the political order in Europe and the role that Germany would play within that order.

Given Russian domination of the relationship, however, the German state's attitude toward Russia has been a complex one. On the one hand, the Germans, for generations, saw Russia as a counterweight to the unified French state and as a vast export market for Germany's skilled labor, its land-hungry peasants, and its minor princes. On the other hand, as Germany's power grew, the overbearing Russian presence was increasingly feared and resented by the unified German state. By the end of the nineteenth century, the history of Russian assertiveness, along with an array of political and economic issues, made the Russo-Germanic alliance through the *Drikaiserbund* untenable.[3]

The rapid industrialization and militarization of Russia in the 1880s and 1890s created anxiety in Berlin. Despite Russia's primitiveness, a pseudo-industrial Russia, given its sheer size, was considered to pose a mortal threat to the German reich.[4] Even at the end of the first decade of this century, when it was clear to many in the German leadership that they faced a coalition of European powers opposed to German expansion, the German elite continued to view Russia as the ultimate threat to Germany's viability. In 1910-12 Georges Bordon, deputy editor of the French daily *Le Figaro,* conducted an extensive study of German political elites, ranging from members of the Reichstag to military officers to Germany's industrial barons. The unanimous conclusion of these interviews was that Germany's true nemesis was presented neither by France nor by the United Kingdom but consisted of the coming struggle between the "Germanic and the Slavonic Race."[5]

This set of conflicting perceptions, coupling traditional reliance on Russia with threat assessments, continued. Thus, for example, General Hans von Seeckt, the Weimar Republic's defense minister and the "father" of the Reichswehr, cautioned in a 1933 pamphlet *(Deutschland zwischen West und Ost)* that Russia remained both the key guarantor of, and main threat to, German territorial integrity. He warned that a Germany that turned its back on Russia would wake up to discover a Polish state extending to the banks of the river Oder[6]—a prediction that materialized in twelve years. Others within the German political elite—ranging from Friedrich Engels to the National Socialists on the Right to the Social Democrats—viewed Russia as the greatest danger Germany faced.

In the aftermath of World War II the German body politic's contradictory perception of Russia was sealed by the installation of the Adenauer ministry in West Germany, which was firmly committed to the concept that Russia posed a mortal threat to a democratic, Western-oriented Germany and which was therefore determined to keep Russia out of West German affairs.[7] Despite some significant changes in West German foreign policy between 1949 and 1989, *Ostpolitik* included, the period may well be characterized by a historical anomaly—the absence of a major Eastern option in Germany's foreign policy. Yet, throughout this forty-year period, a commonly held perception among wide circles in Germany was that the solely Western orientation of Adenauer's policy made it a "one-legged" policy, unnatural and ultimately dangerous to German interests. It was this feeling of confinement that induced Helmut Schmidt to refer to West Germany's *Ostpolitik* as an "act of liberation." During the last two decades, this feeling has apparently deepened, with all West German governments, regardless of party affiliation, continuing to defend the gains of détente, and to do so long after détente ceased to be the preferred policy of the Carter and Reagan administrations. Therefore, despite the political cost to itself, West Germany acquired the role of the Kremlin's prime advocate in Western councils, even when faced with unbridled Soviet aggression and blatant violations of human rights.[8]

The Russian attitude toward Germany is an equally complex affair. From Peter I ("the Great") on, the German states were viewed as an essential barrier to Catholic France and its Eastern extension, Poland. Over the centuries, Russian leaders repeatedly referred to the German states as the critical "roadblock" to seditious ideas from France and the West. Thus, Germany was to Russia both a primary source of human capital and ideas and a conservative filter against the West. From 1792 on, the German states (mainly Prussia and Austria) were also viewed as an indispensable stabilizing force in Eastern Europe and, to a lesser degree, in the Balkans.

Although successive tsars considered the German states both a vital element in Russia's security policy and a model of governance, Russia's policy toward Germany consistently opposed the emergence of a unified German state. The prevailing perception in the Russian court was that Russia could deal with Germany if the latter was dwarfed by Russia's military might and thus reduced to the position of a client. It was with this policy in mind that Alexander I at the Congress of Vienna blocked all attempts by Austria to expand into the rest of Germany, while he limited the expansion of Prussia to the Rhineland and part of Saxony;[9] it was with this policy in mind that Nicholas I helped induce Frederick Wilhelm of Prussia to reject the all-German "crown from the gutter" offered him by the Congress of Frankfurt in 1848 and, further, that Nicholas actually backed Austria in checking Russia's efforts in seizing the initiative in Germany.[10]

It was defeat in the Crimean War (1854-55)—which revealed Russia's backwardness and weakness—and the Polish uprising of 1863 that forced Russia to withdraw its opposition to the Prussian drive for German unification and, in fact, to rely on Germany as an equal partner in upholding both the regional and the European order. Throughout the reign of Alexander II (1855-81) and until 1887, Russo-German relations enjoyed a heyday. The two conservative powers mutually reinforced each other's notions of world order and rapidly became each other's largest trade partner.[11]

As noted previously, Russo-German relations started to come apart even before the fall of Bismarck in 1890. While the Germans increasingly feared that a rapidly industrialized Russia might pose a mortal threat to Germany's national security, the Russians accused the Germans of being responsible for Russia's failures in Bulgaria and were irked by German restrictions on Russia's access to Germany's capital markets after 1887.[12]

It was these tensions and those that were growing between Russia and Austria-Hungary over the Balkans that made the continuation of the Berlin-Saint Petersburg axis untenable. It was this mutual disillusionment and the growing perception that each of the parties was posing a threat to the other that ultimately led Russia to abandon its natural tendency and to ally itself with the country it had historically considered anathema, Catholic, Republican France. The collapse of the alignment between Russia and Germany unraveled the Bismarckian European order and, ultimately, led to World War I.

Russian foreign policy in the interwar period can be viewed as one prolonged effort to reestablish the harmonious partnership that existed between Russia and Germany until 1887. From the Russian perspective, a close relationship with Germany guaranteed the survival of the Bolshevik regime. It was with Germany in mind that Lenin published the secret treaties that predated World War I—treaties that, among other things, forced Woodrow Wilson to offer his Fourteen Points calling for a nonpunitive end to the war.[13] Even after it became clear that no Marxist revolution was likely to occur in Germany, the Soviet regime continued to view Germany as the ultimate restraining power on the successor states that had emerged in Eastern[14] and central Europe, as a stumbling block for a capitalist coalition against Russia, and as a natural source of capital and technology.

If Russia's efforts to reestablish a partnership with Germany were less than a complete success, it was mainly because of Germany's inability to decide whether to favor an Eastern or a Western orientation. Furthermore, the conclusion of the Russo-German Rapallo Agreement (1922) triggered what the United Kingdom's foreign secretary, Austen Chamberlain, called a "struggle for the soul of Germany." With the USSR on the one side, and with the United Kingdom, France, and, to a degree, the United States trying to draw Germany into their respective orbits, Berlin was able to play off both sides. Thus, the Rapallo Agreement between Russia and Germany was followed by the Locarno Accords between Germany and the West in 1925, which in turn were followed by the Treaty of Berlin in 1926. The Treaty of Berlin, reaffirming Germany's link to Russia, was then followed by Germany's joining the League of Nations in 1926—a move that was perceived as hostile to Moscow and that caused Foreign Commissar Litvinov to reconsider the wisdom of Rapallo.[15]

Nevertheless, Germany remained, by far, Russia's highest foreign policy priority. Even during the height of Litvinov's collective security campaign to isolate nazi Germany, few in the Kremlin disguised Russia's preference for an alliance with Germany should the opportunity present itself. As Jiri Hochman illustrates in his scholarly study, throughout Litvinov's campaign, Russia never abandoned the hope that it could restore its partnership with Germany.[16] Accordingly, Moscow never seriously cooperated with the West Europeans to contain Germany and so willingly signed the hastily prepared Molotov-Ribbentrop Pact.

After World War II, Russia's foreign policy toward Germany still did not deviate from its traditional path. The overwhelming evidence suggests Stalin hoped to see the establishment of a united, militarily weak, neutral Germany that would again play the client role it had played before its unification in 1871.[17] Joseph Stalin's goals, however, were dashed when the West opted to create a West Germany firmly grounded in the Western alliance. The West's decision to establish a German state from which Russia was, in essence, completely excluded, forced Moscow to adopt a basically reactive policy that remained faithful to the concept of a united, tractable Germany in the shadow of preponderant Russian military power. Thus, every Western step to integrate its zones into the West provoked a Russian response: the currency reform begot the Berlin blockade; the creation of the Federal Republic of Germany (FRG) prompted the creation of the German Democratic Republic (GDR); and the integration of West Germany into the North Atlantic Treaty Organization (NATO) led to the formation of the Warsaw Pact.

Even after Germany's incorporation into NATO and the electoral victories of the Christian Democratic Union (CDU), the USSR did not tire of promoting the concept of German unification in exchange for disarmed neutrality. It was only after the adoption of the Bad Godesberg Program by the Social Democratic party (SPD) in 1959 that the Soviets finally recognized they would not be able to trade German unity for a weak, neutral, and dependent Germany.[18] It is noteworthy that even after 1959—when the USSR abandoned all hope of recreating the historical role of German dependence on Russia—the Kremlin never signed with East Germany the equivalent of the 1954 Paris treaty, which the West had signed with West Germany and which restored most of West German sovereignty and made the presence of allied troops on German soil subject to the consent of the West German government.[19] Perhaps the reason that the USSR chose instead to continue its presence in the GDR on the legal basis of an occupying power was some residual belief that the Soviet Union could still exchange German unity for neutrality.

The election of Willy Brandt as chancellor and his launching of the SPD's *Ostpolitik* in 1969 were thought by the Kremlin to denote a significant movement toward the creation of a neutralist (if not actually neutral) West Germany. Bonn's implied recognition of the post-World War II territorial settlement, along with its acceptance of the notion of two German states, was perceived in Moscow as a significant movement by West Germany toward the resumption of traditional Russo-German relations. Although the Kremlin failed throughout the 1970s to sever West Germany's link to NATO, *Ostpolitik* and the Soviet response succeeded in restoring not only Germany's traditional role as both the USSR's and Eastern Europe's prime source of capital and technology but also Germany's role as the USSR's chief advocate in the Western councils.

Despite the marked improvement in Russo-German relations during the 1970s, however, the Kremlin never fully surrendered its hope that it could—through sheer intimidation—force a government on West Germany that would be willing to play the role of a Soviet client at least in security matters. The Soviet Union's decision in the 1970s to continue to increase its conventional presence in Europe and its decision to deploy huge numbers of SS-20 surface-to-surface mid-range missiles were part of a concerted Kremlin effort to coerce the West German government toward a more neutralist position.[20] Given the strong opposition of German public opinion to the deployment of Pershing and Cruise missiles on German soil, the Soviet leadership firmly believed that Chancellor Schmidt's "double-track" approach would ultimately be scuttled by the pressure within the SPD. Some Soviet spokesmen made no secret of their belief that the Schmidt ministry would fall and that a "Red-Green" coalition would form the next government of Germany and block the deployment of U.S. missiles on German soil.[21]

Whatever the motivations for the USSR's policy toward Germany, that policy had clearly failed by 1983. The fall of the Schmidt cabinet did not result in a shift to the Left, as the Soviets had hoped it would; rather it brought the return of a pro-American, CDU-dominated government. A series of conservative victories in the United Kingdom and the United

States and among pro-NATO Socialists in France inspired Germany with renewed determination to go through with the deployment of mid-range U.S. nuclear weapons.[22]

Mikhail Gorbachev's ascent to power in March 1985 was in many ways analogous to the ascent of Alexander II to the throne in 1855. Much as the Crimean War had shattered the Russian-designed European order created after the defeat of Napoleon, the defeat of the USSR's armies in Afghanistan shattered the world order that had been imposed on Europe by the Kremlin since 1945. Not only did the Afghan Mujaheddin destroy the myth of Russian invincibility, but they undermined the will of the Soviet army to play the role of the praetorian guard of the Soviet-installed regimes in Eastern Europe, a role the army had played in East Berlin (1953), Budapest (1956), and Prague (1968). As one Soviet analyst stated, "The decision whether or not to crush [Poland's] Solidarity movement by military means was decided in the mountains of Afghanistan." Much like Alexander II—who was faced simultaneously with a military defeat abroad, a crisis of confidence at home, and an incipient explosion in Eastern Europe—Gorbachev, after two years of indecision, decided to make Germany Russia's partner in its quest to revive its own economy and to restore political stability in Eastern Europe.

Recognition that Brezhnev's aggressive foreign policy had accomplished little for the USSR—and that it had, indeed, led to a coalescence of virtually every important country for the purpose of opposing Soviet expansionism—led the Soviet regime to enunciate the "new thinking" in Soviet foreign policy. Among other things this included the de-ideologization of Soviet foreign policy and an attempt to integrate the Soviet Union into the international economic order. The military counterpart of "new thinking" was a shift in Moscow's military doctrine, which dropped the traditional Soviet insistence on across-the-board superiority in all spheres, as advocated by Tukhachevsky's "deep-strike" doctrine since the 1920s, and opted for a "reasonable sufficiency."[23]

In 1987 Gorbachev took several dramatic steps that signaled the Soviet Union's readiness to elevate Germany to the role of an equal partner rather than continue the futile effort to deal with Germany as a dependent client. The first step that shook the entire postwar order in Europe was Gorbachev's sudden acceptance of the "double-zero" proposal, which had been offered by President Ronald Reagan several years earlier. The West reacted with surprise and even dismay over the Soviet move, but in reality the Reagan proposal was not very different from the Rapacki Plan floated by the Soviets and rejected by the West in the late 1950s.

It should be noted that Gorbachev's bold initiatives did not receive uniform support from the Soviet political and military elites. Conservative military men, such as Marshal Sergei Akhromeev, believed that any fundamental change in Soviet-German relations would ultimately result in a loss for the USSR and for socialism. The Defense Ministry's publication *Voenno-Istoricheskii Zhurnal* took upon itself the publishing of excerpts from Hitler's *Mein Kampf* in order to alert the Soviet public to the imminent German threat. Gorbachev's liberal foreign minister, Eduard Shevardnadze, however, saw improved relations with Germany as a key to integrating the Soviet Union with Europe. Some liberal *"institutchiki"* started to justify Soviet withdrawals from Europe by using the German SPD's doctrine of "non-offensive defense" (a doctrine whereby security is attained not through the ability to attack an enemy's territory but through the ability to blunt an attack and exhaust the enemy in the process).[24]

The new arms control initiative, it is true, compelled the Soviet Union to dismantle far more missiles than the United States, but the Kremlin had succeeded in fundamentally altering the relationship between Bonn and Washington. In the past the nuclear connection to the United States had been a source of security for the Germans. The withdrawal of the mid-range missiles from Europe and the reliance on short-range nuclear weapons only revived German fears of "singularity" and brought into question the entire nature of the NATO defense doctrine.

The second dramatic step that Gorbachev took in his effort to restructure Moscow's relations with Bonn was the extension of a personal invitation to the conservative prime minister of Bavaria, Franz Josef Strauss, to visit Moscow in December 1987. The symbolic significance of the visit cannot be overstated. By inviting Strauss, Gorbachev made clear that the Soviet Union had abandoned its goal of inducing a leftist government to its liking and that it was ready to deal with Germany as an equal partner with any government the Germans happened to have in power. Gorbachev's last dramatic gesture toward Germany was his December 1988 announcement at the United Nations in which he stated the USSR's decision to reduce drastically its theater forces in central Europe, in effect denying itself the capacity to launch a blitzkrieg-style offensive across the North European plain.

At the same time that Gorbachev was upgrading his relationship with Bonn, the USSR started to distance itself from East Berlin. Articles criticizing the rigidity of the prewar German Communist party appeared in Soviet journals in 1986. In 1987 "Germanists," such as Kvitsinsky, Falin, and Portugalev, were promoted by the new foreign minister, Shevardnadze, and soon thereafter they floated trial balloons concerning the possibility of a "new look" at the "German Question." Even more daring were several articles by Dashchev in *Literaturnaia Gazeta.*

Gorbachev's triumphal visit to West Germany in the summer of 1988 prompted a harried visit by General Secretary of the East German Communist party Erich Honecker to Moscow, where Soviet-East German tensions became more apparent than ever. Then, in the summer of 1989, when Hungary lifted its segment of the iron curtain and a massive flight of East Germans ensued through Austria to West Germany, the Kremlin informed Hungarian foreign minister Horn that it had no intention of intervening in an internal Hungarian matter. Similarly, when the regime in East Berlin was directly challenged by street demonstrators in Leipzig, Moscow made clear that its troops would not take part in suppressing the demonstrators. The most dramatic Soviet disassociation from East Germany, however, occurred during Gorbachev's September 1989 visit to the GDR on the occasion of its fortieth anniversary. During the celebration, Gorbachev publicly rebuked Honecker for his unwillingness to reform. Some have suggested that Gorbachev not only refused to come to Honecker's aid but actually conspired with the former Stasi boss, Markus Wolf, to force a fundamental reform in East Germany, a process that they lost control of and that led to the collapse of the East German regime.[25]

Regardless of Gorbachev's original plans, Moscow was clearly shaken by the speed of the GDR's disintegration and collapse. Similarly, Moscow had not anticipated the victory of the Christian Democrats in the only free elections in the history of the GDR, having believed that the German northeast would follow prewar electoral patterns and support the Social Democrats. Once it became apparent, however, that German reunification was inevitable, the USSR's leadership never seriously questioned Germany's right to complete sovereignty and self-determination. Even the Kremlin's objections to the membership of a united Germany in NATO never elicited a coherent Soviet counterproposal. Rather, a barrage of semi-serious proposals were put forward, proposals that Gorbachev must have realized would have little hope of being accepted by either West Germany or its NATO allies.[26]

With the conclusion of the Zheleznovodsk Accords in July 1990, Russo-German relations came full circle. Moscow accepted a united Germany, albeit with some military limitations, as a member of NATO. Germany agreed both to pay for the Soviet troop withdrawal from the former GDR, and to sign a treaty of "good neighborliness," which, among other things, included in paragraph III an implied neutrality clause. The signing of the Zheleznovodsk Accords signaled an end to a century of almost uninterrupted Russo-German struggle. By signing the accords, the Soviet Union accepted Germany as an equal, in essence abandoning its forty-five-year effort to form a client German government. Germany, by agreeing to limit the size of the Bundeswehr and to renounce access to chemical, nuclear, and biological weapons, conceded to the Soviet Union the position of the premier military power on the European continent and, in essence, agreed not to challenge that status quo.

The key question that the accords raised in most Western capitals concerned the nature of the Soviet-German relationship in the post-cold war era. A frequently stated misconception was that the Soviet Union and Germany were on a path toward a new Rapallo-like agreement. This notion was totally mistaken. Rapallo, signed in 1922, was a conspiratorial agreement between two pariahs of the international community, both hoping either to undermine the world order at the time or to use each other as a ticket into the international community. This is certainly not the situation in the 1990s; Germany is prosperous and totally integrated into the international community, and Russia is poor and eager to join the international community rather than to undermine the world order.

What is true, is that, in a somewhat analogous situation to the 1920s, both Moscow and Bonn sought to use their reestablished link to alter their predicament within the international community. For Gorbachev's USSR, closer links to Germany were a means by which to weaken U.S. opposition both to technology transfers to the USSR and to Soviet membership in such international bodies as the World Bank and the International Monetary Fund. For Helmut Kohl's Germany, closer links to Moscow meant the possibility of attaining German reunification and ending

Germany's inferior political position vis-à-vis France and the United States. If Gorbachev saw a means of forcing the kind of a change in the international order that would enable the USSR to become part of that system, Kohl envisioned an end to the German paradox of being "an economic giant and a political dwarf."

Bonn was further convinced that only through dealing with Gorbachev's USSR could Germany attain reunification cum stability in Europe. Consequently, the Kohl government went to extraordinary lengths to bolster the increasingly weakened Gorbachev regime. Not only did Germany provide more than half of all aid given the USSR (nearly DM 60 billion),[27] but Chancellor Kohl traveled to Kiev in July 1991 to help President Gorbachev prepare his case before he was to present it at the G-7 meeting in London. This eagerness to help Gorbachev in part reflected German concerns about seeing the Soviet troop withdrawal completed by the end of 1994 and in part were owing to a strong personal commitment to Gorbachev on the part of many Germans.

West German efforts in support of Gorbachev went beyond the economic sphere as well, with the Kohl-Genscher team going to great lengths to protect Gorbachev from embarrassment. Thus, after the massacre at the Vilnius television tower in January 1991, the German government went out of its way to absolve Gorbachev, and it urged the Lithuanians to take many small steps rather than a few large ones. Similarly, when Ukraine's Leonid Kravchuk visited Bavaria, the government in Bonn made a point of stressing its commitment to the integrity of the USSR. During the April 1991 meeting between Federal German president Richard von Weizsaecker and Leonid Kravchuk, the German host stressed that Germany was interested in the success of reform "in the USSR as a whole." It should be also noted that while the Germans emphasized that Kravchuk was a guest of Bavaria, Chancellor Kohl invited President Tudjman of the yet unrecognized Croatia as a guest of Germany. Even after the failed August coup, when it became abundantly clear that the three institutions holding the Soviet empire together—the army, the security apparatus, and the Communist party—were damaged beyond repair, Bonn continued to champion the unity of the USSR. Thus, despite the universal agreement that the Baltic states' incorporation into the USSR was an illegal result of the Molotov-Ribbentrop Pact, Bonn did not recognize the independence of these states until Boris Yeltsin's Russia did so. In the case of Ukraine, as late as November 1991 Foreign Minister Genscher urged Kravchuk to remain in the Union, stating: "Diplomatic recognition of Ukraine is out of the question."[28]

It should be noted that Germany's determined support for preserving the Soviet Union derived from several sources aside from the goodwill toward President Gorbachev felt by many Germans. These included worries about the short- and long-term effects of a collapse of the USSR. Now Germany must confront possibilities it had hoped to avoid. In the short term the USSR's demise poses serious questions for Germany, questions arising from concerns about the safety of the Soviet nuclear arsenal, proliferation, and a successor government's willingness to carry out the obligations undertaken by Gorbachev in Zheleznovodsk. It was with those concerns in mind that Bonn used its economic leverage to press Ukraine to agree to become a nuclear-free state and abandon plans to create a 400,000-man army.

The breakup of the Soviet Union may create serious long-term security problems for Germany as well. It is clear that nationalism and territorial irredentism will remain a basic threat to the territorial integrity of the Soviet "successor states" and that of the neighboring countries, especially given the increasingly evident outbreak of assertive nationalism in Eastern Europe. With every former Soviet republic containing huge minority ethnic populations within its borders, the dissolution of the Soviet Union may yet cause mass population movements reminiscent of those that occurred on the subcontinent following the partition of India in 1947. Such a development would be made more likely if the former Soviet Union and other states of the region, in addition to suffering a wave of competitive nationalism, were undermined by economic decline. The primary destination of such a migration would be Germany; the scale of such a migration is potentially so large that it could overwhelm Germany's resources and political stability.

Furthermore, since virtually no border in Eastern or central Europe is accepted by all concerned as a legitimate demarcation, the reopening of any territorial dispute in the region might well undermine the entire frontier system imposed on the region at the Potsdam Conference. The reopening of the question of frontiers in central and Eastern Europe would have serious consequences for the former Soviet Union and its East European neighbors; it would seriously threaten the political stability of

Germany. Not only could Germany be awash with waves of unwanted immigrants (already an intractable issue in internal German politics), but the entire question of Germany's acceptance of the Oder-Neisse Line, including the rights of the postwar German "expellees," would be bound to revive in some form. This is not to suggest that many in Germany, beyond a tiny political fringe, contemplate another *Drang nach Osten* to recover the territories Germany lost as a result of the last world war. However, with about 2 million ethnic Germans in Poland clamoring for cultural and group rights, with the Russian grip on the isolated Kaliningrad (Konigsberg) district apparently weakening, and with a strong expellee lobby in the Bundestag, along with an increasingly xenophobic eastern Germany, it appears certain that these groups would raise the question of redressing what they consider historical wrongs. The difficulties that the Kohl government encountered in trying to pass the German-Czechoslovak friendship treaty through the Bundestag owing to the intense lobbying of expellees from the Sudetenland, is but a harbinger for the difficulties that could arise. Even if these groups remain a fringe minority—which will almost certainly be the case—they nevertheless may be able to force the national body politic to deal with an issue that it would rather avoid, much as Jean Marie Le Pen has managed to force France's major political parties to deal with the highly charged question of non-European immigration. A situation in which central Europe's frontiers appear to be open to change, accompanied by ethnic turmoil, could clearly give them this ability.

Should the question of Germany's postwar frontiers or the rights of expellees become a political issue within Germany, much of the goodwill that Germany has amassed since 1949 would be questioned in short order, reawakening suspicions that could only harm Germany as well as its neighbors and partners. The increased concern voiced by the governments of Poland and Czechoslovakia, arising from Moscow's opening of the Kaliningrad Oblast to a German presence, is a symptom of the anxiety that is growing in the region as the postwar demarcations come under increased question. Apparently, it was with this in mind that Chancellor Kohl, after the January 1991 massacre of civilians in Vilnius, delivered a warning to...the Lithuanians. In a sense, until the August coup attempt in Moscow, the Soviet-German policy in Eastern Europe was a repeat of the policy of the two countries between 1863 and the 1880s, when both saw it to their advantage to enforce stability in this volatile region, however unjust this enforced stability might be to the smaller nations. German government officials appeared cognizant of the fact that East European security can be better assured if Germany counterbalances its inevitable predominance in the region by subsuming itself in NATO and the European Community, and by assuring regional stability through supporting peaceful democratization of the Soviet Union or Russia.[29]

Of even greater importance for Germany and the Soviet Union, however, has been the emerging geostrategic relationship. Now, with the end of the cold war and an almost certain decline in the U.S. presence in Europe to the level of a "trip wire," Germany will face two immediate and critical security concerns, both intimately tied to its relationship with the Soviet Union. The first is the future stability of the newly democratic states of Eastern Europe. The second is what role the former USSR will play in the European theater now that it has abandoned its role as an enforcer of European order.

The basis for a security link between Germany and the USSR was, of course, not limited to the two powers' mutual abhorrence of an uncontrolled disintegration of order in Eastern Europe. A far greater factor in the relationship was Germany's own security concerns. Whereas, NATO will most probably continue to function, albeit on a much smaller scale, and whereas France may reenter some integrated defense structure under the fig leaf of the Western European Union, Germany will always have to contend with the issue of how to deal with its unstable and residually powerful eastern neighbor. It will always have to wonder about the depth of its allies' commitment to come to its defense, especially since Germany's defense needs can no longer be met through mere military deterrence, as was the case during the cold war. The status of German vulnerability was legally enshrined in the Zheleznovodsk Accords, whereby a united Germany forswore all nonconventional weapons and agreed to reduce the Bundeswehr permanently to 370,000 men. Even without these agreements, however, Germany seems virtually condemned to a position of military weakness when its comes to dealing with Russia.

In considering Germany's security options, it is important to look at the viability of a program to build a German nuclear weapons arsenal. What must be said first is that despite Germany's obvious ability to produce nuclear weapons, it is difficult to see how these weapons could enhance German security. Even if Germany ever opted to produce nuclear weapons, given the limitations on Germany, it can be a power only in the league of the United Kingdom or France; it lacks the continental size and many other prerequisites to join the league of superpowers. In fact, any attempt by Germany to enter the nuclear club would more likely provoke than deter. Not only would a move by Germany to acquire nuclear weapons upset its neighbors—both East and West and lead to Germany's isolation within the international system, but it might even incite an impoverished and unstable Poland to attempt to produce a crude nuclear weapon, as presidential candidate Tyminski suggested during the 1990 presidential election campaign. It might even revive mini-entente between France and Poland. Reading the statements made by Presidents Lecha Walesa and President Francois Mitterrand during the former's visit to Paris, one could think that the mini-entente never ceased to exist anyway. Therefore, it is hard to see how Germany could enhance its security by acquiring nuclear weapons; it is even more difficult to imagine a German government taking such a course. According to Egon Bahr, Germany's budgetary and demographic problems, and reduced threat perceptions owing to the fact that the former Soviet Union will be separated from Germany by a truly independent Poland, make it doubtful that Germany will be able even to sustain the armed force of 370,000 allowed under the Kohl-Gorbachev agreement.

Thus, the first order of business for any German government—given the objective limitations, given the relative as well as absolute decline in Germany's population compared with the population of the USSR (and that of virtually all other potential rivals),[30] given all the above constraints faced by Germany along with the explosive mix of Russian military strength and political and economic instability—has been to find as much common ground with the Soviet Union as possible. What Germany has energetically tried to avoid is the emergence of what Stephen Sestanovich referred to as a "Weimar Russia," a Russia that feels excluded from the European mainstream and pushed to where Josef Pilsudski always dreamed of—across the Urals.

Germany is much like Japan, which understands that it cannot conduct a normal existence if its giant neighbor, China, perceives itself as a sallow power outside the international system—a perspective that makes Japan willing at times, such as after the brutal repression in Tiananmen Square, to defy its Western allies in order not to offend China. As was the case at the Houston Conference of the G-7, Germany will therefore, on the one hand, continue to rely on the United States for its ultimate source of defense and to opt for what William Odom called the "Atlantic House" rather than the "European House" (which will include the former USSR).[31] On the other hand, given the potential degree of complementarity between the German and Russian economies; given the pivotal importance that the preservation of Europe's current frontiers and that overall stability in Eastern Europe have for the security of both powers; and given that, to Russia, Germany will always remain the litmus test of Russia's ability to join the international system—and that, to Germany, Russia will remain a residual threat, it will be in the interests of both parties to develop their special relationship. As Chancellor Kohl stated, it is vital for Europe's peace and prosperity to "bring Russia into Europe."[32] It was a reflection of these realities when Germany, alone among the countries of Europe, signed with the USSR a treaty of good neighborliness that included a de facto neutrality clause reviving France's Tauroggen Complex, and it was a reflection of these realities when Germany continued to support the USSR as a unified entity, even when the USSR's ability to continue functioning as a unitary political entity was seriously in doubt.

It may, then, be said that Germany and Russia have long had a special relationship, one that has at times expressed itself in struggle and at other times in strong cooperation. During Gorbachev's tenure, a symbiotic relationship between the two countries was supported by perceptions in both capitals. If the Kohl government had a clear preference for Gorbachev's Soviet Union, the feeling in Moscow was more than reciprocated. The perception among many of the Gorbachev-era Soviet elite was that Germany was far better positioned to bring the USSR into the international system than either the United States or Japan. The prevailing Soviet view was that Germany, unlike the United States, did not allow superpower competition to color its intercourse with Moscow.

Soviet analysts never tire of noting that even at the height of the cold war, in the late 1970s and early 1980s, the Germans were willing to defy the United States and go through with the natural gas pipeline from Siberia. The United States, which has an open mechanism for forming foreign policy and a proliferation of interest groups with a gripe against the USSR, might choose to hold economic links to the USSR as a hostage (an approach that the Kremlin has found both humiliating and at times puzzling). All relevant segments of the German body politic, however, support the expansion of economic links with Russia, and they do not provoke political controversy. Furthermore, with the exception of some specialized areas of industrial activity, such as petroleum recovery, aircraft engines, and some aspects of computer technology, much that the United States has to offer (in terms of infrastructure projects) represents neither the latest technology nor the cheapest price. Thus, the fundamental base for U.S.-Russian trade is smaller than it may appear.

A no less complicated set of difficulties awaits any massive expansion of the Russo-Japanese economic relationship, even assuming that the Northern Territories dispute could be overcome. The burden of history between the two countries and cultures is one of relentless hostility. It is hard to imagine a very warm reception for Japanese capital among Russia's primitive and xenophobic masses. In the past, whenever the possibility was raised that Japanese capital might take part in the development of the Soviet Far East, the common reaction was one of undisguised xenophobia and racism. Even the liberal Soviet press maintained that Russia could deal with Japan only from a position of strength, and that to turn to Japan at a time of economic weakness would be a national humiliation that would yield little good.[33] Thus, whereas a greater German presence in former East Prussia was treated by most Russians as a positive development, concessions to Japan regarding the Northern Territories received almost uniform scorn in the Soviet media.

Even if these problems could be overcome with better education, some very practical problems would remain. Japan's committing itself in any major way to the Russian economy would entail severe strains in its two key relationships. Both the United States (which accounts for almost 35 percent of Japan's trade and which is Japan's military protector) and China (Japan's pivotal ally in Asia) would take a very dim view of any intimacy between Tokyo and Moscow. It is hard to imagine the kind of benefit that the Kremlin could bestow on Japan to make a relationship with Russia attractive. Furthermore, the Russians admit freely that many of Japan's technological exports are far too expensive and sophisticated for their needs. Although Moscow could envision a closer economic relationship with Japan in the energy sector, most Soviet efforts in the Far East have been concentrated in South Korea and Taiwan. For the

Russians, the constraints on a deep economic relationship with the United States and Japan, along with a cognizance of the historical relationship, make Germany appear as a natural partner.

For Moscow, the rationale for a special relationship with Germany went beyond the Kremlin's desire to gain greater acceptance within the international system. A stable geostrategic relationship with Germany was also vital. Although Germany was not in a position to threaten the Soviet Union, it was only through an intimate relationship with Germany and the United States, Gorbachev and Shevardnadze believed, that Moscow would be able to demilitarize the Soviet economy—an essential step if the economy was to recover. Thus, despite the preoccupation of both powers with their internal difficulties, which may still make the relationship appear marginal, "Soviet-German bilateralism" may be considered the cornerstone of both Gorbachev's and Kohl's European policy.[34]

The failed August coup attempt and the subsequent demise of the Soviet Union have profoundly changed the relationship between Bonn and Moscow. From the German perspective, the former Soviet Union has become less important, if for no other reason than that six[35] newly independent states between the Baltic and the Black Sea now separate Germany from Russia instead of an independent Poland. Given the poverty of these new countries and their desperate need for German trade and capital, and given the decision of both Ukraine and Belarus to enter the international system as nonnuclear countries with independent armies of their own, the immediate threat to German security posed by Russian military might has greatly diminished. The most serious security problem that Germany potentially faces from the East is a civil war within the Russian Republic or a conflict among members of the Commonwealth of Independent States (CIS), either of which could send a torrent of refugees heading westward. The other potential problem is the failure of Russia or other members of the CIS to complete the withdrawal of the remaining 200,000 former Soviet troops from Germany.

Although it is possible for Germany to contribute to the stability of the CIS through economic aid, pursuing a course similar to that followed vigorously by the Kohl government, the immediate needs within the CIS are so great that Germany—and perhaps even the entire West—would not be able to cover them. Germany is also seriously limited in its ability to affect events in the former USSR. It should be borne in mind that many of the economic problems faced by Russia and the other states are a direct outgrowth of the internal political situation in the CIS. The process of stabilizing this situation is one in which outside players can play an important, yet a fundamentally marginal, role.

The immediate prospects for growth in the Russo-German economic relationship are poor for several reasons. Not only has the sorry state of the post-Soviet economy resulted in the collapse of Soviet trade with Germany, but German banks and Germany's national treasury wound up as the world's largest holders of currently uncollectible Soviet debt. Furthermore, the costs of reviving the economy of the German Five New Länder have been unexpectedly high, and there are many competing demands for German capital from Eastern Europe. Against this backdrop and the decline of the Soviet or Russian military threat to Germany, the German appetite for additional forays into Soviet markets has declined sharply.

A further complicating factor in Russo-German relations is the absence of the special rapport occasioned by President Gorbachev, who had a reservoir of popularity in Germany as well as a warm personal chemistry with Chancellor Kohl. Yeltsin and Kohl do not share a mutual sympathy, nor has the Russian president succeeded in persuading German political and economic circles that he has a clear vision of how to move Russia from its current economic predicament. Therefore, whereas the German media routinely described Gorbachev in the most flattering of terms, Yeltsin, during his visit to Bonn, was described as a courageous yet "ungainly" figure.

If Russia has lost for Germany some of its previous importance, a similar process is taking place in Russia as well. Many factors that made Germany such a critical partner in the past have diminished in importance, and few in Moscow today make a case for Germany as a pivotal future partner for Russia within the international system. To begin with, Germany's unique position as Moscow's "advocate" in the councils of the West declined in significance when the USSR, collapsing at the end of 1991, ceased to be a global rival of the United States. Moscow's ambition to join the International Monetary Fund, the World Bank, and other institutions is no longer blocked by the United States or any other major international player.

In contrast with the Gorbachev era, which saw efforts to establish closer links to Germany as a means to "open" the international system to the USSR, the Yeltsin team is far less enthusiastic over an overly close association with Germany. Some Russian analysts point out that a close association with Germany carries historical baggage identified by most Europeans and Americans with a strong "anti status quo" tendency, an impression Moscow is eager to avoid. According to this argument, given the history of the Holy Alliance, Rapallo, and Molotov-Ribbentrop pacts, any real or perceived alliance with Germany would heighten anxiety in Eastern Europe, France, and even the United States. Since the Yeltsin regime equates its economic and political success with Russia's ability to integrate itself into the international system, any posture that might appear contrary to such efforts is to be avoided.

Consequently, although the Yeltsin government pursued its plans for the Kaliningrad Oblast (former East Prussia and an area in which the German presence is rapidly expanding)—plans, that is, to turn it into an "amber" free trade zone—it repeated Shevardnadze's assurance to Poland that the Volga Germans would not be resettled there. Responding further to nationalist pressures at home, Yeltsin reneged on Gorbachev's promise to resettle large numbers of Germans, even in the area around Saratov, a region from which Stalin expelled these people in August 1941. In addition, whereas Gorbachev floated the idea of a permanent German seat on the United Nations Security Council, the Yeltsin team has shown no interest in the idea. Even more significant was Russia's open displeasure with Germany's assertive manner in ramming through the recognition of Slovenia and Croatia. Yeltsin, in part fearing a "Slavophile" nationalist backlash in Russia against German encroachment into the Slavic Balkans, chose to follow the U.S. rather than the European lead and to withhold immediate recognition of the former republics of Yugoslavia.

The logic emanating from Yeltsin, and even more clearly from his U.S.-oriented foreign minister, Kozyrev, is this: now that Russia has abandoned its pretensions to being a global power, and indeed sees itself as a pro status quo power, there is a great deal of mutuality of interest between Moscow and Washington. The United States is no longer viewed as an obstacle to Russia's entry into the international system but rather as a supporter of it. Therefore, to continue to pursue a German-oriented policy that is bound to annoy Russia's East European neighbors, France, and to a degree, the United States is no longer in Russia's interest. In fact, all major powers, with the possible exception of Japan, find it difficult to adjust themselves to deal with a Germany that is demanding political stature commensurate with its economic weight: Russia being anxious to join the international system would not want to be identified with a country perceived as challenging the international status quo. Further, as noted earlier, given Russia's changed global position, Moscow no longer needs Germany as a key to open the doors into the international system. It is also true that certain of Germany's actions of late have displeased Moscow. For example, Germany's flirtation with the offer of Ukraine's president Kravchuk[36] over the issue of resettling the Volga Germans in the disputed Crimean Peninsula and the Russian-speaking southern rim of Ukraine, although not drawing an official response from the Kremlin, clearly annoyed the Russians. Yet perhaps the most important source of Russia's reluctance to conduct a policy focused on Germany lies in the present "correlation of forces" between the two powers, which is clearly tilted in Germany's favor. Whereas Germany seems to be regaining its hegemony in what Friedrich Naumann called *Mitteleuropa,*[37] Russia since last August has been shorn of the territorial gains it had made since the early eighteenth century and has been driven to the periphery of Europe. Given the history of Russo-German relations, and given the rising tide of Russian nationalism, it would be difficult for Russia to maintain an intimate relationship with Germany from a perceived position of inferiority.

The Yeltsin team seems to believe that the United States, needing Russia as a critical pillar of the World Order (as illustrated by Russia's cosponsorship of the Arab-Israeli peace talks), will assume the role of Russia's key advocate in international forums. Furthermore, Yeltsin's Kremlin seems to believe that it can draw in Japan as a main source of capital to develop the mineral base of Russia's Far East—even before the resolution of the territorial dispute over the four Kuril Islands, a development that would enable the two countries to sign a peace treaty formally ending World War II. Japan's response thus far has been contradictory and inconsistent. Japan's Foreign Ministry has maintained that Japan will not grant Russia any large-scale aid until the question of the islands is resolved; however, its Ministry of International Trade and Industry did allow Mitsui to take a lead role in a $7 billion project to recover natural gas off the island of Sakhalin.

Even in Europe, where Germany has been Moscow's key partner for the last decade, Yeltsin, significantly, has stressed improved relations with

Italy and France to a degree equal to or perhaps even greater than relations with Germany. This is not to suggest that relations between Moscow and Bonn are either bad or declining. Nevertheless, it is significant that whereas Gorbachev's first major foreign treaty was with Germany, Yeltsin's first accord was the treaty of friendship with France—a treaty that symbolically renewed the 1894 accord, when the two joined together to rein in Germany's rapidly expanding presence in Eastern Europe and the Balkans.

Despite all this, the current coolness between Moscow and Bonn should be viewed as a temporary phenomenon. As far as Russia is concerned, there is no more natural trading partner than Germany. Not only is there a millennium of German economic activity in Russia, and far greater familiarity with the quirks and conditions of operating in that enigmatic country than what any other country can claim, but Germany is also far more adaptable to Russia's needs than any other supplier because of its ability to produce large infrastructure and turnkey operations. This inherent German strength is bound to be further enhanced by Germany's current efforts to restore the infrastructure of the former GDR as well as parts of Eastern Europe.

Russia will continue to cultivate its relationship with the United States and the dynamic economies of the Pacific Rim, but there are inherent limitations to those relationships. The United States, aside from the fact that it is itself a net borrower country and thus limited in its ability to provide capital, has other major distractions. As the Western Hemisphere moves toward an economic bloc, U.S. economic attention will increasingly concentrate on one of two key targets. Either it will stay in the Western Hemisphere, or it will be invested in Western Europe in anticipation of a single European market that may not be open to overseas products. The absence of cultural links to, and traditions in, Russia will hinder U.S. investment there, much as it hinders U.S. investment in the rest of Eastern Europe. Thus, while it is likely that U.S. energy concerns, telecommunications outfits, information management companies, and segments of the service industries will make significant investments in Russia, it is doubtful that the most dynamic element of the capitalist economy—the middle-sized firm (with an annual turnover of less than $100 million)—will find Russia very attractive.

As far as Japan and the Pacific Rim countries are concerned, there are, again, severe limits on the degree of intercourse between the parties. Even if all parties could overcome Russia's historical racism and xenophobia, particularly toward Japan, there is little in Russia that interests Japan in the foreseeable future aside from the exploitation of Siberia's energy resources. Japan, apart from its aggressive investment program in choice assets in the developed world, is concentrating its investments almost entirely in Southeast Asia, with massive investments in such huge, unsaturated markets as Indonesia, Malaysia, and Thailand (Vietnam recently becoming of greater interest). From the Russian perspective, large-scale Japanese investment presents problems. Given Russia's inherent fear that Asian powers in the Far East are interested in detaching Russia's littoral provinces in the Pacific, and given the growing separatism among some groups in Siberia, it is doubtful that large-scale Japanese investment would be possible without provoking a nationalist backlash or suspicion in Moscow. Furthermore, the history of mutual antipathy between Russia and China makes it unlikely that Japan would be able to invest heavily in Russia without arousing Chinese disapproval.

The interest in closer economic relations between Germany and Russia should have a strong resonance on the German side as well. On the one hand, the German economy is apparently robust, and this year Germany regained its place as the world's largest trader. On the other hand, however, there are several serious structural problems in the German industrial base that cause severe angst among some German industrialists, such as Ezhard Reuter of Daimler-Bentz—problems that will make *Osthandel* an area of growing importance to the German economy.

What is of particular significance is that Germany's spectacular export performance over the last forty years has been built almost exclusively around the concept of competence rather than innovation. Relying on an excellent apprenticeship system and a highly efficient and disciplined labor force, German producers were able to win a large market share on the strength of the quality and timely delivery of their products, and on prompt after-service. Unlike the case in the early decades of this century, when Germany pioneered a whole array of industrial products and processes, post-World War II Germany fell behind the United States, Japan, and even the United Kingdom (although the British have rarely managed to turn their spectacular innovations into efficient industrial production) in actual innovation and technological breakthroughs.

The long-term problem for Germany is that this model of success is coming under severe strain. Increasingly, German producers are facing competitors who may well be as competent as they and who are far more innovative and have a more flexible labor force. Competition, primarily from the Pacific Rim of Asia, is placing greater pressure on the German industrial establishment. During the last twenty years the Germans have nearly been driven out of such traditional German domains as optics and consumer electronics; they have been wounded in the area of popular automobiles; and they are now challenged even in the luxury car sector (an area that was almost an exclusive German preserve only five years ago). It is instructive that in the North American market, where trade barriers showed neither a favorable nor an unfavorable bias between Germany and Japan, German imports have been systematically eliminated by Japanese and other Asian competitors.

Germany's exports, although they continued to grow at an impressive rate throughout the 1980s, also became increasingly concentrated on fewer markets and fewer goods. By the late 1980s, almost two thirds of Germany's trade was within the European Community. In North America the German share of the market has actually declined, and while it has shown some growth in the Far East, Germany's deficit with Japan continues to expand. It may well be a symptom of Germany's (and perhaps even Europe's) decline as an innovative power that with the exception of the UK-based ICL (now Japanese-owned), not one European computer company is profitable—and that, despite massive state support.

The long-term prospects for Germany's success, however, are particularly troubling. Other industrial powers may have been injured by Japan's industrial might, but no other economy competes with the Japanese to the same degree that Germany's economy does. Furthermore, no economy in the Organization for Economic Cooperation and Development (OECD) is more dependent on foreign trade than Germany's economy. With almost 40 percent of Germany's Gross National Product derived from foreign trade (compared with about 20 percent for Japan and 10 percent for the United States), Germany's prosperity is tied directly to its ability to maintain its global market share. The pressure on Germany to continue to run a current account surplus is all the more severe because the deutsche mark has become a reserve currency, accounting for 20 percent of the world reserve holding. (This is a very high figure, given the size of the German economy. Although the U.S. economy is more than four times the size of Germany's, the U.S. dollar accounts for 60 percent of the world reserve; Japan's yen is less than 10 percent.)

Although the rapidly growing markets of the Iberian Peninsula within the European Community as well as limited growth in Eastern Europe will provide some relief for the German economy, Germany will need to find large new markets (and ultimately improve its innovative ability) if it is to avoid the difficulties witnessed recently by the Swedish economy. It is noteworthy that whereas in 1990 the German economy grew by nearly 4 percent, by early 1992 Germany was suffering from the highest interest rates in its postwar history and was experiencing only an anemic growth of 1.3 percent. Perhaps the best illustration of the long-term structural problem can be seen in the fortunes of Germany's famed machine tool industry, where German leadership, despite the losses in other industries, appeared to be unassailable. For the last 100 years Germany has been the undisputed leader in the production of machine tools. Yet even in this vital industry Germany has increasingly been forced to yield to more efficient, and at times more innovative, competitors along the Pacific Rim, which have forced the German share of the global market to decline from 31 percent in 1970 to 24 percent in 1990.[38]

It is in this context that *Osthandel* with Russia is very important. Russia is, and will remain for many years to come, the world's largest market for large infrastructure projects as well as for machine tools—both areas in which Germany still retains a competitive advantage. Geography makes the prospective relationship between the two powers even more likely. For example, Germany, in response to its ecological concerns, will move to reduce its dependence on nuclear energy and soft coal. The most feasible substitute for these sources of energy is increased shipments of Russian gas pumped through the pipelines across Eastern Europe. Even in the current climate of confusion in Russia, and despite bitter disputes between Russia and Germany over Russian debt repayment as well as German payment for the property left behind by Soviet troops, Germany's economics minister, Moellemann, has repeatedly stressed that Germany is willing and indeed eager to play an important role in the recovery of Russia's oil and gas resources. In general, Germany (with the most mineral-intensive industrial base within the OECD) is relying on an increasingly chaotic and unreliable mineral base from the Third World. It will naturally drift toward the vastness of Russia, especially if the latter reciprocates with large-scale imports of German capital equipment.

Although it is true that the current level of Russo-German trade is low—and even that much of it is fueled by German credits aimed at averting the total collapse of the East German economy, which depends on exports to the former USSR—it would be a mistake to conclude that Germany's economic interest in Russia is part of a short-term strategy to facilitate the withdrawal of Soviet troops from its territory and provide short-term relief to the crumbling East German economy. The two countries' economies have a vast degree of mutuality, which will increasingly manifest itself as both recover from their current internal travails. The Russo-German economic relationship might not reach the high point achieved at the end of the nineteenth century, but it will become of growing importance to both countries. It may well be true that trade with Russia will never account for more than 10 percent of German trade and that Germany's trade will remain oriented toward Western Europe.[39] Given the very high concentration of Russian imports from Germany's increasingly challenged heavy industries, however, the importance of that trade should not be underestimated. It is interesting to note that German banks, historically the pioneers of German investment in the USSR, continue to expand their presence in the East. In addition to Deutsche Bank, which has been active in Moscow since the early 1960s, Dresdenr Bank has established its presence by opening branches in Alma-Ata, Kiev, Moscow, and Saint Petersburg. It was against this background that Economics Minister Mollemann traveled to Russia to assure that country that Germany would still rely on Waggonbau (formerly of East Germany) to secure continued Russian purchases. Foreign Minister Genscher went further, speaking of an "economic, environmental, and transportation zone" from the Atlantic to Vladivostok that would "diversify Western Europe's supply sources while strengthening the safety of those supplies."[40] Similarly, Chancellor Kohl's insistence that Yeltsin be invited to the forthcoming G-7 meeting in Munich, as well as Kohl's "co-announcement" with President Bush of the joint decision to create a $24 billion fund to stabilize mainly the Russian economy, is a reflection of Germany's continued interest in Russia's economic potential.

The special Russo-German relationship, furthermore, can be expected to strengthen along other than merely economic lines. With the end of the cold war and the disintegration of the Soviet outer and inner empires, it is Russia and Germany that will be most directly affected by the rise of nationalism in Eastern and central Europe. Indeed, Bonn and Moscow will have to cooperate closely if that kaleidoscope of peoples between Russia and Germany is not to become—once again—the source of European instability. Tacit cooperation has, in fact, already started to emerge. Germany, despite Ukraine's objections, took a lead in recognizing Russia as the successor state to the USSR, and it backed Moscow's claims to sole control over the former USSR's nuclear weapons as well as to the USSR's seat in the Security Council. Russia, in turn, brushed aside Polish and Czechoslovak complaints about the growing German presence in the Kaliningrad district.

For Russia, Germany will always remain the window to Europe, a continent that Russia feels a part of and considers its cultural home. For Germany, much of its peace and stability will depend on how Russia evolves. Thus, Russia will remain a priority of its foreign policy. Although Russia in its current "times of trouble" is hardly capable of playing a substantial role in the international system, few doubt that Russia will eventually regain its internal equilibrium and again assert itself as a Great Power.[41] The question for Germany and the world is whether Russia, at last, will join the family of nations and become a normal country, or whether it will resort to yet another messianic crusade aimed at upsetting the international system. In 1919, at the height of the Russian civil war, Winston Churchill observed: "Russia like any great nation is indestructible. Either she must continue to suffer and her suffering will disturb or convulse the world or she must be rescued.... You may abandon Russia, but Russia will not abandon you.... You cannot remake the world without Russia." What was a truism for Great Britain in 1919 is certainly true for Germany at the end of our century.

Notes

1. *Helmut Schmidt, A Grand Strategy for the West (New Haven: Yale University Press, 1985),* 26.

2. See Walter Z. Laquer, *Russia and Germany: A Century of Conflict* (New Brunswick, N.J.: Transaction Publishers, 1990), chaps. 1-3.

3. See David Calleo, *German Problem Reconsidered: Germany and the World Order, 1870 to the Present* (New York: Cambridge University Press, 1978), chap. 2.

4. A symptom of the changed German perception of Russia's military power can be gauged from the evolution of German military plans. Von Moltke, in 1880, believed Russia could be eliminated through a series of hammer blows, thus enabling Germany to throw its weight against France. By 1890 von Schlieffen had reversed Germany's strategy, believing that France should be eliminated first so that Germany could concentrate all its might against a more threatening foe, Russia. See Gordon A. Craig, *The Politics of the Prussian Army 1640-1945* (New York: Oxford University Press, 1979), 277-81.

5. See Georges Bordon, *The German Enigma* (New York: E.P. Dutton & Co., 1912). It should be noted that this view of pre-World War I Germany is not universally accepted. There is a school of prominent historians, such as A. J. P. Taylor and Paul Kennedy, who ascribe the origins of the war to the Anglo-German maritime competition.

6. See Edward Hallett Carr, *German-Soviet Relations Between The Two World Wars 1919-1939* (Baltimore: The Johns Hopkins University Press, 1951), 104.

7. See Wolfram F. Hanrieder, *Germany, America, Europe: Forty Years of German Foreign Policy* (New Haven: Yale University Press, 1989), chap. 5.

8. For example, Chancellor Schmidt refused to condemn the arrest of Nathan Sharansky, noting that the Soviets had "17 million German hostages"; similarly, whereas the Nixon and Carter administrations saw China as a counterweight to an aggressive USSR, Schmidt compared this to pushing a bamboo stick into a bear's cage.

9. See Hugh Seton Watson, *The Russian Empire: 1801-1917* (Oxford: Oxford University Press, 1990), 142-52.

10. See Nicholas V. Riasanovsky, *A History of Russia* (New York:

Oxford University Press, 1984), 335.

11. This is not to say that the relationship was without tensions. Russia's diplomatic defeat at the Berlin Conference of 1878 resulted in a burst of anti-Bismarck polemics in Russia.

12. For an excellent treatment of the period, see George F. Kennan, *The Decline of Bismarck's European Order* (Princeton: Princeton University Press, 1979).

13. See Arno Meyer, *Wilson vs. Lenin* (New York: Meridian Press, 1967).

14. Both Germany and Russia perceived themselves as victims of Poland's territorial ambitions.

15. See R. M. Mayl, D. S. Morris, and A. R. Peters, *German-Soviet Relations in the Weimar Era: Friendship from Necessity* (Totowa, N.J.: Barnes & Noble Books, 1985), 145.

16. See Jiri Hochman, *The Soviet Union and the Failure of Collective Security* (Ithaca: Cornell University Press, 1984). For a book that derives virtually the opposite conclusion, see Jonathan Haslam, *The Soviet Union and the Struggle for Collective Security* (London: Macmillan & Co., 1985).

17. See D. Melnikov, *Bor'ba Za Ediniui Nazavisimuiu, Demokraticheskuiui, Miroliubivuiu Germaniu* (Moscow: Gospolitizdat, 1951).

18. For a Soviet analysis, see M. S. Voslenskii, *Vneshnaiia Politika i Partii FRG* (Moscow: IMO, 1961).

19. For the comparative text of treaties, see Dieter Blumenwit, *What is Germany? Explaining Germany's Status after World War II* (Bonn: Kulturstiftung Verlag, 1989).

20. Some analysts, such as Michael Sodaro, believe that the Soviet placement of the SS-20 was merely meant to keep the level of tension in Europe high and thus enhance the alliance cohesion in Eastern Europe.

21. See Josef Joffe, "The Revisionists: Germany and Russia in a Post Bi-Polar World," in *New Thinking and Old Realities,* ed. Michael Clark and Simon Serfaty, (Washington, D.C.: Seven Locks Press, 1990).

22. See Jeffrey Werf, *War By Other Means: Soviet Power, West German Resistance and the Battle of the Euro-missiles* (New York: The Free Press, 1991).

23. For a good analysis of the change, see Raymond L. Garthoff, *Deterrence and the Revolution in Soviet Military Doctrine* (Washington, D.C.: The Brookings Institution, 1991).

24. See Marian Leighton and Robert Rudney, "Non-Offensive Defense: Toward a Soviet-German Security Partnership?" *Orbis*, Summer 1991, 377-93.

25. See Jeffrey Gedwin, *The Hidden Hand: Gorbachev and the Collapse of East Germany* (Lanham, Md.: University Press of America, 1991).

26. For a good discussion of Soviet negotiating tactics during the German unification negotiations, see Elizabeth Pond, *After the Wall: American Policy Toward Germany* (New York: Priority Press, 1990).

27. See *New York Times*, 23 January 1992.

28. Foreign Broadcast Information Service, *Daily Report on the Soviet Union*, 18 October 1991.

29. Professor George Liska has suggested that Czechoslovakia may be best served through the creation of close economic links to Germany, balanced by a military relationship with the USSR. See George Liska, *Fallen Dominions, Reviving Powers: Germany, the Slavs, and Europe's Unfinished Agenda* (Washington, D.C.: The Johns Hopkins Foreign Policy Institute, 1990).

30. In 1905 Germany's population was almost half that of the Russian empire (61 million vs. 125 million), and the German economy was actually larger. By 1990 the population of a united Germany was marginally about a quarter that of the USSR (79 million vs. 292 million), and the size of the German economy was about two-thirds that of the Soviet economy.

31. William Odom, "The German Problem: Only Ties to America Provide the Answer," *Orbis* 34 (Fall 1990): 483-504.

32. See Helmut Kohl, "Voice of Harmony That Stills National Rivalry," *Financial Times*, 29 October 1990.

33. See S. Agafonov, "Moskva-Tokio: Vozmozhny li Varianty?" *Izvestia*, 29 and 30 March 1990 and 1 April 1990.

34. The term was first used by Jerry Livingston during a presentation in Washington, D.C., on 20 November 1990.

35. The countries are Belarus, Estonia, Latvia, Lithuania, Moldova, and Ukraine.

36. See *Der Spiegel*, 3 February 1992.

37. This was originally perceived as an anti-Russian alignment of Germany and the smaller countries separating it from Russia.

38. See *The Economist*, 16 November 1991, 88.

39. For an excellent analysis, see Heinrich Vogel, "Die Vereinigung Deutschlands und die Wirtschaftinteressn der Sowjetunion," *Europa Archive,* no. 13 and 14 (1991).

40. John Tagliabue, "When the Best Customer—the Ex-Soviet Union—is Broke" *New York Times* 5 April 1992.

41. See Bruce Porter, "The Coming Resurgence of Russia," *National Interest* (Spring 1991).

3

Poland, Czechoslovakia, and Hungary: The Triangle in Search of Europe

Andrew A. Michta

S ince the 1989 disintegration of the Yalta system on the Continent, Poland, Czechoslovakia, and Hungary have faced a unique opportunity to overcome their historical position as pawns in the Great Power competition between Germany and Russia. In geopolitical terms the reunification of Germany has placed the "Triangle" states of Poland, Czechoslovakia, and Hungary at the critical eastern periphery of the emerging new Europe, while the demise of the Soviet Union has given them a chance to redefine their relations with the Soviet successor states. These new conditions in Europe have brought together the national interests of Poland, Czechoslovakia, and Hungary to an unprecedented degree, transcending past differences and forging the consensus in Warsaw, Prague, and Budapest that the three nations ought to work jointly to accelerate their "return to Europe." The collapse of the Warsaw Pact and the demise of the USSR have left the former Soviet satellites in east central Europe in a security vacuum. The reunification of Germany within the framework of the Western security system, Moscow's retreat from Europe, and the disappearance of the East-West divide of the cold war period have been accompanied by a new distribution of power and influence between the developed northwestern core of the Continent, centered around Germany and France, and the areas lying to the east and south.

The fundamental challenge for the Triangle governments is to ensure that east central Europe eventually becomes fully included in central Europe as an important part of the Western-dominated pan-European economic and security systems. The prospects for the success of this endeavor, while by no means assured, are better now than at any time in this century. The task will require political vision and firmness on the part of the Triangle states, as well as assistance from the developed countries. To reintegrate with the West, Poland, Czechoslovakia, and Hungary must build good working relations with Germany and the Soviet successor states. In addition to these bilateral relations, the Triangle needs to forge a workable common agenda in the area of economic and security policies that will accelerate its entry into established Western European institutions. In the words of Hungarian foreign minister Geza Jeszenszky, cooperation among Poland, Czechoslovakia, and Hungary rests "on important similarities in their internal developments and on the three states' shared aspirations to rejoin the European community to which they belong by virtue of history, intellectual relations and economic ties."[1] This has been increasingly recognized by the West, which has treated the Triangle as a region distinct from the rest of the former Soviet bloc. In turn, Poland, Czechoslovakia, and Hungary have responded to the growing Western commitment to include them in the pan-European architecture by developing and strengthening trilateral regional cooperation. If Czechoslovakia fragments into independent Czech and Slovak states, as appears likely gauging from the results of the 1992 parliamentary elections, the Czech Republic has expressed its determination to continue the policies of market capitalism and reintegration with the West. The program was outlined by the federal government in 1990-91, and reaffirmed by new Czech Prime Minister-designate Vaclav Klaus in 1992.

Among the multitude of problems facing east central Europe in the wake of the 1989 anticommunist revolutions, arguably the two most critical challenges are (1) a successful economic transformation, and (2) the creation of an effective security system capable of providing the three countries with the requisite stability along their periphery. The two issues are interrelated, for their resolution will ultimately define the success of the Triangle's "return to Europe" that is, the success of democracy at home and the inclusion of east central Europe in the new, post-cold war European order. Here the interests of the Triangle states and the West meet. The eventual success of market reform in Poland, Czechoslovakia, and Hungary depends on an effective solution to the region's security dilemmas; in turn, the reform's success is essential to the creation of a stable regional and, ultimately, pan-European system.

Economic Policies

Poland. Poland, by virtue of the size of its territory and population and the scope of the economic devastation inherited from forty-five years of communist mismanagement, holds the key to the region's stability. In 1990 and 1991 the country was in the forefront of postcommunist economic reconstruction, with the Polish government implementing an economic stabilization program developed with the assistance of Western economists and the International Monetary Fund (IMF). Introduced on 1 January, 1990, the so-called "Balcerowicz Plan," named after the country's finance minister, Leszek Balcerowicz concentrated on fighting hyperinflation, which by that time had reached close to 1,000 percent per annum. It also aimed at making the Polish zloty convertible and began the process of privatizing the economy. In January 1990 Warsaw freed the prices, imposed a wage freeze, and all but eliminated government subsidies; by the end of 1991 the subsidies constituted less than 5 percent of the government's budget. In short, the Poles opted for a shock treatment to resuscitate their decrepit economy.

The Balcerowicz program has been a qualified success. The inflation rate was brought down from 1,000 percent in 1989 to less than 50 percent by the end of 1990. Today, the Polish zloty is fully convertible internally, with an exchange rate reflecting the currency's real value against principal Western currencies. The swift transition to the convertible zloty has been a remarkable achievement, for it was brought about without the government's having to draw on the $1 billion currency stabilization fund set aside by the IMF.

Since the implementation of the Balcerowicz plan, and as the markets have begun to work again, the Polish economy has undergone a remarkable change. The removal of government controls has led to a surge of economic activity in Poland. Thousands of new small businesses sprang up in the country during 1990 and 1991. Polish merchants imported food, clothing, durable goods, and even gasoline,[2] thereby increasing supply, lowering prices, and undercutting the monopoly of state-owned enterprises Employment in the private sector of the Polish economy grew from only 7 percent in 1988 to 16 percent in 1990, with its share in industrial output increasing from 3.9 percent to 11 percent. In addition to the growth of the industrial private sector, in 1991 the traditionally private Polish agriculture began to undergo a painful transformation toward greater consolidation and efficiency in response to market forces. Within the year the perennial food shortages of the communist period were eliminated, while the new open pricing mechanism resulted in a surplus of food in Poland by the end of 1990.

The Balcerowicz program also contributed to the revitalization of Polish trade with the West. In 1990 Poland achieved a $2.2 billion trade surplus from its convertible currencies exports.[3] Furthermore, in 1991 Warsaw succeeded in devising a formula that may eventually revitalize its Eastern market. On 24 December, 1991 Poland and Russia signed a trade agreement covering "strategic commodities." The deal is valued at $1.4 billion for each side. According to the agreement, Poland will provide Russia with coal and sulphur, as well as $500 million worth of food and $400 million worth of medicines. In return, Russia will supply Poland with natural gas and oil. The December trade deal with Russia was a major coup for Poland because the expected Russian gas deliveries will cover all its needs in 1992, while the oil deliveries will supply 50 percent of the projected Polish oil consumption in 1992.[4]

Despite these undeniable successes, problems remain. In contrast with the successful macroeconomic stabilization policies and the transition to the convertible zloty, the large-scale privatization of Polish industry in 1990 and 1991 was a failure, partly because of the political pressures leading up to the October 1991 parliamentary election. The various interim proposals, including a voucher system suggested by the Polish government in 1991 to privatize 8,000 state-owned enterprises, were never fully implemented.

Direct sales of government-owned assets to foreign investors also proved disappointing. Polish privatization minister Janusz Lewandowski admitted in the spring of 1991 that although the government had planned to sell at least sixty majority stakes in Polish companies to Western firms by the end of the year, as of May 1991 only the French Thomson Consumer Electronics and the Dutch Philips electronic company had concluded such agreements.[5] The privatization schemes developed under the Balcerowicz plan were put on hold until the October 1991 election, as the Polish government feared that it lacked the popular mandate to implement a radical privatization program that would force thousands of workers out of their jobs. The Polish economy was paying for the delays in completing the process of ridding the country's politics of the remnants of its communist past.

In 1991 Poland completed its 1989 anticommunist revolution with a two-year delay; the October parliamentary election was its last chapter. The new Sejm (parliament) elected in late October replaced the so-called "contract parliament" of the April 1989 "round table accord," in which 65 percent of the seats had gone to the Communists. Paradoxically, however, the prospects for the privatization program looked even worse after the 1991 election than they did before. Adhering to the principle of proportional representation, the new Sejm consisted of deputies from twenty-nine political parties, including such marginal groups as the Party of the Friends of Beer. The results of the election were the recipe for chronically weak government, as the coalition cabinet could hardly claim the majority mandate to implement a rapid privatization program. Amidst the growing disenchantment of the Polish population with the hardships associated with economic reform, radical market solutions found ever fewer advocates. Shortly after the election, the very idea of rapid, large-scale privatization came under attack in the parliament and in the press, with a growing number of parliamentary and opinion leaders calling for a gradualist approach to the problem.[6] The five political parties that garnered the most votes in the October election have put forth economic programs often completely at odds with one another on such key issues as privatization and agricultural policy.[7] As of early 1992 the privatization phase of the Balcerowicz plan has reached an impasse.

The inconclusive outcome of the 1991 parliamentary election also set the stage for a confrontation between the legislative and the executive branches of the Polish government. Thus, in addition to weakening the government's commitment to the Balcerowicz program, the election led to an increase in the importance of the office of the president in the day-to-day running of the country. In 1991 a number of Sejm deputies charged that the president had sought excessive executive powers and that, as a result, Poland was drifting toward a de facto government by decree, in which Lech Walesa would eventually combine the office of the president and of the prime minister. By the end of 1991 the conflict between the president and the Sejm had contributed to the progressive paralysis of the Polish government and a deadlock on the issue of the new constitution. In 1992 the political controversy over the new constitution (Poland still uses the communist-imposed constitution from 1952) and the attendant succession of weak coalition governments created a virtual administrative deadlock at the top, resulting in the progressive alienation of the citizenry and delaying the implementation of further economic reforms.

On balance, however, despite the slowing down of large-scale privatization and the squabble between President Lech Walesa and the parliamentarians, Poland has made remarkable progress on the road to democracy and market capitalism. Most important, the country's political elite has remained committed to the basic premise that the political and economic future of Poland depends on its successful integration with the West. The economic program for 1992, outlined in the newspaper *Rzeczpospolita* in November 1991, emphasized Warsaw's continued commitment to privatization, banking and insurance reform, a new housing policy, and a new regional policy directed at the development of the country's infrastructure.[8]

Poland also has several unique assets that will continue to facilitate the transition to market capitalism. Throughout the communist period Poland was the only Soviet satellite to preserve the private ownership of land. Polish agriculture, albeit grossly inefficient, has been since 1989 a cornerstone of the new market system. Furthermore, under communism Poland developed a large black market for Western goods and currencies, which today has found its way to the mainstream of the country's business life. On the political side, the experience of the ten years of Solidarity in the 1980s has resuscitated civil society in Poland, and it remains the foundation of the country's nascent democracy. Finally, since 1945 Poland has been an ethnically homogenous nation-state. This condition has all but eliminated the danger that the collapse of communism might revive the sort of ethnic passions that since 1989 have bedeviled other former Soviet satellites in postcommunist Eastern Europe.

Czechoslovakia. Czechoslovakia has moved more cautiously than Poland, choosing a gradualist approach to economic change for fear that a radical reform program may endanger the integrity of the federation. Prague began implementing market reforms a year after the Polish program had been put in place. Introduced in January 1991, the Czechoslovak plan constitutes a scaled-down version of the Balcerowicz program, but in contrast with the Polish approach it has opted for the gradual removal of price subsidies while holding down wage increases. The Czechoslovak plan calls for a two-year transition period, during which the country's price system will be readjusted to fall in line with the world market prices, the Czechoslovak koruna will become internally convertible, and the privatization program in industry and agriculture will begin in earnest. Prague expects to have the key reforms in place by the end of 1993, with positive results apparent by the second half of the decade.

In 1991 Czechoslovakia's gradualist approach to reform was both praised for lowering the social cost of economic reform (especially when compared with the shock therapy administered to Poland by the Balcerowicz plan) and criticized for retarding the necessary economic adjustment process and prolonging the painful transition period. Czechoslovakia managed to hold down inflation to less than 30 percent in the first half of 1991, and the decline in the standard of living was less pronounced than in Poland. At the same time, however, the plan for large-scale privatization became caught up in bureaucratic infighting, with Finance Minister Vaclav Klaus remaining a staunch proponent of a rapid transition to the market, while the social-democratic members of the federal administration, the Federal Assembly, and the government of Slovakia called for continued gradualism. The Slovaks were especially concerned about the unemployment that would inevitably accompany the radical privatization of industry. Since most of the Czechoslovak heavy defense industry is concentrated in Slovakia, the republic would bear the brunt of the social cost of unemployment if the course advocated by Finance Minister Klaus was adopted. Prague feared that such a powerful shock to Slovakia's economy would fuel the separatist pressures and might contribute to the collapse of the Czechoslovak federation. In addition, various privatization schemes discussed in Prague in 1991 had to take into account the heavy indebtedness of Czechoslovakia's industry, especially that of its heavy, inefficient enterprises. Reportedly, as of spring 1991, Czechoslovak heavy industry plants owed in excess of 15 billion korunas—close to 25 percent of all of their earnings in 1990.[9]

Large-scale privatization, announced in the government's 1991 reform program, has meant in practical terms the sale of Czechoslovakia's heavy industry to foreign investors. In 1991 several of the more profitable Czechoslovak enterprises were bought up by Western firms, as seen, for example, in the acquisition of the Skoda car manufacturing plant by Volkswagen. In early 1991 it had already become apparent that if the current trends continued, most of the foreign investment in Czechoslovakia would come from the Federal Republic of Germany. In the summer of 1991 the Japanese also began purchasing selected Czechoslovak industrial plants. Skolunion, the country's largest glass company, was acquired by the Japanese-controlled Glaverbel of Belgium. Although the actual German and Japanese equity investment in both Skoda and Skolunion, respectively, is relatively small, the deals include the long-term commitment by Volkswagen and Glaverbel to invest in new equipment and to open new markets for Czechoslovak-made goods.

In 1991 Germany and Austria held the majority share of foreign investment in Czechoslovakia, with France and Holland falling far behind the two. In January 1992, however, the French made some strides when the French BSN and Swiss Nestle groups each obtained approval from the Czechoslovak government to buy 21.5 percent of Cokoladovny Prague, Czechoslovakia's biggest confectionery. According to Czech privatization minister Tomas Jezek the BSN/Nestle deal is worth close to $100 million.[10]

In the first half of 1991 the total direct foreign investment in Czechoslovakia amounted to $500 million; the projection was that it would go up to $1.5 billion by the end of the year and to $3 billion by the end of 1992.[11] Paradoxically, the privatization program's success became a source of discord within the government as the pattern and source of foreign investment proved to be a contentious political issue on the federal and republic levels. Since in 1991 most direct foreign investment in Czechoslovakia was concentrated in the Czech lands, Slovakia charged that it was being left out of the process.

The growing friction between the Czech and Slovak governments in 1991 over the distribution of direct foreign investment was, however, only one aspect of the growing unease at the federal level regarding the impact of foreign acquisitions on Czechoslovakia's future. The relative success of foreign investment projects in Czechoslovakia in 1991 also caused fears in Prague that the continued, uncontrolled inflow of foreign capital might eventually compromise the country's newly regained independence. Prague grew increasingly worried about the long-term impact that such large-scale acquisitions of Czechoslovak assets by foreign interests would have on the country's ability to make autonomous foreign and domestic policy decisions, especially if the 1991 trend toward the majority German investment in Czechoslovakia continued. In the spring of 1991 the Czechoslovak government began to review the so-called "reasonable economic dependency proposal," submitted by the Foreign Ministry's Planning and Analysis Department in May of the same year, which called for limiting foreign holdings of Czechoslovak assets by an individual country to less than 50 percent of the total foreign investment in the country.[12] Critics of the proposal, especially the Ministry of Finance, charged that if the proposed program became official state policy, large-scale privatization through direct Western purchases of Czechoslovak assets would most likely end.

Throughout 1991 the Czechoslovak economic reform program seemed to lack the kind of unequivocal commitment to the free market principles that characterized the Balcerowicz plan in Poland during the first year of its implementation. In January 1991, following a devaluation of the koruna and the removal of some price subsidies, Prague imposed a 20 percent tariff on all industrial imports to protect the country's large, inefficient industrial enterprises from foreign competition. As a result, the Czechoslovak market remained protected, and the large enterprises retained their monopoly position. The Ministry of Finance strongly opposed the new tariffs. To increase market competition, increase output, and, it was hoped, break the monopoly position of the large enterprises, on 1 May, 1991 Finance Minister Klaus pushed through a 2 percent tariff reduction. The "import surcharges" went down from 20 percent to 18 percent, with the short-term goal being to reduce the tariffs to 15 percent by June 1991.[13] Resistance in the federal government notwithstanding, Klaus has remained committed to his goal of exposing the Czechoslovak industry to the competitive pressures of world markets.

In sum, the 1991 Czechoslovak reform was limited, as was the price the country paid for it. In the first half of 1991 about 200,000 Czechoslovakians were unemployed—or approximately only 3 percent of the labor force—and the government expected that the unemployment rate would not exceed 8 percent by the end of 1991. On the negative side, the policy of continued protectionism through import tariffs hampered the development of the markets. In the first half of 1991 Czechoslovakia's heavy industry remained effectively shielded from outside competition. This began to change in the second half of the year, when in June 1991 the government put up for sale fifty leading Czechoslovak enterprises. The decision was taken by Prague upon the strong recommendation of London's Bankers Trust International, the principal adviser to the Czechoslovak government on the question of privatization. The plants put up for sale cut across Czechoslovakia's industrial spectrum, including engineering, chemicals, building materials, paper, printing, textiles, electronics, and metal processing.[14] It appeared that Finance Minister Klaus was going to prevail after all.

The greater opening to the West and the privatization program were nevertheless more than offset by the breakdown of Czechoslovak-Soviet trade. As were the other Triangle countries, Czechoslovakia was hit hard by the collapse of the Eastern market, which was caused by the January 1991 transition to convertible currency trade as well as the rapid disintegration of the Soviet economy after the failed putsch of August 1991. Even before the Soviet coup attempt, in the first half of 1991 Czechoslovak trade with the USSR dropped by more than 50 percent.[15]

The disintegration of Czechoslovakia's trade relations with the Soviet Union in 1991 presented a particularly difficult challenge to the country's entire economic reform program, and it had an indirect impact on Prague's relations with the West as well. Czechoslovakia has been 90 percent dependent on energy supplies from Russia.[16] The need for diversification of the country's oil supplies was brought home in November 1991, when Russian president Boris Yeltsin announced the suspension of all oil sales abroad in order to meet the domestic demand for energy faced by his republic in the winter of 1991.

Czechoslovakia has continued to search for ways to increase the deliveries of Russian oil and natural gas. Since the former Soviet Union owes Czechoslovakia about $5 million in unpaid bills for goods delivered in accordance with past bilateral trade agreements, in early 1992 Finance Minister Klaus tried to negotiate a debt repayment schedule with the

Soviet successor states in the form of guaranteed oil and natural gas deliveries to Czechoslovakia.[17] The negotiations have underscored Prague's efforts to ameliorate its difficult energy situation in the face of considerable uncertainty about the final settlement of the Soviet imperial succession.

As chaos in the former USSR increased, Prague strove in 1991 to purchase oil and natural gas from other sources, including nations belonging to the Organization of Petroleum Exporting Countries. Because of the chronic shortage of foreign exchange (Czechoslovakia continues to import more from the West than it exports), the Czechoslovak government negotiated a series of barter swap agreements with oil-producing countries. In April 1991 Czechoslovakia agreed to supply Nigeria with L-39 trainer jets, as well as the requisite maintenance shops and spare parts, in return for 100 million tons of Nigerian oil.[18] Prague expected to secure additional deliveries of Nigerian oil for 1992 by building and starting up an ammunition manufacturing plant in Nigeria. At the time, the Nigerian weapons-for-oil deal was presented by the government as part of Czechoslovakia's policy of diversifying its energy suppliers sufficiently to become within two years practically immune to economic dislocations at home in the event that Moscow terminated its oil and natural gas supplies.

The barter swap agreements trading Czechoslovak weapons for oil proved a two-edged sword, for Prague risked alienating the West, especially the United States, over continued weapons sales to the unstable areas of the Third World. The 1991 deliveries of Czechoslovak arms to countries in the volatile Middle East led to open U.S. disapproval and contributed to growing tensions in Czechoslovak-Israeli relations. In May 1991 Israeli prime minister Yitzhak Shamir demanded unequivocally that Prague stop its tank sales to Syria and Iran.[19] Pleading for understanding, Prague nevertheless asserted that arms sales would have to continue until the country's precarious energy position had sufficiently improved and substitute industries had been developed in Slovakia to replace the defense plants. Despite strong U.S. pressure, in September 1991 Czechoslovakia agreed to supply Syria with 300 new tanks. Tank sales to Syria have continued in 1992 and have included the shipment of 16 T-72 Czechoslovak tanks through the Polish port of Szczecin as well as the contract with Syria for an additional delivery of 150 Czechoslovak armored personnel carriers.[20]

Economic reform in Czechoslovakia still has a long way to go before the goal of restoring a free market economy is completed. On balance, however, the country managed to do fairly well in 1991, considering the complexity of its domestic situation, the inherited bureaucratic structure, and the pressure of Slovak separatism. Partial macroeconomic stabilization in Czechoslovakia in 1991 was achieved at the price of a 10 percent drop in real incomes and a considerable decline in output and exports. Despite Western purchases of selected Czechoslovak assets in 1991, privatization at the level of small businesses has not worked as expected, in part because during the first half of 1991 small businesses still operated under the old tax code, which imposed an excessive burden on small entrepreneurs. A report issued by the Organization for Economic Cooperation and Development on 7 January, 1992 praised Prague's ability to keep inflation down, but warned that prospects for continued progress toward market capitalism in Czechoslovakia remained uncertain, subject to the successful sale of state industries.[21]

Unlike Poland, Czechoslovakia is a two-nation federation, and the threat of Slovak separatism has been a constant concern for the Czechoslovak decisionmakers. The government's fear that the integrity of the federation may be put in jeopardy by social dislocations associated with radical economic reform has already exacted a price by slowing down the necessary market adjustment process. In light of a strong secession movement in Slovakia, manifested by popular support for Slovak Prime Minister-designate Vladimir Meciar's program for the creation of an independent Slovak state, this concern has been fully justified. If Czechoslovakia breaks up, as it now appears imminent, the Czech Republic will be free to accelerate its market reform program. The selection of Vaclav Klaus as the republic's future prime minister and the continued popularity of President Vaclav Havel among the Czechs are encouraging signs that, after Slovakia has left the federation, the Czech Republic will continue on its "road to Europe." More poignant, the German, Austrian, French and Japanese investment in the Czech lands is an unmistakable message of Western confidence that the Czechs will eventually shed the remaining vestiges of their communist past.

Hungary. In contrast with Poland and Czechoslovakia, Hungary has gone about postcommunist economic reform in a much more eclectic as well as effective fashion. Building upon more than two decades of experimentation with the market, the dramatic liberalization of trade and investment laws introduced by Budapest in 1989 and 1990 began to show results in 1991. Crucial among the changes were the 1989-90 liberal new laws on direct foreign investment in Hungary. The new policy generated a dramatic rise in the level of the purchases of Hungarian assets by Western corporations. In 1990 direct foreign investment in Hungary for the year stood at between $750 million and $1 billion, or half of all foreign investment in Eastern Europe, including the investment in eastern Germany.[22] Compared with the figure for 1989, this was a dramatic increase in the flow of Western capital into Hungary. As reported by the Hungarian Central Statistical Office, the number of joint ventures registered in Budapest by the end of March 1991 was 7,500, compared with only 900 such ventures in 1989. In addition to the growing number of joint ventures, in 1990 1,200 Hungarian companies attracted substantial foreign stakes.[23] Even more significant than the absolute volume of direct foreign investment in Hungary was the increasingly diverse pool of investors interested in acquiring Hungarian assets. In 1990 and 1991 Hungary managed to attract investors from several Western European countries, as well as the United States and even Japan.

Although in 1990 and 1991 Hungary performed admirably well in the area of direct foreign investment, it was plagued by problems typical of all postcommunist societies, including a decrepit infrastructure, a cumbersome state bureaucracy, inefficient plants, and distorted pricing. The imbalances in the economy and the artificial price structure could be corrected only at the cost of market price adjustment and unemployment. The inflation rate in the first half of 1991 stood at 30 percent, and it would increase further once most of the government subsidies were removed. On 1 June, 1991 Budapest implemented dramatic increases in domestic energy prices, with the average price going up by as much as 285 percent; the average price of coal, the main energy source in Hungary, went up by 176 percent.[24] This was followed in 1992 by a new round of price increases, introduced on 2 January, which raised the price of cosmetics and household chemicals by about 20 percent and the price of selected wines by as much as 50 percent. In addition, the government announced that it would again raise the price of gasoline and public transportation as well as the price of milk and dairy products.[25]

Budapest has been consistent in its commitment to policies aimed at the restoration of market capitalism. On 7 January 1992 the Hungarian parliament approved a law that allows for the privatization of cooperatives in agriculture, industry, and services and that outlines the privatization procedures.[26] The new law is bound to have a dramatic impact on Hungarian agriculture, for it allows the former owners to acquire land that was confiscated by the Communists after World War II. Also in January 1992 the government announced that it intended to accelerate the privatization process further through the creation of new financial institutions to provide credit to the new private companies.[27] The new credit system will be in place by the end of the year.

In 1990 and 1991 Hungary was hit hard by the loss of its Eastern market, as its trade with the Soviet Union collapsed. In mid-1991 the Soviet Union owed Hungary 1.7 billion transferable rubles, which, according to Lajos Berenyi, deputy state secretary for the Ministry of International Economic Relations, Moscow flatly refused to repay or renegotiate.[28] The disintegration of the Soviet state in December 1991 made the prospect of Hungary's ever recovering even a portion of the money questionable at best.

The collapse of Hungarian-Soviet trade in 1990 and 1991 threatened to undermine the Hungarian economy. To compensate for the complete disintegration of its Eastern market, Hungary therefore redoubled its efforts to stimulate trade with the West. In 1990 Hungary managed to increase its exports to the West almost as fast as its exports to the East were falling; in the first quarter of 1991 Hungary earned a $150 million current account surplus in its trade with the European Community (EC).[29] However, while in 1990 Hungary made up for the rapid loss of the Eastern market with increased sales to the West, it was much less likely to perform the same feat in 1991 unless Western Europe absorbed more Hungarian goods. From the Hungarian point of view, the EC's commitment to open its markets to Polish, Czechoslovak, and Hungarian imports, outlined in the 15 November 1991 agreement on the Triangle's associate EC membership, was a most welcome and timely development.

In addition to the goal of attaining full membership in the EC, Hungary has promoted an economic cooperation program between developed Western democracies and postcommunist states within the Pentagonal group. The Pentagonal is a coalition of states in the Danubian basin that agreed in 1989 to collaborate in the area of trade and economic development. Originally it consisted of Austria, Czechoslovakia, Hungary, Italy, and Yugoslavia. In July 1991 the group was expanded when Poland joined the Pentagonal with Hungarian support, transforming the Pentagonal into the Hexagonal and extending the zone of cooperation from the Danubian basin north to the Baltic Sea. The group's project proposals in 1990 and 1991 focused on improving the road and railroad transport, air transport, telecommunications (including the building of a fiber-optic regional network), waste management, nuclear safety, scientific research and development, and ecology.[30]

Although at present its work is stalled due to the war in the Balkans and the uncertainty about the future of the Czechoslovak federation, the Pentagonal/Hexagonal group provides a formula for cooperation across the former East-West divide of the cold war era. It gives east central Europe access to Italian and Austrian technology and capital. It augments the Warsaw-Prague-Budapest Triangle by demonstrating the viability of the economic integration of complementary economic regions across the state boundaries in Europe, regardless of the present disparity in the level of economic development among its members. Ambassador Istvan Koermendy, director of the Hungarian Foreign Ministry's Department for Cooperation in Europe suggested that the Pentagonal could "reestablish the traditional economic links which were cut after the end of World War II."[31]

Hungarian commitment to regionalism aside, full membership in the EC has remained the highest priority of Budapest's economic and foreign policies. Early on, during his visit to Brussels in July 1990, Hungarian prime minister Jozsef Antall made it public that Hungary hoped to gain associate membership in the EC by 1 January 1992, to be followed by full membership by 1995.[32] On 15 November 1991 Hungary signed an agreement with the EC, which has opened the door for its becoming, together with Poland and Czechoslovakia, an associate member of the organization.

To conclude, Hungary's history of experimentation with the market dates back to Janos Kadar's failed "New Economic Mechanism" reforms of 1968. Since the collapse of communism Hungary has demonstrated its unswerving commitment to full integration with the West. The long history of Hungary's close political and cultural ties to Austria, Germany, and Italy are bound to ameliorate the painful process of postcommunist economic reconstruction. The small size of its territory and of its population (barely more than 10 million) makes the scale of Hungary's adjustment problems manageable in comparison with the task facing the former Soviet Union. Finally, Hungary's geographic proximity to the developed West (with Budapest only a few hours' train ride from Vienna) makes the country a natural partner for Germany as the latter develops its economic relations with the Soviet successor states, specifically Ukraine.

The common objective of the Polish, Czechoslovak, and Hungarian economic policies since 1989 has been to find the most direct road to integration with the economic structures of the developed northwestern core of Europe. For economic reform in east central Europe to succeed, the Triangle needs a period of sustained economic growth. The long-term solution to the Triangle's current economic woes, especially after the total collapse of the Soviet market, lies in access to the markets of Western Europe. This view appears to have been generally accepted in the West. In April 1991, as a result of combined diplomatic pressure from the Triangle countries, the EC foreign ministers agreed that (1) the Triangle will be in a second wave of new EC members after the European Free Trade Association countries join in the mid-1990s, (2) the condition of a midterm review during the ten-year phasing in period will be dropped, (3) the Triangle will have more time to develop a tariff system, which will then be progressively dismantled, (4) extra concessions on farm exports, which will allow the Triangle to sell more fruit, vegetables, pork, and game, will be granted, although cereals, beef, lamb, and dairy products will continue to enjoy the full protection of the Common Agricultural Policy, and (5) all textile tariffs will disappear over the next ten years, and steel import duties and quotas will go within five years.[33]

The main focus of the EC foreign ministers' meeting in Brussels in April 1991 was to emphasize the movement toward nondiscrimination against the Triangle and the intention of the West to integrate east central Europe with the EC markets. In terms of east central Europe's economic future, the most important development of 1991 came in November when the Triangle negotiated successfully with the EC an agreement granting it associate membership in the organization, which will translate into greater access for Polish, Czechoslovak, and Hungarian exports to the Common Market. In 1992 Poland, the Czech Republic within the Czechoslovak federation, and Hungary remained committed to market capitalism.

Hungary proved quite successful in attracting foreign investment, but investment in Poland suffered because of administrative inertia at the top as the country struggled to create an effective coalition government. In Czechoslovakia the economic programs espoused by the two republics increasingly diverged: Slovakia's Vladimir Meciar argued for the slowing down of the reform and for greater state intervention in the market, while the Czech Republic's Vaclav Klaus vowed to accelerate the transition to a market economy. Judging from the two programs, the Czech Republic appears determined to speed up its integration with the EEC, while the future independent Slovak state may ultimately find itself outside the Common Market.

Regional Security Issues

The dramatic decline of the threat of general war in Europe, occasioned by the collapse of the Soviet Union, has been accompanied by a surge of militant nationalism in the former USSR and in the Balkans. Regional instability constitutes today a threat to the security of Poland, Czechoslovakia, and Hungary, and it will continue to be so for the foreseeable future as the Soviet successor states either solidify the new Commonwealth of Independent States or emancipate themselves to become fully independent countries.

The former Soviet Union and the Balkans are likely to remain a major area of instability and low-level violence on the Continent. The fall of communism and its aftermath have made Poland, Czechoslovakia, and Hungary the "frontier states" on the eastern periphery of Europe; they face along their borders the danger of continued nationalist turmoil set against the background of residual Soviet military power. Instability in the former USSR continues to pose the primary challenge to the security of all the Triangle states. Hungary's security position, however, has been made even more precarious by the protracted war in former Yugoslavia and by its historically strained relationship with Romania. If Czechoslovakia breaks apart, Hungary may also have problems in its relations with the future Slovak state on account of some 600,000 ethnic Hungarians living in Slovakia. As it became apparent in June of 1992 that the federation may indeed fragment, the Hungarian minority in Slovakia seemed determined to demand complete autonomy.[34]

The 1991 demise of the Warsaw Treaty Organization (WTO) has left east central Europe in a partial security vacuum, with Soviet power no longer present and with the West still hesitant to make the Triangle a member of the existing security structures. Under these conditions, the Triangle's security policies have been aimed at ameliorating the negative effect of being in a "grey zone" of Europe. These policies listed here in a descending order of priority have followed three directions: (1) the quest for a direct Western security guarantee—including future membership in the North Atlantic Treaty Organization (NATO), to be augmented by cooperation with other Western security institutions, especially the Western European Union (WEU), (2) the negotiation of bilateral friendship treaties and regional trilateral cooperation agreements in east central Europe and the Danubian basin, and (3) support for the Conference on Security and Cooperation in Europe (CSCE) process. Whereas before the summer of 1991 the Triangle placed a greater emphasis on bilateral and trilateral cooperation and the CSCE, the failed Soviet coup of August 1991 and the December 1991 demise of the Soviet Union have accelerated the three governments' search for closer ties to the North Atlantic Alliance, including associate membership in NATO, and the future full integration of the Triangle in its security system.

The region's security continues to depend primarily on each country's success in improving relations with its regional neighbors. This political aspect of security will remain the decisive factor determining east central Europe's relative security position for the rest of the decade, especially as the crisis in the Balkans and in the former Soviet Union continues to unfold.

Polish Security Dilemmas

Historically, Poland's basic security dilemma has stemmed from its geographic location between Germany and Russia. Since the collapse of communism in 1989 the overriding policy objective for the Polish government has been to supersede the legacy of hostility with its neighbors. The continued Western orientation of united Germany, the collapse of communism, and the disintegration of the Soviet Union in 1991 have presented Poland with a unique opportunity to build the country's future security on the basis of existing Western institutions. Germany's strong commitment to NATO has been a powerful assurance to Warsaw that history need not repeat itself.

In 1990-91 Polish policy toward Germany had two principal objectives: (1) to obtain a firm German commitment to the Oder-Neisse Line as the permanent border between the two countries and (2) to negotiate a new bilateral friendship and cooperation treaty with Germany that would begin the process of overcoming the legacy of mistrust. Since 1989 the Polish government has remained committed to developing good neighborly relations with Germany, based on the premise that Germany will pose no threat to Poland so long as it remains anchored within the Western security system.[35] Warsaw has hoped that Polish-German relations will continue to improve, reflecting the growing bilateral trade and contacts.

The Polish-German border treaty, which confirmed the existing borders, was signed in November 1990. The new Polish-German bilateral treaty on friendship, cooperation, and good neighborly relations was signed in June 1991. The friendship and cooperation treaty has extended broad legal protection to the approximately 200,000 ethnic Germans living in Poland, explicitly guaranteeing their religious, cultural, and educational rights. The Germans reciprocated by extending the same legal protection to the Polish minority living in Germany. Bonn also promised to support Poland in its bid for full membership in the EC. Polish foreign minister Krzysztof Skubiszewski, the architect of his country's German policy, described the two treaties as a "breakthrough in Polish-German relations"[36] and the first necessary step toward overcoming the legacy of hostility.

In contrast with his well-articulated German policy, Skubiszewski has faced a much more difficult task in dealing with the former Soviet Union, in part because of the continued chaos in the East and the attendant breakdown of Moscow's administrative authority. As a result, Polish-Soviet negotiations of the new bilateral treaty, which began with an October 1990 meeting between Soviet foreign minister Eduard Shevardnadze and Polish foreign minister Krzysztof Skubiszewski, proved to be a difficult and often acrimonious process, and they eventually deadlocked in the first half of 1991.

Before the demise of the Soviet state, Poland pursued a "two-track" Eastern policy, aimed at both maintaining good relations with the center in Moscow and attempting to develop better ties to individual Soviet republics. This delicate balancing act proved difficult to sustain in the long run, as both Moscow and republic leaders regarded it as a disingenuous effort on Warsaw's part to keep all alternatives open. The official

Polish policy vis-à-vis the Soviet Union was based on the principle of noninterference; throughout, however, the government and the majority of the Poles expressed their strong sympathy for the national independence movements within individual Soviet republics.

Since the demise of the USSR Warsaw's Eastern policy has faced new challenges. Prospects of regional instability along Poland's eastern border have been increasing since 1989 proportionately to the decline of the now hypothetical threat of direct Soviet invasion. Since 1 January 1991 Poland has no longer bordered on a multinational, Russian-dominated empire; instead, it faces the task of building good relations with its four neighbors: (1) Lithuania, (2) Ukraine, (3) Belarus (Byelorussia), and (4) Russia (the Kaliningrad region).

Polish-Lithuanian relations have remained strained, and have been even more tense since Lithuania regained its independence. Several Lithuanian political and cultural leaders have expressed concerns about alleged Polish interference in Lithuania's domestic affairs. The historical legacy of interwar hostility between the two countries has done little to improve the present relationship.

Polish-Lithuanian relations are further complicated by the presence of an 800,000-strong Polish minority in Lithuania.[37] In December 1991 Polish foreign minister Skubiszewski expressed his government's strong dissatisfaction with Lithuania's treatment of its ethnic Polish minority, which has included the government's redrawing of electoral districts, allegedly to discriminate against the Poles, and its decision to discontinue the Polish language program on Lithuanian television. Skubiszewski maintained that mistreatment of the ethnic Poles by Lithuania was the reason he postponed his visit to Vilnius, originally planned for November 1991 until January 1992. He also disclosed that Polish president Lech Walesa wrote a letter to Lithuanian president Landsbergis, presumably addressing the issue of the status of the Polish minority in Lithuania.[38] Even as the Polish and Lithuanian sides worked out the details of the joint declaration on friendly relations and a new consular convention, to be signed during Skubiszewski's January 1992 visit to Lithuania, Warsaw and Vilnius faced the prospect of difficult relations. One of the intractable problems is a potential territorial dispute. The Lithuanian allegations that Poland harbors claims to the city of Vilnius/Wilno, which before World War II belonged to Poland but which historically has also been claimed by Lithuania, have remained an explosive issue.

Polish-Byelorussian relations have fluctuated, reflecting Byelorussia's new and growing assertiveness within the former Soviet empire. Today some Byelorussian nationalists consider Poland a threat to the republic's future independence on par with that posed by Russia itself. They often point to the 1921 Treaty of Riga, which ended the Polish-Soviet war of 1919-20 and led to Byelorussia's partition, as a prime example of Polish and Russian duplicity. To make matters worse, Byelorussia's extreme nationalists harbor territorial claims against Poland, in particular, claims to the Bialystok region in eastern Poland. Skubiszewski was reminded of Byelorussia's alleged rights to Bialystok during his October 1990 visit to Minsk.[39] Today Poland faces the difficult task of ameliorating the legacy of mistrust between the two nations while establishing working state-to-state relations with the newly independent Belarus (Byelorussia).

Polish-Ukrainian relations are burdened with a history of mutual hatred and atrocities committed by both sides. A segment of the Polish society has retained a strong sentimental attachment to the city of Lwow/Lviv in western Ukraine, which belonged to Poland before the war and which has traditionally been considered the cradle of Polish culture in the East. In 1991 the leadership of the Ukrainian Independence Movement *(Rukh)* charged that the Poles were harboring revisionist designs on western Ukraine and pointed to the activities of the Polish Association of the Aficionados of Lwow *(Towarzystwo Milosnikow Lwowa)* as proof that Warsaw might some day attempt to reclaim western Ukraine.[40]

The relationship between Poland and the state of Ukraine is further complicated by the question of the Ukrainian minority living in Poland and the Polish minority in Ukraine. In 1991 the Ukrainian minority in Poland launched a political campaign for the restoration of its minority rights and for a "moral and material compensation to those Ukrainians who had suffered discrimination [in the past], as well as [for assistance to] those Ukrainians who may want to resettle on the formerly confiscated land."[41] In turn, the Polish minority in Ukraine complained of discrimination by the Ukrainian government, including government interference with three Polish associations set up in Lwow/Lviv to promote Polish culture among the tens of thousands of ethnic Poles living in and around the city. Recognizing the potential for tension between Poland and Ukraine, in 1992 the governments of the two countries made a concerted effort to improve bilateral relations. In May 1992 Ukrainian president Leonid Kravchuk made a ground-breaking official visit to Warsaw, raising hopes of a new era in Polish-Ukrainian relations.

The future status of the Kaliningrad district, a remnant of former East Prussia that was incorporated into the Russian republic after World War II, presents a potentially divisive issue for Polish-Russian as well as Polish-German relations. In 1990 Bonn and Moscow briefly entertained a scheme of resettling the approximately 2 million Volga Germans in the district, a plan that Poland staunchly opposed on the grounds that it would recreate the prewar conditions.[42] In 1991 the Polish government effectively blocked the Kaliningrad district resettlement plan. Warsaw informed Moscow and Bonn that it would view the plan's implementation as a direct threat to Polish security, as the plan would in effect recreate the Polish "corridor" running in between Germany proper and an area that would be tied to Germany politically and economically.

The demise of the Soviet Union has raised the prospects of continued instability along Poland's eastern border. The Poles are well aware that the new Commonwealth of Independent States, put in place of the former USSR, may ultimately fail to provide the Soviet successor states with a working central government. The creation of the Ukrainian national military forces was an indication that the CIS may eventually break up.

In addition to its bilateral relations with Germany and the Soviet successor states, Poland has been an active proponent of regional and pan-European security cooperation. Since the fall of communism Warsaw has consistently viewed the continuation of NATO, and the attendant U.S. presence in Europe, as a necessary precondition of Poland's security and of stability on the Continent. It has regarded NATO as the only Western security organization capable of keeping Germany firmly anchored in the West and of offsetting the residual Soviet military threat in central and eastern Europe.

Polish overtures to NATO have been partially successful. In May 1991—following a working visit by Poland's defense minister, Rear Admiral Piotr Kolodziejczyk to NATO's headquarters in Brussels—NATO's Secretary-General Manfred Woerner declared that the Atlantic Alliance would expand its military contacts with Poland to include the exchange of officers and the exchange of information on military doctrine. Woerner assured the Poles that NATO had made a commitment to take into account

Poland's security needs.[43]

Czechoslovak Supranationalism

There is no fundamental difference between Czechoslovakia and the other two Triangle states as far as the overall definition of the future regional and pan-European security is concerned. The differences are more a question of emphasis than of substance. Since the collapse of communism Czechoslovakia has placed greater stress on collective security in Europe, as embodied by the CSCE than have Poland and Hungary. Czechoslovak security policy, outlined by Foreign Minister Jiri Dienstbier, has emphasized collectivism and mutuality as the path to a regional and pan-European security system.[44] The general security policy objective of the Czech and Slovak Federal Republic has been to develop a cooperative pan-European security system within the broad context of the CSCE process and to "transfer security on the Continent from a bloc basis to an all-European one."[45] Dienstbier has argued for the creation of a "confederated Europe" enmeshed in a web of shared economic and security interests. In practical terms Czechoslovakia has outlined the following three security policy objectives: (1) bilateral treaties, (2) cooperation with NATO, the WEU, the Council of Europe, and the European Economic Community, and (3) CSCE.[46]

Since the second half of 1991, and in light of the growing instability in the East, Czechoslovakia has renewed its efforts to become an associate member of NATO. In April 1991 Havel made a highly symbolic visit to NATO's headquarters in Brussels to explore the extent of Czechoslovakia's possible association with the North Atlantic Alliance—in particular political and military cooperation between Czechoslovakia and NATO. At the time, Prague received a cautiously worded pledge of limited Western cooperation. Further, the Czechoslovak Federal Assembly has become an associate member of the European Parliament. And in 1991 Czechoslovakia submitted, as did Poland and Hungary, formal letters of intent asking for close association with the WEU, NATO, and the European Economic Community.[47] Havel was encouraged by the 7-8 November, 1991 NATO decision, taken during a summit in Rome, to open the doors for direct consultations between Czechoslovakia and NATO as part of the new NATO formula for direct consultations with former Warsaw Pact countries.

In addition to the residual threat from the East—in particular, regional instability along its eastern border—Czechoslovakia faces the growing pressure of Slovak separatism.[48] In 1991 the demand by Slovak prime minister Jan Carnogursky that "in 1992 Slovakia join the new Europe under its own banner" generated enough concern in Prague to prompt the Czech parliament to consider a contingency plan for Bohemia and Moravia if the federation fragmented. In May 1991 Czech prime minister Petr Pithart submitted to the Czech parliament a contingency plan for his government's action in the event of the breakup of Czechoslovakia.[49] If Czechoslovakia breaks up, the Czech Republic is likely to redouble its efforts at integration with the existing Western security system. It remains to be seen if an independent Slovakia would be able to build equally strong ties to the West.

Hungary's Commitment to NATO

In contrast with the occasional equivocation on the part of Poland and Czechoslovakia, Hungary has been a clear advocate of NATO membership as a panacea for the Triangle's security dilemma. Hungary was pivotal in forcing the dissolution of the Warsaw Pact. More than a year before the collapse of the Soviet military bloc, Budapest stated openly that it was interested in future membership in NATO. On 20 February 1990 Hungarian foreign minister Gyula Horn told the audience at the Hungarian Political Science Association that within a few years Hungary should become a member of NATO's political structures.[50] The issue was pressed further by Geza Jeszenszky, Hungary's current foreign minister. On 28 June 1990, during a visit to NATO's headquarters, Jeszenszky asked directly whether Hungary could become a member of the alliance.[51] Despite the lack of Western encouragement, in 1990 and 1991 Budapest continued to push for closer cooperation between NATO and the Triangle. On 17 May 1991 on the eve of the Bologna meeting of the Pentagonal, Jeszenszky reaffirmed his country's commitment to the North Atlantic Alliance as the "cornerstone of security and stability in Europe."[52]

Budapest has supported, as have the other two members of the Triangle, the development of bilateral relations within the region and with the West, as well as the pan-European CSCE process. In December 1991 it broke new ground by initiating military consultation with Ukraine. On 20 December Hungarian defense minister Lajos Fur and Ukrainian defense minister Konstantin Morozov signed in Kiev a declaration of intent to establish regular consultations between their countries' military leaders and experts with the goal of improving mutual trust and regional security.[53] However, these were clearly of secondary importance compared with Hungary's commitment to the "common transatlantic home" idea. Increasingly the Hungarians view NATO as the essential "peace-keeping capability of the CSCE."[54]

Since the collapse of communism the Hungarian military has worked to create a strong professional relationship both with NATO armies and with the armies of Poland and Czechoslovakia. In 1991 the Hungarian Ministry of Defense signed military-technical cooperation agreements with the Polish and Czechoslovak defense ministries. The two agreements cover the areas of information exchange and weapons maintenance. Intra-Triangle military cooperation has been supplemented by defense ministry-to-defense ministry agreements between Hungary and several NATO countries. The Hungarian military has also tried to improve the historically hostile relationship between Hungary and Romania. In 1991 the Hungarian Ministry of Defense concluded an "open skies" agreement with the Romanian Ministry of Defense; the agreement was signed in early May of that year. The Hungarian-Romanian "open skies" convention provides for confidence-building overflights of the two countries' respective air spaces.[55] On 28 June 1991 the first overflight of Hungarian territory was carried out by an aircraft of the Romanian air force equipped with French sensors. On 29 June 29 1991 a similarly equipped Hungarian jet overflew Romanian territory.[56]

Today Hungary faces an unstable and potentially explosive situation on its northern, eastern, and southern borders, owing to the unresolved problems of the Magyar ethnic minorities in Czechoslovakia (Slovakia), Romania (Transylvania), and the defunct Yugoslav federation (Vojvodina). Prague and Budapest have been able to manage the question of the Hungarian ethnic minority rights in Slovakia through negotiation, but the impending break up of Czechoslovakia has raised questions about future Hungarian-Slovak relations on this issue. Relations between Budapest and Bucharest have remained particularly tense, with the Hungarian side angrily charging Romania with human rights violations in dealing with its Magyar minority in Transylvania.[57] In turn Bucharest has accused Hungary of pursuing policies designed to isolate Romania internationally by barring its future entry into the Pentagonal.

Hungary faces potentially intractable problems in its relations with the Yugoslav successor states over a Magyar minority in Vojvodina, especially if war engulfs the entire former Yugoslav federation. Although officially Hungary has remained committed to the policy of non-interference with respect to the Yugoslav crisis, the relationship between Budapest and Belgrade was rocked in 1991 by the disclosure of Hungarian weapons deliveries to Croatia.

*   *   *   *

Between 1989 and 1991 the Triangle's quest for Western security guarantees intensified in proportion to the decline of Moscow's influence in the region. Poland, Czechoslovakia, and Hungary were instrumental in the dismantling of the Warsaw Pact's military organization and in the elimination of the treaty itself in 1991. The armies of the three countries have been reformed in line with their new military doctrines, which emphasize primarily the deterrent and defensive role of military force. Each country is in the process of redeploying its troops in new military districts to provide for a balanced defense of the national territory along the country's entire periphery.

In 1991 the defense ministries of Poland, Czechoslovakia, and Hungary signed a series of technical military cooperation agreements. Although these fall far short of being full-fledged defense commitments, the ministry-level agreements provide for the exchange of military expertise within the Triangle as well as for mutual assistance in maintaining the large stock of Soviet-designed weapons. The Triangle states have signed agreements with a number of NATO armed forces, including the German, British, and U.S. armies, to allow for the training of their officers in Western military academies. The armies of Poland, Czechoslovakia, and Hungary hope to develop close ties to NATO, with the goal of their future reequipment with Western weapons and integration into NATO's military structures.

In November 1991 the NATO summit in Rome opened up the possibility of bringing the Triangle closer to the Atlantic Alliance by allowing former members of the Warsaw Treaty Organization to join NATO's new consultative council. More important for Warsaw, Prague, and Budapest, the Rome summit raised the possibility that the Western alliance might renegotiate the original 1949 Washington treaty, perhaps to allow for the stationing of NATO's troops outside the territory of the original NATO member states, as well as for out-of-area military operations. The ongoing restructuring of NATO's political objectives and military doctrine, intended to make them more "European," is viewed by the Triangle as an important first step on the road to opening NATO to new members in the future.

Prospects for the Triangle

Poland, Czechoslovakia, and Hungary, the postcommunist Triangle "successor democracies," harbor few illusions about their prospects for independence and sovereignty outside the Western security system. The great unknown in the region is the future of the former Soviet Union—that is, whether the Commonwealth of Independent States formula will succeed in replacing the defunct central administration in Moscow. Whatever the outcome in the East, it is apparent that both economically and politically Russia and the other Soviet successor states will not be ready to become a part of the new Europe until well into the next century. In practical geopolitical terms, if the current trends hold, by the end of the decade Europe's eastern frontier will have shifted from the Oder-Neisse Line to the eastern borders of Poland, Czechoslovakia (or the Czech Republic if Slovakia abandons democratic and market reforms) and Hungary.

The reunification of Germany and the speedy change now under way in the three successor democracies have already charted a new direction in Europe's political geography. It is no longer the question of whether, but only when, the new Europe—built around the northern industrial core, with Germany and France at the center—will bring Poland, Czechoslovakia, and Hungary into its fold. Associate EC membership for the Triangle became a reality in November 1991; full membership may come as early as 1995. On 7 November 1991 an important step was taken in that direction when the EC reached a compromise on steel imports from Eastern Europe and thus removed the last obstacle delaying the issue of associate EC membership for Poland, Czechoslovakia, and Hungary.[58] All three accords were signed on 15 November 1991. In short, Western Europe has already demonstrated that it intends to treat the Triangle as a group and that it plans to bring these countries into the Community jointly.

The Triangle can reasonably expect to become fully integrated in

Europe's economic and security system. Poland and Czechoslovakia constitute a natural bridge between the West and the former Soviet Union, and Hungary also borders on the Balkan tinderbox. Stability in Poland, Czechoslovakia, and Hungary is today more than ever before an important factor of European security; to Germany it has become a question of a broadly defined national interest. Largely owing to German pressure, the West accepted the idea of bringing the Triangle into the EC. The integration of the region's security system with that of the West presents a much greater challenge.

While membership in NATO remains their first priority, Poland, Czechoslovakia, and Hungary have worked to build a network of regional cooperation within the Triangle. In 1990 and 1991 regional cooperation was fostered by the geopolitical conditions, which brought these nations' interests together. In addition to the early plans for Poland's entry into the Pentagonal, on 15 February 1991 Poland, Czechoslovakia, and Hungary concluded an agreement (during a regional summit meeting in Visegrad, Hungary) on long-term economic and environmental cooperation.[59] Regional collaboration within the Triangle has increased in response to several practical military considerations, such as the need for cooperation in the area of weapons maintenance and joint efforts to modernize military equipment through the joint purchases of Western weapons systems. This regionalism needs to be anchored in the restructured NATO alliance.

Only a security system built around the core of Western industrialized nations and reinsured by the transatlantic connection can give east central Europe the requisite regional stability. The Triangle's "return to Europe," that is, the inclusion of east central Europe in the emerging pan-European order, rests on the development of a working security system that can link the Triangle to the post-cold war West.

Notes

1. Geza Jeszenszky, *Security in the New Central Europe,* Occasional Paper No. 67 (Bologna: The Johns Hopkins University Bologna Center, 1991), 9.

2. Polish Television, Channel 1 News, 12 January 1991.

3. *Financial Times,* 3 May 1991.

4. RFE/RL Daily Report, 30 December 1991.

5. "French Join Poles for TV Venture," *Financial Times,* 23 May 1991.

6. "Antyrecesyjny zwrot: Balcerowicz proponuje korekte polityki gospodarczej," *Zycie Warszawy,* 15 November 1991.

7. "Pojedynek na gospodarcze programy," *Kurier Polski,* 28 November 1991.

8. "Kontynuacja i nowosci: Polityka gospodarcza w roku 1992," *Rzeczpospolita,* 7 November 1991.

9. Cestmir Konecny, interview with author, Institute of International Relations, Prague, Czechoslovakia, 2 May 1991.

10. RFE/RL Daily Report, 9 January 1992.

11. "Czechs Hang 'For Sale' Sign on 50 of Republic's Key Companies," *Financial Times,* 14 June 1991.

12. Jiri Pavlovsky (deputy head, Planning and Analysis Department, Federal Foreign Ministry), interview with author, Prague, Czechoslovakia, 30 April 1991.

13. Foreign Broadcast Information Service (hereinafter FBIS)-EEU-91-099, 22 May 1991, 16.

14. "Czechs Hang 'For Sale' Sign on 50 of Republic's Key Companies," *Financial Times,* 6 June 1991.

15. "Czech Bank Chief Appeals for More Aid," *Financial Times,* 16 April 1991.

16. *Atlas of Eastern Europe* (Washington, D.C.: Central Intelligence Agency, August 1990), 11.

17. RFE/RL Daily Report, 30 December 1991.

18. RFE/RL Daily Report, 29 April 1991.

19. "'Stop Czech Arms Sales to Syria' - Shamir," *Financial Times,* 7 May 1991.

20. RFE/RL Daily Report, 2 January 1992.

21. RFE/RL Daily Report, 8 January 1992.

22. "Hungary Takes the Lead on Foreign Investment," *Financial Times,* 14 May 1991.

23. Ibid.

24. "Hungary to Raise Energy Prices," *Financial Times,* 18 and 19 May 1991.

25. RFE/RL Daily Report, 3 January 1992.

26. RFE/RL Daily Report, 8 January 1992.

27. RFE/RL Daily Report, 7 January 1992.

28. "Official on Trade Problems With USSR," FBIS-EEU-91-099, 22 May 1991, 18.

29. "Hungary Goes West with a New Urgency," *Financial Times,* 2 May 1991.

30. *The Pentagonal Initiative: Program of Work, 1990/1992* (Venice: 1 August 1990).

31. Dr. Istvan Koermendy (director of the Department for Cooperation in Europe, Hungarian Foreign Ministry), interview with author, Budapest, Hungary, 10 May 1991.

32. RFE/RL Daily Report, 18 July 1990.

33. "Brussels Opens its Doors to Trade with Eastern Europe," *Financial Times,* 19 April 1991.

34. Stephen Engelbert, "Careful Breakup in Czechoslovakia," *The New York Times,* June 21, 1992, A7.

35. "Jeden Dzien z Januszem Onyszkiewiczem," *Zolnierz Rzeczypospolitej,* 1/3 June 1990.

36. "Wielkie zmiany," *Sztandar Mlodych,* 19/21 April 1991.

37. Ibid.

38. RFE/RL Daily Report, 23 December 1991.

39. According to Poland's deputy defense minister, Janusz Onyszkiewicz, the question of the future of Bialystok was raised in private discussions between Foreign Minister Krzysztof Skubiszewski and his Byelorussian hosts, but it was kept off the official agenda. (Janusz Onyszkiewicz, interview with author, Warsaw, Poland, 8 January 1991).

40. "Nasi w Kijowie," *Sztandar Mlodych,* 5 November 1991.

41. "Zadania Ukraincow," *Rzeczpospolita,* 22 March 1991.

42. "2 Million Volga Germans Pose Settlement Issue for Bonn, Moscow," *Washington Post,* 4 February 1991.

43. RFE/RL Daily Report, 24 May 1991.

44. Jiri Dienstbier, "Central Europe's Security," *Foreign Policy,* (Summer 1991).

45. "Statement by the Deputy Prime Minister and Minister of Foreign Affairs of the Czech and Slovak Federal Republic Jiri Dienstbier in the Federal Assembly on April 9, 1991" (Prague: Ministry of Foreign Affairs, 1991), 3.

46. Svatopluk Buchlovsky (director of the Department of European Security, Czechoslovak Foreign Ministry), interview with author, Prague, Czechoslovakia, 30 April 1991.

47. Svatopluk Buchlovsky, interview with author, Prague, Czechoslovakia, 30 April 1991.

48. "Press Reacts to Havel's 10 December Proposals," FBIS-EEU-90-244, 19 December 1990, 13.

49. RFE/RL Daily Report, 23 May 1991.

50. Alfred Reisch, "The Hungarian Dilemma: After the Warsaw Pact, Neutrality or NATO," *Report on Eastern Europe,* vol. 1, no. 15 (Munich: RFE/RL, 13 April 1990), 17.

51. RFE/RL Daily Report, 29 June 1990.

52. Jeszenszky, *Security in the New Central Europe,* 11.

53. RFE/RL Daily Report, 23 December 1991.

54. Janos Matus, "The Future of European Security and the Role of the Institutions: Views from Hungary," *Report of a seminar for senior academics in The Hague,* June 17/22, 1991, organized by the Clingendael Institute in Cooperation with the NATO-Information and Press Office (The Hague, October 1991), 8.

55. Colonel Tibor Koeszegvari (director of the Defense Research Institute, Hungarian Ministry of Defense), interview with author, Budapest, Hungary, 8 May 1991.

56. RFE/RL Daily Report, 24 June 1991.

57. Istvan Koermendy, interview with author, Budapest, Hungary, 10 May 1991.

58. "EC Removes Last Obstacle to East European Accords," RFE/RL Daily Report, 8 November 1991, 6.

59. *Commercial Appeal,* 15 February 1991.

4
Balkan Insecurities

Daniel L. Nelson

P owder keg or Achilles' heel—the southeastern peninsula of Europe has been bestowed with descriptive phrases that connote turmoil, ferment, and disruptive potential. During the past century and a quarter, wars involving major European powers, devastating rebellions and civil wars, and dictatorships of the Right and Left have all afflicted this corner of Europe, most often referred to as the Balkans.

Today, in the last decade of this century, the Balkans once again pose a challenge. The closely related strategic retreat of Soviet/Russian power and the demise of Communist party regimes throughout Europe's eastern half have engendered an acute security crisis in the Balkans. Intrastate and interstate conflicts are numerous and intense, presenting ample opportunity for heightened tension and animosity during this and the next decade.

This regional survey concentrates on the four previously communist states of Albania, Bulgaria, Romania, and Yugoslavia, although considerable mention is also made of Greece and Turkey. An assessment of historical contributions to the region's unsure security environment is a necessary, initial part of this survey. Second, this chapter briefly highlights the issues within and between the states or emerging states of southeastern Europe, issues that may imperil the peace and well-being of one nation or the entire peninsula.

Beyond such a country-specific endeavor, one must consider the core issues of the Balkans' security dilemma as well as policies by which to ameliorate factors that are most associated with an increase in the frequency or intensity of conflictual issues. No one can prescribe an elixir sure to rid the Balkans of conditions that disrupt these nations' peaceful development. Nevertheless, larger goals of U.S. and European foreign policies—to ensure that the cold war victory is not ephemeral and that nascent democracies become true partners in a "Europe whole and free"—require that the community of nations ignore neither the threats to such goals from a Balkan imbroglio nor the conditions that exacerbate the region's instability.

Living in a Threat-Rich Environment:
Bitter Legacies of Empires

In early 1990 this author wrote that "[t]he historical cleavages of Southeastern Europe have...penetrated and 'overcome' the veneer of late-twentieth century alliances."[1] Two years later, such an assessment has been overtaken. Historical cleavages have, indeed, recurred. No longer, however, is it appropriate to speak of alliances being "overcome"; the Warsaw Pact has disbanded, and the raison d'être of the North Atlantic Treaty Organization (NATO) has been recoded and recalibrated in an effort to keep the venerable alliance alive.[2] The erstwhile cold war divide in the Balkans between states in the Warsaw Pact (Bulgaria and Romania) versus NATO members (Greece and Turkey) and the "nonaligned" (Albania and Yugoslavia) now seems, to outside analysts and to citizens of Balkan countries, a receding memory.

Far more lasting, however, are conflicts that predate both modern ideologies and the alliances that were created in their name. Hungary and Romania dispute the treatment of ethnic Hungarians in Transylvania within Romania—an issue that has roots, most recently, in the 1920 Treaty of Trianon, but that may be traced back centuries earlier.[3] Animosity between Greece and Turkey has been heightened by contemporary problems—Cyprus, control of airspace and the continental shelf in the Aegean, and so on. Yet this too is a conflict of centuries' duration.

At the confluence of empires, Europe's southeastern corner has been forced to deal with the legacy of conquest.[4] In the past five hundred years the Turks, Hapsburgs, Germans, and Russians have all established their "turn" with the Balkans. The Ottoman Turks, of course, established the most lengthy presence, lasting (in the case of Bulgaria, Macedonia, and Thrace) more than five centuries. Hapsburg rule was brief in the Austro-Hungarian Empire's extremities, but the effects were powerful insofar as the economic ties with Vienna and Budapest created profound transformations.[5] Similarly, a German military occupation, confined to the few years of World War II, was nevertheless preceded by decades of Berlin's economic suzerainty. Russian control, sought during the heyday of pan-Slavism in the late nineteenth century, was effected by the Red Army in late 1944; although Albanian, Greek, Turkish, and Yugoslav territories were never occupied by Soviet forces, Moscow's insertion into the Balkans was heavy-handed and ominous to all.

The waxing and waning of these empires, and their battles with each other and against indigenous peoples, fashioned the Balkan Peninsula of today. Obvious, yet overlooked by external analysts, is the legacy of imperial conquest throughout the eastern half of Europe, and particularly in the Continent's southeastern corner. The distribution of ethnic groups, languages, and faiths is a direct consequence of migration—often because of imminent threat—and colonization owing to conquest.[6] The landowners, administrators, and clergy of victors moved in behind their armies, while those among the existing population who were able tried to flee.

The residue of empires are the diasporas of every nation and the irredentist claims of every state. An intermingling of peoples and borders leaves a high-threat environment for today's low-capacity states. Without exception, the Balkans have been an arena from which human and material resources were extracted while the indigenous conditions decayed. Poor, underdeveloped, and having Europe's highest population growth rates, the Balkans' potent admixture is an invitation to instability.[7]

Efforts to address these problems have been inconsistent and desultory. After gaining independence from the Turks and Austro-Hungarian Empire after World War I, Balkan elites added to their nations' difficulties by concentrating on "military preparedness and national expansion over internal development"[8] Military coups, royal dictatorships, fascist and communist agitation meant that sovereignty gained in 1918 remained disassociated from security. Underdeveloped and without self-governing experience, they were ripe for domination by larger European powers and for destabilization by extremist ideologies.

The cycle of weakness, dependence, and conquest is characteristic of peripheral systems. That one imperialism ends matters little; in the wake of empires lie institutions and societies too fragmented to avoid a quick return to dependence.

At the end of the twentieth century, the principal news from Europe's eastern half would appear to be the demise of communist regimes and the disintegration of the Soviet Union. This is not, however, a perspective common to the Balkans, where there has been little time to celebrate the lifting of yesterday's repression or threat. In the Balkans there is little enthusiasm for commemorations. Instead, a desperate search is underway for twenty-first century institutions that will constrain nineteenth century conflicts.

Western indifference to this search is fraught with risk. From the standpoint of the North Atlantic community, southeastern Europe may appear less able to achieve a stable democratic future and thus merit less of an "investment." But the threats that will emanate from an unstable Balkan Peninsula will not leave the rest of Europe unaffected. The prognosis for Hungarian democracy, Austrian and Italian prosperity, Ukrainian nationalism, and so on will all be influenced immediately by Balkan conflagration.

Further, far beyond these pragmatic issues, there lies the wider concept of a new security for all of the Euro-atlantic community. At Helsinki in 1975, and again in the Paris charter of November 1990, all states in the Conference on Security and Cooperation in Europe (CSCE) committed themselves to a new vision of human rights and security from the "Atlantic to the Urals." The testing of this vision began in the Balkans as nations within Yugoslavia warred against each other in 1991. A belated Euro-atlantic response to Serbs and Croats' bilateral suicide and, ultimately, the "pass" of this intractable conflict to the United Nations, do not engender confidence about the community of nations' collective resolve.

Country-Specific Conditions

Albania. Albania is insecure and is itself a source of regional insecurity because of its poverty, population growth, and political instability. The death of Enver Hoxha in 1985, after more than forty years of one-man, one-party, one-clan rule, left Albania bereft of any political alternatives.

Under Hoxha, Albania's foreign and defense policies continued the practice of interwar years—operating within the dominance of outside powers or seeking such an overwhelming presence to "balance" other ominous threats. Italian suzerainty and occupation were resisted by Hoxha's partisan forces during World War II. Hoxha was highly dependent on Yugoslav Partisans, however. From the war's end until July 1948, Josip Broz Tito exerted mastery of almost all things Albanian.[9] When Joseph Stalin expelled Tito from Cominform in 1948, Hoxha was thrown into Stalin's arms, and he remained closely linked to the Soviets until 1961, providing important military facilities to the USSR while Moscow invested in Albanian industrial development.[10]

The Sino-Soviet rift and mutual recriminations between Nikita Khrushchev and Enver Hoxha led to a sudden Soviet departure and the arrival of the Chinese.[11] As a new, distant, and poor patron, China nevertheless showered Albania with whatever it could—until Deng Xiaoping's "revisionism" also led to a rupture with Hoxha in 1978. For perhaps seven or eight years it appeared that Albania had become the world's most isolated state, throwing invectives at virtually every state.[12]

Hoxha's death brought change, however, and Albania renewed ties with France, Germany, Greece, Italy, the United Kingdom, and other countries.[13] CSCE membership was finalized in 1991. Among these relations, the Italian bond has developed most fully—and Europe seems quite willing to have Italy "handle" Albania's difficulties. The Italian connection, however, is no solution, and Albania's capacity to become a harbinger of regional instability should not be underestimated.

Albania's Democratic party, the best developed party without a communist past, joined the Socialist party (formerly the Party of Labor, that is, communist) in a June 1991 to December 1991 coalition government. A victory by the Democratic party, with other smaller parties (those of the Social Democrats, Republicans, and so on) in 22 March 1992 elections, will still leave a large constituency fully alienated from the government and all of its policies. Democratic party leader Sali Berisha is no more likely than is Ramiz Alia (president of Albania and principal figure within the Socialist party) to bridge the gap between urban and rural voters, a gap that was painfully clear in Albania's first free election in late 1990. A split within the Democratic party makes a clear political consensus even less likely; Gramoz Pashko, a cofounder of the party with Sali Berisha and a deputy premier in the coalition government, severely criticized the latter for contributing to chaos by withdrawing support from Prime Minister Ylli Bufi.[14] And Berisha is even less likely to be able to control the *Segurimi* (secret police from the communist era) or the armed forces.

Workers' strikes, disturbances on university campuses, and additional violence related to food distribution will confront the next government. Vicious attacks on democratic politicians or others who speak out on behalf of movement toward a plural, competitive democracy are likely to continue or worsen. (An example of such violence was the attempt to kill Voice of America Albanian Service Director Eliz Biberaj and his wife in the fall of 1991 when they visited the country.)

This political environment and an extremely desperate economic condition will be strong incentives for anyone who can leave to try to do so. Food riots in late February 1992 augur poorly for a stable period during which an Albanian democracy might develop. Egregious suffering, for which anyone in authority will be blamed, is unlikely to be assuaged by elections or new laws that protect personal or political rights.[15]

States neighboring Albania—especially Greece and Italy—are not sanguine about such a prospect. Greek concerns are heightened by the long-standing claim that much of today's Albanian state lies within North Epirus and is, with its large ethnic Greek minority, part of historical Greece. Not infrequent border incidents, with people trying to flee Albania being detained, injured, or killed by Albanian guards, have added to the tension.

Italy has already had to confront the "boat people" of Albania, who crossed the Adriatic in anything that would float. The exodus in the summer of 1991, reaching a level of perhaps 20,000 people, led to exceedingly difficult circumstances for the Albanian refugees and to diplomatic and political embarrassments for the Italian government.[16] The Italian government reacted to protect its fragile political coalition, throwing a cordon of *carabinieri* and military police around the ports of Bari and Ascona, where most Albanians landed, and holding the Albanians until arrangements could be made for their return. Although there were exceptions, most Albanians were transported back to Tirana. The Alia government's acceptance of these repatriated Albanians, however, was smoothed by an Italian agreement to provide food, medicines, and other essentials—and a small contingent (800) of Italian military personnel to guard and distribute these items *inside* Albania.[17]

But a return to dependency—particularly a renewed dependence on Italy—is no solution. If each country in the Balkans was allotted, by default if not by design, to a particular major power as primarily its concern, the prospects for anything approaching free market democracy in the region would still be gloomy. Italy, for example, will secure itself *from* Albanian threats—principally, from uncontrolled migration. Yet Italy's security will not enhance Albania's capacities to meet threats—from domestic upheaval owing to popular desperation or from Serbia. And unless a country is secure, the chance to nurture democracy will be minimal indeed.

Bulgaria. From Sofia, the post-cold war security horizon that has dawned is discomfiting. Bulgaria, instead of gaining clear and prompt assurances from the West about its role in democratic Europe, has been slow to appear on the screens of Western political radar. When U.S. Deputy Secretary of State Lawrence Eagleburger finally addressed Bulgarian concerns in early March 1992, on the eve of Prime Minister Philip Dimitrov's first visit to Washington, D.C., he characterized Bulgaria as Europe's "best kept secret"—a newfound discovery of democratic progress, apparently, for U.S. policymakers.[18]

Bulgaria must grapple with a new regional disorder that has visceral effects on its well-being. The realities of Yugoslav civil war, Soviet dismemberment, and a cascade of NATO weapons from central Europe to flanks (particularly to Turkey) have been among the principal events creating knots in the stomachs of Sofia's new policy planners.[19]

External threats are not imminent but have enormous potential. Turkey has been an adversary for centuries. Although there is now no expectation of an armed conflict, and assiduous efforts have been made to develop bilateral confidence and security-building measures, Bulgarian military officials still compare their force structure and weapons with those of Turkish armed forces. Most often these comparisons are subtle—referring, for example, to "military imbalances remaining from the time of bloc confrontation."[20] Such comparisons have become more vociferous as excess weapons, including Abrams M1 tanks, have been provided to the Turks by the United States and other NATO allies. Considerable Bulgarian effort has been directed at achieving a reduction of Turkish troop and equipment strength in Eastern Thrace (European Turkey, bordering Bulgaria), where the Turkish First Army is deployed.[21]

With more than 10 percent of Bulgaria's population being of Turkish background, the Islamic faith, or both, there is an omnipresent feeling of sociocultural division. Ethnic Bulgarians regard such a Turkish diaspora as dangerous, and strong resentment is stirred when egalitarian policies are pursued by the government, regardless of that government's political identity. Perhaps a half million Gypsies also live in Bulgaria, although their political position is far weaker.[22] Todor Zhivkov, in his waning years as a communist dictator, pulled out the "Turkish card" and sought to clothe himself and the Bulgarian Communist party in the mantle of Bulgarian nationalism. A 1984-89 campaign to assimilate forcibly Turks and Pomaks (Bulgarian Muslims) included an insistence that these people adopt Bulgarian surnames, a prohibition on Turkish-language broadcasts and classroom instruction, and constraints on Islamic religious observance.

Serbia and its national communist leader, Slobodan Milosevic, have become threatening because of Belgrade's role in regenerating Macedonia as a regional issue. Bulgarians see Macedonia as generically Bulgarian, and they suspect strongly that Serbs have again been trying since the late 1980s to foment the claims of Macedonians to part of Bulgaria—a claim vehemently rejected by Sofia. The "Ilinden" Macedonian nationalist organization in Bulgaria is proof enough of such covert Serbian involvement, according to many in Sofia. Ilinden's goal is to strip away "Pirin Macedonia" from Bulgaria and to incorporate that territory into an independent Macedonia. That Bulgaria recognized an independent Macedonia in January 1992 over strenuous Greek opposition is understandable from one respect; an independent Macedonia is far preferable to Sofia than having that territory remain within a rump, Serbian-dominated federation. With an independent Macedonia, notwithstanding severe limitations on Skopje's ability to act autonomously, Bulgaria can do more to counter Serbian efforts to dominate this core of the Balkans.

A border that had been deceptively quiet to the north has now become far more tense. Bulgarian concerns about air pollution emanating from Romania were raised, and even for a time encouraged by the Zhivkov regime, in the 1980s.[23] The Bulgarian Danube city of Ruse had (and still has) exceptionally foul-smelling air. That the pollutants seemed to be carried across the Danube from Giurgiu, Romania, made the matter more unpleasant. After governments changed in 1989, this issue expanded rather than contracted. Bulgarians continued to charge the Romanian side with willful pollution that endangered lives, to which the Romanians responded with charges of their own about Bulgarian nuclear power-plant safety violations, especially regarding the Kozlodoy plant, which provides more than a third of all Bulgarian electrical-generating capacity.

None of this may be the "real" issue at hand, however. In environmental concerns such as these there *are* serious and potentially deadly violations occurring.[24] Yet, both countries have economic and territorial issues in mind—most notably, Dobrudja, which changed hands several times between the late nineteenth and mid-twentieth century—for which the environmental disputes may be a stalking-horse.[25]

Bulgarians and Russians have residual affinity derived from tsarist support against Ottoman Turks. No communist regime was closer to Moscow over the decades after World War II than that of Todor Zhivkov. To see the Soviet ruin today is discomfiting even to the most ardent anticommunist Bulgarians because Russians, and the USSR, had been an immense economic partner. Because of the USSR's dominant role in Eastern Europe, 80 percent of Bulgarian trade in the mid-1980s was within the Council for Mutual Economic Assistance.[26] This interweaving of the Bulgarian economy was so thorough that as the Soviet market collapsed, the Bulgarian economy suffered (proportionately) the largest contraction in Eastern Europe.

Further, Bulgarians have long looked to Moscow for security guarantees vis-à-vis external threats (against Serbia and Turkey, for example). In the 1990s, suddenly released from the Soviet grip, Bulgarians found that there was nothing on which to lean. Bulgaria's scramble to develop close associations with NATO, the United States, France, and other countries outside the Balkans is no surprise.[27] The blatant appeals of some groups in Sofia for Western attention, however, will not elicit guarantees from Brussels or Washington.[28]

Yet the Bulgarian president, Zhelyu Zhelev (reelected rather narrowly in early 1992), and other new noncommunist leaders seem convinced that external threats may be secondary to their country's greatest danger, Bulgaria's own nationalism. In this author's interviews with principal Bulgarian policymakers in late 1991, there was no doubt that external perils were dangerous primarily because extremist forces could use them to enhance their own appeal within Bulgaria. In addition, and somewhat ironically, the former Communists (now members of the Bulgarian Socialist party or BSP) have become a principal source of nationalist rhetoric. In both the parliamentary elections of October 1991 and the

February 1992 presidential vote, BSP candidates stressed the threats to Bulgaria from external and internal enemies.

The Bulgarian army's history raises the question of its nationalist and authoritarian potential. For now, younger officers and the Union of Democratic Forces (UDF) are making progress in depoliticizing the military, although the BSP continues to criticize reforms as weakening the country's defense capacity.[29] To ensure its orientation toward a democratic polity, however, will take both the retirement or isolation of Communists *and* careful monitoring for any signs of extreme right-wing cells. A critical step toward ridding the army of communist-era leadership was taken in the summer of 1991 when a wholesale turnover of the general staff was instituted on the orders of President Zhelev, with a dozen officers brought in from lower ranks. The chief of the general staff, General Minchev, was among those who departed. When the UDF government of Philip Dimitrov was elected in October 1991, changes in the Ministry of Defense were accelerated; the first civilian defense minister, Dimitur Ludzhev, was named (as General Mutafchiev was moved to the post of chief inspector of the armed forces), and numerous posts were eliminated within the ministry to enable Ludzhev to clean house.

In Bulgarian society generally, fertile ground may develop for chauvinistic appeals as the pain of marketization intensifies. To the public squalor of Bulgaria's communist era is now added burdensome debt payments, high inflation, severe recession, and mounting unemployment (which reached more than 10 percent by December 1991).[30] Politicians' diverting attention by highlighting external threat is a tactic with a perilous logic, given that once nationalism is encouraged, there are few means by which to control it.

Such linkages endanger more than Bulgaria and southeastern Europe. If small, weak countries such as Bulgaria cannot be secured sufficiently in the new Europe, the old rhetoric and behavior of Balkan nationalism may be expected to gain ascendancy.

Romania. Romanian insecurity originates within the country. Yet Romania's external environment makes any resolution of domestic turmoil far less likely.

Although international sympathy for Romania was considerable in the weeks immediately following the December 1989 fighting that overthrew the Ceausescu tyranny, the country's image was tarnished badly during the first half of 1990. The National Salvation Front (FSN) government was accused by urban intellectuals and students of stealing the revolution and of being run by crypto-Communists. Then, a mid-March 1990 confrontation between Hungarians and Romanians in Tirgu-Mures left several dead, and the videotape of such fighting implied a rapid deterioration of public order. The first postcommunist election in May 1990 saw an overwhelming FSN victory that, notwithstanding a fair vote, was clouded by incidents of intimidation and media manipulation during the campaign. Then, in mid-June 1990, the government of President Ion Iliescu made matters worse by ordering the forcible eviction of demonstrators who had occupied a central Bucharest square for two months. A violent reaction to such police action led the Iliescu government to appeal for support from loyal elements of organized labor. Coal miners from the Jiu Valley responded with wanton abandon, beating demonstrators and ransacking opposition offices.

Taken together, these episodes (plus such images as infants infected with AIDS, and towns suffocating on air pollutants) spawned a decidedly negative reaction in the West to Romania's plight. Whether or not the West ought to have taken punitive action may be debated.[31] The ostracism of Romania in 1990-91, however, was clear; Romania, alone among postcommunist Eastern Europe, was considered unworthy of U.S. and (for the most part) Western largess.

With the door to Western attention barely ajar until the end of 1991, conditions that contribute to Romania's insecurity remained largely unattended. First, heterogeneity in the Balkans heightens insecurity. When one adds the Hungarians (roughly 2 million), Gypsies (conservatively figured to number another 2 million), and other, smaller minority groups within Romania, at least 17-18 percent of the population is non-Romanian. Because ethnic Hungarians are the biggest component of a diaspora to which Hungary's current government makes frequent reference, and since the Gypsy population may be increasing at more than 3 percent annually, the minority issue is highly volatile.

A sense of peril and the potential for unrest, however, do not arise merely from the numerical strength of minorities. Instead, Romanians and any government in Bucharest recognize clearly the appeal of the Hungarian state to ethnic kin inside the Romanian state. This attraction is particularly strong insofar as Hungary offers more economic, cultural, or educational opportunities. Romanians suspect, not without historical cause, that such appeal will detract from Bucharest's control over Transylvania. Budapest's efforts to strengthen its cultural or economic presence within Transylvania are, thus, resisted by Romanian governments, regardless of their place on the ideological spectrum.

These threatening inferences have been made more troublesome by the creation of rabid anti-Hungarian, anti-Semitic political organizations, such as *Vatra Romaneasca*.[32] The ethnic hatred fanned by *Vatra* is opposed by most Romanians and by responsible elements of the political spectrum.[33] Yet the growth of *Vatra*, and its apparent organizational efforts within the Romanian army and other institutions, could have destabilizing effects, even if most citizens reject the idea of voting for such a position.[34]

Disastrous economic conditions, not ethno-nationalism, are at the core of Romania's domestic insecurity. Extremism and the appeal of holding out scapegoats would be negligible if the well-being of many Romanians was not being threatened by impoverishment and malnutrition.

Ceausescu's policies left the country with no "cushion" in its living standard; his forcible austerity squeezed from the population the money to repay his own regime's foreign loans, leaving no hidden savings, and no family treasures, to sell.[35] Efforts to convert Romania's highly Stalinist economy of 1989 into a free market have been arduous and destabilizing. Huge cost of living increases, as price controls were ended, were registered from late 1990 through late 1991. Opening the country to imports, while exports dropped precipitously, quickly created massive balance of payments deficits. And as privatization was begun, unprofitable enterprises began to close. All of this led to strikes, an erosion of the National Salvation Front's support (especially in cities) and a rise of "economic fear."[36]

Unease within Romania about the residual presence of Ceausescu's *Securitate*, inside and outside the new Romanian Intelligence Service (SRI), and the dubious loyalty of the army to democratic ideals both fuel domestic insecurity.[37] These institutional uncertainties, however, might be handled by a government that had the unquestioned legitimacy of economic performance, Western support, and an untarnished electoral victory. Romania is unlikely in the near future to achieve all these desiderata at once.

Externally, Romania must deal with strained relations with Hungary, violence in Moldova that endangers the ethnic Romanian majority of that newly independent country, tension with Bulgaria, and concerns about the emergence of a Greater Serbia. The Transylvanian issue, as noted earlier, seems intractable. From the standpoint of the government in Bucharest, almost regardless of its political orientation, statements by Prime Minister Jozsef Antall of Hungary (that he was to be prime minister of all fifteen million Hungarians, that is, a number including the entire diaspora) and by Defense Minister Lajos Fur (regarding Budapest's responsibility to defend Hungarians elsewhere) are bound to be interpreted in a threatening manner. Although the militaries of Romania and Hungary seem to have every intention of avoiding any mistake that could lead to conflict, politicians have been less cautious. The early 1991 "open skies" accord between the two countries was important for its symbolism, not its military significance. Because it allows only four overflights per year, without any surprise inspection option, there are unlikely to be any militarily interesting observations. Yet, transparency is served by such gestures.

Meanwhile, politicians who began to meet on the issue of a basic Romanian-Hungarian treaty—long sought by Budapest—quickly encountered a sizable roadblock in their first series of meetings in early 1992. Romania wants an unequivocal written statement in the treaty by which Hungary renounces any territorial claim in Transylvania—a demand that Hungary rejects as being unnecessarily provocative, given that both countries have already signed the Helsinki Final Act and the Paris charter. Romania's position is adamant; if Budapest really has no claims, let it put this guarantee in writing.[38] Hungary's pages of detailed minority rights demands are, in turn, rejected by Romania as being intrusive—constituting an infringement on sovereignty.[39] The negotiations, although scheduled to continue, will be arduous.

Sustained fighting between Moldovan police and irregulars of the breakaway "Dniester Republic" (where the majority are Russian and Ukrainian) began in March 1992 and elicited calls from Romanian political parties of the center and Right for a more forceful Romanian role.[40] During the late spring or early summer 1992 national elections, the fate of Moldovan kin is certain to be among the principal issues around which the nationalist "credentials" of parliamentary and presidential contenders are tested.

Romanian-Bulgarian acrimony is often couched in the language of ecological concerns but, in fact, has lasting roots in the irredentist issue of Dobrudja.[41] Both sides began, in 1991, to raise the territorial issue defensively, accusing the other of bringing it up first. This jockeying for a position concerning what may become a tendentious issue for the latter 1990s is not surprising, but adds to a Romanian calculus of external threat. In none of these cases are there imminent military threats. Rather, each represents a further strain on a country that has ample internal insecurities and significant constraints on its ability to respond to threats. Romania has not cut the size of its military to the same degree as Czechoslovakia or Hungary, retaining an active-duty force of 170,000. The low degree of effectiveness of Romania's army, however, cannot be overestimated; high-ranking military officials themselves admit to doubtful combat readiness of troops and equipment.[42]

But Romania's principal route to security will have little to do with its armed forces—a fact recognized by the National Salvation Front's leadership in 1990-91. Regional and multilateral security ties—with the European Community (EC), a Danubian basin cooperative group, the Black Sea Economic Cooperation zone, and other endeavors—form a vision of interlocking "harmonious relationships amidst the new all-European architecture and its sub-regional components" sought by the FSN government.[43] Romania's future governments will have little choice but to continue this multifaceted approach to their country's security.

Yugoslavia. Yugoslavia died violently in 1991. Ten thousand martyrs, and monuments such as the rubble of Vukovar, will remind future generations of Serb and Croat enmity that erupted into a kind of bilateral suicide. After Marshal Tito's death in 1980, and the end of a Soviet threat, no "Yugoslav" institutions were sufficient to hold the disparate state together. A Communist party discredited long ago by its corruption and an army that was primarily an instrument of its Serbian-dominated officer corps were inadequate centripetal forces in the face of historical and cultural distinctions, ethno-nationalism, and socioeconomic inequalities.

Against the clear potential that "progressive internal disintegration" would be manipulated by external forces,[44] Tito had pursued greater stability in the region while he cast a much wider net for Yugoslav security. The Non-Aligned movement was that broader framework, in which Marshal Tito, Jawahralal Nehru, and Gamal Abdel Nasser played the formative roles at the 1961 Belgrade conference. Nonalignment, as opposed to neutrality, enhanced Yugoslav visibility and brought an element of respect and assistance that Belgrade might not have otherwise obtained. By the mid-1970s, the Non-Aligned movement began to splinter, with more radical Third World voices pushing the "message" toward North-South divisions rather than the dangers of superpower-led military alliances.[45]

In the aftermath of warfare during 1991, however, no remnant of the old Yugoslav federation will play a significant international role. Obtaining security for a rump Yugoslavia, consisting of Serbia and Montenegro, or for independent states of Bosnia-Hercogovina, Croatia, Macedonia, or Slovenia will bear little resemblance to Tito's security policies. None of these smaller entities, notwithstanding the higher living standards of Slovenia or the larger population of Serbia, have the capacity to act outside the confines of contiguous areas.

Unquestionably, however, the territory and peoples that constituted Yugoslavia now require new sources of security and will be perceived by those around them as a source of regional insecurity for years to come. A 24 February 1992 meeting between Bulgarian Foreign Minister Stoyan Ganev and Romanian president Ion Iliescu, for example, focused on (in addition to bilateral relations) the need for both of their countries to avoid any action that would unsettle the delicate movement toward a UN peacekeeping force to end Serb-Croat fighting. Specifically, there was agreement that Bucharest and Sofia would renounce any territorial claims and consider a regional collective security enterprise for guaranteeing borders.[46]

Slovenia, having expelled the federal (that is, Serbian) army in the early summer of 1991, is not under an imminent military threat. The strong support of Germany for Slovene and Croat independence resulted in EC (and, by spring 1992, U.S.) recognition. High-visibility trips by figures such as Hans Dietrich Genscher to Slovenia and Croatia in February, 1992, in which he called for immediate UN and CSCE membership for both states, underscore a commitment to Ljubljana's security.[47]

But the Christian democratic government of Prime Minister Lojze Peterle is highly insecure, and in February 1992 it was confronted with a parliamentary test of no confidence demanded by independent and Democratic party deputies, which it survived by a slim margin. Unrest owing to a steep economic decline in a country accustomed to high living standards is very possible, as few of the immediate benefits of independence have become apparent.

For Croatia, the warfare against Serbs in Krajina and Slavonia, supported by the Serbian-led federal army, carried an extremely high cost. The vast majority of an estimated 10,000 deaths from July 1991 through the end of January 1992 were Croats. In Vukovar alone, perhaps 2,000 civilians died during the prolonged siege. The Zagreb government of Franjo Tudjman lost control of virtually all of both Krajina and Slavonia and substantial portions of the southern Dalmatian Coast, together amounting to roughly a third of the prewar Croatian territory. The Croatian economy suffered, apart from the physical destruction of towns, roads, bridges, and other infrastructure, an enormous disruption of commerce, which will not easily be resumed.

The deployment of 14,000 United Nations troops in disputed zones of Croatia, authorized by the Security Council on 21 February 1992, ensures that no further territorial losses will take place. Yet the presence of UN troops also risks the de facto separation of these lands from Croatia. Tudjman's vacillation on accepting UN forces reflects a frustration among members of the Croatian military that they were nearing a point when a counteroffensive could have been begun to retake lost territory. At the same time, Tudjman's own leadership had suffered considerably during the fighting, and his vow that "Croatian legal order" would be reestablished, even in areas where Serbs are not disarmed, is a posture that his weak political position seems to demand. It is also, however, a position that directly contradicts the commitment of UN Secretary General Boutros Ghali to deploy forces in Krajina and Slavonia without a return to Croatian administrations.

That the UN action will provide no lasting security for Zagreb's control over Croatian territory as defined before the war—even if all Serb military units are withdrawn—is understood by Croats and outside observers. Enlarging Croatian military capacities is being undertaken;[48] but this, too, would assume that the military balance would change sufficiently to enable a decisive Croat counteroffensive. Much more likely is that a Croatian buildup would engender a Serbian preemptive attack, particularly given the desire to avoid a repetition of Serbian tactical errors experienced during 1991 fighting.[49]

For the Serbs, a respite from fighting in Croatia will not produce assured peace and well-being. Serbs in Bosnia-Herzegovina may be involved in the next Yugoslav battleground if Croats and Muslims in that republic try to implement fully a late February 1992 referendum for independence. Within Serbia, the Albanian population concentrated in Kosovo has been denied any autonomy owing to constitutional changes imposed by Slobodan Milosevic's nationalist government in Belgrade. The chance that this conflict, too, may surge back toward significant violence is always on the minds of Serbian leaders.

Recognizing that future confrontations are more likely than not, Milosevic has sought to ensure "normal" relations with other neighbors. His 21 February 1992 visit to Bucharest, for example, was a clear attempt to obtain commitments from the Romanians that they would continue their policy of uninterrupted commercial relations, which allow a supply of oil and other commodities critical to Serbia's economic survival. On the heels of EC action, Romania had also recognized Slovenia, Croatia, and Milosevic's trip was an attempt—largely successful—to maintain access to critical supplies via Romania.[50]

Bosnia-Herzegovina rests dangerously on the precipice of internecine warfare with potentially tragic consequences. At issue in this complex republic is the challenge by two of its three principal ethno-religious groupings—the Croats and Muslims—to join Slovenia and Croatia in the march toward independence. The republic's Serbs, about 31 percent of the 4.3 million inhabitants, resist such a notion, and they boycotted the referendum. They appear to be willing to use violence to oppose the republic's departure from Yugoslavia, and armed Serbs threw up roadblocks around Sarajevo on 1-2 March in a temporary blockcade of the city. Two days of violence left several people dead. Sufficient weapons and armed groups exist throughout the republic to engage in fierce combat; the army has many important bases, weapons depots, and military-industrial sites to defend; and Croat paramilitary units have proliferated in the first months of 1992.

Macedonia's independence is further along but challenged from within by Albanians (about a third of the republic's population) and from outside by the displeasure of Greece to find the name "Macedonia" associated with a state to be governed from Skopje. Bulgarian recognition of a Macedonian state, which caused considerable upset in Athens, was, as mentioned earlier, undertaken primarily because Sofia considers an independent Macedonia is preferable to a manipulated republic under the control of Serbia. As a state that no one else really wants to see succeed, however, Macedonia will have a rocky future.

In what was Yugoslavia, there is little about which to be sanguine. Peace will be, for now, merely the absence of daily combat in several republics, with a precarious calm in Croatia dependent on the presence of UN troops there. Elsewhere, fear that one or two deaths might precipitate a far wider war may constrain most individuals from acting violently. But such a condition can hardly be equated with security.

Postcommunist Transitions and the Balkan Security Dilemma

Throughout this abbreviated survey, there are several common themes. In a region of very few capacities—political, economic, or military—there is little chance that insecurities can be resolved by a resort to war or confrontation. No state, even if temporarily victorious, will be able to defend and keep the spoils of conflict.

Further, one can see rather clearly that political units within a region troubled by interwoven peoples and borders, poverty, and high population growth rates among some groups will be unable to obtain lasting solutions to their region's security needs. Whenever there is no imposed hegemonic "solution," outside guarantors have always been sought. For the Balkans, these outside guarantors of the past have been European powers—Russia, Germany, the Hapsburg empire, Italy, France, or the United Kingdom. After World War II, Soviet hegemony and U.S. influence, in part exercised through NATO,"secured" Balkan states by imposing an East-West veneer over the region's intrinsic disputes. Regardless of direction, however, the Balkans fell into behavior typical of peripheral systems wherein weakness and dependency reinforce each other.

At the core of these debilitating conditions is the erroneous equating of security with power. This is a region where any attempt to obtain or enlarge military or economic strength will threaten others, requiring protection from elsewhere, the resort to authoritarian solutions domestically, or both. Each of these systems exhibits a high degree of internal insecurity, which heightens greatly the sensitivity to perceptions of external threat. The attempts by any state to enlarge security via enlarged capacities or through the aid of an external benefactor thus initiates a threat cycle—a slippery slope of perceived peril and fearful reaction that resolutely pulls the Balkans back into the cauldron of its past.

Balkan insecurity is deeply rooted in the historical uncertainty of political boundaries, the high degree of heterogeneity within each political unit, underdevelopment relative to the rest of Europe, high population growth rates among some groups, and the absence of stable, legitimate government. In the Balkan environment these conditions have been strongly associated with a high frequency or intensity of intrastate and interstate conflict.

Such threats, in turn, damage the prognosis for plural, open political systems. Democracy is characterized by demagogues of the Right and Left as a frivolous luxury, with free speech and other liberties attacked. Where democracy cannot be nurtured during a prolonged infancy, its survival is doubtful. The advantage of democracy for Balkan security is clear insofar as democracies are unlikely to initiate war on their neighbors. Unfortunately, the high level of insecurity within the Balkans makes the achievement of stable democracies far more difficult. A vicious circle of authoritarianism and insecurity cannot be broken solely from within the Balkans.

Moreover, conditions that foster insecurity are not amenable to within-region control. These states, regardless of political leadership, cannot adjust borders, move people or monitor the well-being of all minorities, finance developmental programs, and so on. Outside frameworks and processes are essential foundations for Balkan security.

As things now stand, those frameworks and processes are absent. UN peacekeeping forces were deployed in Croatia *after* thousands had died, while Lord Carrington seeks a political settlement on behalf of the European Community. One should not expect, however, the UN-EC combination to end other conflicts that could arise throughout Southeastern Europe, or that Yugoslav wars will remain permanently in remission.

The Balkans require ways in which to *avert* war and costly confrontations, not to halt the killing after thousands have died and cities have been destroyed. Additional martyrs and monuments cannot be viewed as an acceptable outcome in a Europe envisioned by the Charter of Paris, signed in November 1990.

An ongoing system of Euro-Atlantic collective security, not a last-ditch peacekeeping effort by the United Nations coupled with desperate political intervention by the European Community, is the Balkans' best hope. Another attempt at a Balkan Union or merely a number of bilateral arrangements will never suffice. A holistic approach to Euro-Atlantic security, adopted in the Helsinki Final Act and refined by the Charter of Paris, underscores that the inviolability of borders, rights of minorities, transparency of military activities, and other principles are the business of everyone. Unless these principles are enforced externally by an entity far better endowed than the Balkan states can ever be, the region will be unable to avoid calamity.

Notes

1. Daniel N. Nelson, *Balkan Imbroglio* (Boulder, Colo: Westview Press, 1991), 29.

2. The degree to which this effort has been successful is debatable. For a critique, see Daniel N. Nelson, "NATO—Means But No Ends," *Bulletin of the Atomic Scientists* 48, 1 (January-February 1992).

3. A Romanian view of the Transylvanian issue—with a strong emphasis, of course, on both the territory's integral link with the rest of the contemporary Romanian state and the specious nature of Hungarian claims—is Miron Constantinescu et al. eds., *Unification of the Romanian National State: The Union of Transylvania with Old Romania* (Bucharest: Academy of the Socialist Republic of Romania, 1971).

4. Among the best histories of the region is a two-volume work, Barbara Jelavich *History of the Balkans* (New York: Cambridge University Press, 1983).

5. The pronounced role of the Austro-Hungarian Empire in bringing industrialization to Bosnia, for example, which was in Vienna's control only after 1878, is discussed in Peter Sugar *Industrialization of Bosnia-Hercegovina, 1878-1918* (Seattle: University of Washington Press, 1963).

6. Although the region's heterogeneity cannot be detailed in this brief discussion, one can consult geographies of Eastern Europe, such as Roy E. H. Mellor *Eastern Europe* (New York: Columbia University Press, 1975), for greater specificity.

7. Albania's rate of population increase exceeds 3 percent per year; Turkey has averaged 2.4 percent over the 1980s. The Albanian population

in Yugoslavia has increased at a rate of close to 3.4 percent per year. The basis for such statistics can be found in a data source such as the Central Intelligence Agency *Handbook of Economic Statistics* (annual) (Washington, D.C.: CIA, Directorate for Intelligence).

8. Jelavich, *History of the Balkans,* vol. 2, 3.

9. *Ibid.,* 273-75, discusses Yugoslav control over the Albanian Communists, especially in 1943-48.

10. A comment about Soviet naval installations in particular, the submarine base at Valonais in Michael McGwire *Soviet Naval Developments* (New York: Praeger, 1975), 345.

11. The 1950s and events leading to the break with Moscow are detailed in William E. Griffith, *Albania and the Sino-Soviet Rift* (Cambridge: MIT Press, 1963).

12. The Chinese-Albanian relationship and the rupture in 1978 are considered fully in Berhard Tonnes, *Sonderfall Albanien* (Munchen: F. Oldenburg, 1980).

13. For a view of Albania's post-Hoxha reemergence, see Louis Zanga, "Reform Albanian Style," in *Soviet-East European Survey,* 1986-87, ed., Vojtech Mastny (Boulder, Colo: Westview Press, 1988), 297. See also Alez Biberaj, "Albania After Hoxha: Dilemmas of Change," *Problems of Communism* 34 (November-December, 1985), 41-46, especially.

14. See the Pashko accusation in a Radio Tirana broadcast of 5 December 1991, as reprinted in Foreign Broadcast Information Service, *Daily Report: East Europe* 91-235, 6 December 1991, 3-4.

15. A report on these events of early 1992 is given by Louis Zanga, "Albania Reduced to Total Dependence on Foreign Food Aid," RFE/RL Research Report, no. 8, 21 February 1992, 46-48.

16. See, for example, Haig Simonian, "Italy Acts to Repel Influx of Albanians," *Financial Times* 9 August 1991, and "Italy Begins Sending Albanians Home," *Financial Times,* 10 August 1991.

17. See the report on the Italian army deployment in Albania in *Corriere della Sera, '1* January 1992.

18. Eagleburger's speech, given in Washington, D.C. on 4 March 1992, was reported in Sofia on 5 March in the daily *Demokratsia.*

19. Ministry of Foreign Affairs and political party officials, (of both the Bulgarian Socialist Party and the Union of Democratic Forces), interviews with author, Sofia, Bulgaria, September and December 1991.

Concern about Bulgarian insecurity due to these and other matters weighed very heavily in most of the following discussions.

20. President Zhelyu Zhelev, Address to an international conference on "The Army in Democratic Society," in *Bulgarska Armiya,* 18 November 1991, 1.

21. The first deputy chief of the Bulgarian General Staff, for example, went to Turkey in November 1991 for the specific purpose of discussing such a drawdown of Turkish forces. See reports on this visit in *Bulgarska Armiya,* such as the interview with General Stoyan Topalov on 20 November 1991, 1 and 4. The Ministry of Defense spokesman comments with some frequency about the disposition of Turkish forces. For example, see the text of a news conference by Major General Stoimen Stoimenov on 28 November 1991, as reported by Bulgarian Telegraph Agency, and reprinted in Foreign Broadcast Information Service, *Daily Report: East Europe* 91-231 2 December 1991, 6-7.

22. See Luan Troxel, "Bulgaria's Gypsies: Numerically Strong, Politically Weak," RFE/RL Research Report, vol. 1, no. 6 March 1991, 58-61.

23. For a discussion of the Bulgarian ecological protests in the late 1980s, and related examples elsewhere in Eastern Europe, see Daniel N. Nelson, "The Rise of Public Legitimation in the Soviet Union and Eastern Europe" in *Adaptations and Change in Eastern Europe,* S. Ramet (Boulder, Colo.: Westview Press, 1992).

24. Bulgarians report fully on these dangers. See, for example, "Kozlodoui Nuclear Plant: Few Pros, Many Cons," *The Bulgarian Watcher,* 30 January-5 February 1992, 22.

25. This, at least, was the opinion of Romanian foreign minister Adrian Nastase concerning Bulgarian environmental complaints. (Foreign Minister Adrian Nastase, interview with author, Bucharest, Romania, November 1991). Stefan Tavrov, in an interview two months before he was named Bulgaria's deputy foreign minister, offered a parallel assessment of Romania's motives.

26. In 1987, for example, about only $2.8 billion of Bulgaria's almost $17 billion in exports went to non-CMEA states, while a little more than $3 billion of over $17 billion in imports came from non-CMEA sources. Central Intelligence Agency, *Handbook of Economic Statistics,* 1988 (Washington, D.C.: CIA Directorate for Intelligence, 1988), 168 and 169.

27. An example of this Bulgarian full-court press for security guarantees was President Zhelev's trip to France in February 1992, during which the president was accompanied by Foreign Minister Ganev. The Bulgarians signed a treaty of friendship and cooperation that included provisions for security cooperation and full French endorsement of Bulgaria's integration with the European Community.

28. An "Atlantic Club" with NATO membership as its goal was created in early 1991 in Sofia with the blessing of the UDF. NATO Secretary General Woerner has visited Sofia, and numerous NATO delegations have been in the country. Membership, however, remains distant.

29. A representative view was expressed by Vasil Popov in *Duma,* 25 November 1991, 4.

30. The litany of Bulgaria's economic problems is often recited. One succinct statement was "Sofia Brauchte Hilfen," *Die Presse,* 17 December 1991, 11, which cited Bulgarian National Bank president Todor Vulchev.

31. Daniel N. Nelson, "Romania Needs Help Not Sanctions," *New York Times* 19 June 1990.

32. *Vatra's* origins and tactics are discussed thoroughly by Dennis Deletant in "Convergence Versus Divergence in Romania: The Role of the *Vatra Romaneasca* Movement in Transylvania," Paper presented at the Society for Southeast European Studies, Seventy-Fifth Anniversary Conference, 8-14 December 1990.

33. See the declaration of the Democratic Anti-Totalitarian Forum, in *Romania Libera* 2 July 1991, 2; also, the Ministry of Culture's condemnation of *Vatra's* publications such as *Romania Mare,* in *Romania Libera,* 24 July 1991, 1.

34. Concerning *Vatra* within the military, see the report by Constantin Vranceanu in *Romania Libera,* 6-7 July 1991, 3.

35. A compelling description of Romania's economic condition in 1990-91 is given by the governor of the National Bank of Romania, in Mugur "Romania's Economic Reform," in *Romania After Tyranny,* ed. Daniel N. Nelson, (Boulder, Colo.: Westview Press, 1992).

36. For discussion of this "interface" between politics and economic change in Romania, see Daniel N. Nelson, in "Romanian Security," *Mediterranean Quarterly* 3, no. 1 (1992). In the local elections of 9 February 1992 the FSN gained a plurality but lost about half of the voter support that it had garnered in the national elections of May 1990. That

this was a local election, of course, makes extrapolation to a national vote quite tenuous.

37. The SRI has tried to create a more benign aura surrounding its activities. See, for instance, the wide-ranging interview of Mihai Stan, the principal deputy director of SRI, in *Tineretul Liber,* 8 and 9 February 1991. Regarding the army's place in post-communist Romania, the best examination is given in Larry Watts, "The Romanian Army After December, 1989," *Romania After Tyranny.*

38. President Ion Iliescu interview with author, Bucharest, Romania, September 1991; Foreign Minister Adrian Nastase, interview with author, Bucharest and Washington, D.C., March 1992; and Ioan Mircea Pascu (Iliescu's foreign policy adviser), interview with author, Washington, D.C., March 1992.

39. Foreign minister Geza Jeszenszky and state secretary Geza Entz, conversations with author, Budapest and Washington, D.C., February and March 1992.

40. See, for example, a discussion of such vocal proponents of greater Romanian commitment to help Moldova in *Tineretul Liber*, 7-8 March 1992.

41. The Bulgarian view of this matter was expressed recently in *The Bulgaria Watcher*, 5 February 1992, 1-2.

42. General Culda and Colonel Vaduva, interviews with author, Bucharest, Romania, September and November 1991. See also Defense Minister Spiroiu's candid admission that equipment and standards for conscripts require urgent attention in an interview by Octavian Andronic in *Libertatea,* 4-5 July 1991, 1-2.

43. Ion Iliescu conveyed this image when he spoke to a seminar on "Perceptions and Concepts of Security in Eastern Europe" in Bucharest on 4 July 1991.

44. James F. Brown, *Eastern Europe and Communist Rule* (Durham: Duke University Press, 1988), 363.

45. Concerning Tito's strategy of nonalignment, see Alvin Z. Rubinstein, *Yugoslavia and the Nonaligned World* (Princeton: Princeton University Press, 1970). Concerning the metamorphosis of the movement into a more radical forum, see Richard L. Jackson, *The Non-Aligned, the U.N., and the Superpowers* (New York: Praeger, 1983), 24-36.

46. Ioan Mircea Pascu, interview with author, Washington, D.C.,

March 1992.

47. Genscher's trip was reported most fully in the *Frankfurter Allgemeine Zeitung,* 24 February 1992.

48. Reports surfaced in February 1992, for example, of Croatian efforts to assemble an air force using former Warsaw Pact MIG-21s and other assorted fixed-wing aircraft and helicopters. See "Croatia to Set Up Air Force," *Jane's Defence Weekly* 29 February 1992, 343.

49. General Veljko Kadijevic, thought to be relatively moderate, and most of the non-Serbs in top military posts (such as Admiral Stane Brovet, a Slovene, and General Zvonko Jurjevic, a Croat), were removed at the end of February. They were blamed for the poor performance of the military and, in all likelihood, suspected as having mixed loyalties that were no longer appropriate for a truly Serbian army.

50. Ioan Mircea Pascu, interview with author, Washington, D.C., March 1992.

5

The Security Policies of the Former Warsaw Pact States: Deconstruction and Reconstruction

Christopher Jones

The cold war began and ended in Eastern Europe. The reconstruction of a new Eurasian security system now awaits the outcome of the ongoing redefinition of military, political, and economic relationships within the zone formerly covered by the Warsaw Pact. The most important and most problematic of these is the Ukrainian-Russian relationship. But one trend of the post-Soviet security order is already clear: a set of nations formerly incorporated within the Soviet empire is seeking full or associate membership in the European Community (EC) and a complementary security relationship with the North Atlantic Treaty Organization (NATO). These states recognize that the prerequisites for membership in the Western community are market economies and democratic political systems. They also see membership in the Western community as a guarantor of their progress toward democratization and marketization.

Hungary, Poland, and the Czech and Slovak Federal Republic were the first to approach the NATO/EC coalition, soon to be followed by Bulgaria. Estonia, Latvia, and Lithuania appear to be following the central European example. The Balts have sought direct ties with both NATO and the EC and have also sought cooperative economic and political relationships with Finland, Sweden and other Nordic states, virtually all of which are moving toward closer economic and even military links with the European Community (which has designated the Western European Union (WEU) as the agency for creating a "European defense identity").

These developments have raised a series of unanswered questions. The first is whether the NATO/EC coalition is able and willing to respond with a common policy toward some or all of the postcommunist states seeking security ties with the West. NATO has invited its former adversaries to join NATO in forming the North Atlantic Cooperation Council (NACC) to manage a post-cold war security system in Europe in conjunction with the Conference on Security and Cooperation in Europe (CSCE) and the WEU. But the prospects for the NACC initiative are still unclear after the first meeting of the NACC in December 1991. NATO appears reluctant to favor one set of postcommunist states over another, mainly out of concern over provoking Russia, still Europe's greatest military power and still the residual focus of NATO's security concerns. But in rejecting the pleas of the central Europeans for an explicit security guarantee, NATO may unintentionally contribute to the failure of the most promising postcommunist experiments in building new democratic states with market economies.

A second question is how many, if any, of the member states of the newly formed Commonwealth of Independent States (CIS) will follow the central European example of seeking institutionalized security and economic ties with NATO and the EC. Ukraine's president has already declared his long-term goal of EC membership.[1] The pursuit of such ties may generate tension with other CIS members. NATO appears to oppose formal security links as jeopardizing NATO's capability to remain an effective alliance for its existing members. But the most crucial question of all is whether political restructuring within the Commonwealth of Independent States will institutionalize the most revolutionary development of the bygone Gorbachev era: the withdrawal of national armed forces from intervention in the regional and domestic politics of the states that used to make up the Soviet empire.

This policy became operational in August 1989 when Mikhail Gorbachev renounced military intervention against the newly-formed Solidarity government in Poland. Within two years, Gorbachev's unprecedented policy on the regional/domestic use of Soviet military forces produced the only enduring results of *perestroika*: the "deconstruction" of the Soviet empire—first in the East European portion of the Warsaw Pact/COMECON (Council for Mutual Economic Assistance) system and then in the Soviet Union itself.

The State Committee for the Emergency Situation, which attempted to mobilize the Soviet military in August 1991 to preempt a new Union treaty, succeeded only in transferring political power to the Union republics, completing the destruction of the Communist party of the Soviet Union, fracturing the Soviet Defense Ministry, and thereby ensuring the final disintegration of the USSR. The central Defense Ministry of the former USSR, revived as the Defense Ministry of the Russian Federation, retained at least nominal control over the nuclear weapons of the CIS, but control of conventional forces was left an open question, as was the possible reentry of military forces into the domestic politics of the former Warsaw Pact zone.

Such intervention, in support of authoritarian nationalist regimes, would likely remilitarize both the foreign and domestic policies in the entire zone between Germany and the Urals. The murderous disintegration of Yugoslavia stands as the worst possible case for the further deconstruction of what Leonid Brezhnev once hailed as "the socialist commonwealth" (*sotsialisticheskoe sodruzhestvo*).

The Four Issues of Reconstruction
in the Post-Warsaw Pact Security System

The emerging security system of the former Warsaw Pact zone is thus being shaped by the unpredictable interaction of four issues: (1) Ukrainian-Russian security relations; (2) control of nuclear weapons of the former Soviet Defense Ministry; (3) the attempt to obtain a special security relationship with the West by the a central European "Triangle" of Hungary, Poland, and the Czech and Slovak Federal Republic and by the adjoining Baltic "Triangle" of Estonia, Latvia, and Lithuania; and (4) NATO's overall response to the breakup of the Warsaw Pact and the USSR.

The first issue is whether the newly established Ukrainian Defense Ministry will preside over the armed forces of a fully-sovereign state or whether it will instead be a component of a confederal defense ministry that will coordinate the defense system of the Russian Federation with that of the other members of the Commonwealth of Independent States. Such a system might act as an effective restraint on Russian military power, just as NATO has acted as an effective restraint on German military potential. Put another way, a confederal CIS army might blunt incipient national militarism the same way the new NATO military structure seeks to preempt nationalist military policies by constructing multinational alliance forces.

Immediately after the formation of the CIS, however, Ukrainian leaders made clear their intention to maintain a Ukrainian military establishment not under the direct command of a CIS defense ministry. At least initially, the issue driving Ukrainian security policy was the role of military power as the symbol and substance of national independence. Ukrainian resistance to Russian-backed proposals for unified CIS military forces recalled the East European joke about the difference between a language and a dialect: unlike a dialect, a language has its own army.

By any standard—population (about 51 million), area, economic power, or military potential—Ukraine, whose parliament declared independence on 24 August 1991, is not merely the second most important republic of the CIS but a potential major power in Europe as well. The resolution of the military, economic, and political relationships between the two giant republics of Ukraine and Russia will in large part determine the nature of regional security relationships both within the CIS and within the entire zone once covered by the Warsaw Pact. This dynamic is a function of Ukraine's size and location. Ukraine shares borders and overlapping ethnic diasporas not only with Russia (with about 10 million ethnic Russians living in Ukraine) and Belarus but also with the central European "Triangle" of Poland,[2] Hungary, and Czechoslovakia (where a significant Slovak independence movement threatens to break up the republic).

Ukraine also borders on Moldova (formerly Moldavia), a state that is already a target of Romanian irredentist policies, which are supported by a pro-Romanian faction within Moldova.[3] Furthermore, Romania has raised claims to areas annexed to Ukraine by Joseph Stalin.[4] Within

Moldova itself, a substantial Russian minority has sought Russian support for a "Dniester Republic." In addition, a Turkish minority has rallied for a "Gagauz Republic."[5]

In the election of early December 1991 Ukrainian citizens voted for full secession from the USSR and also elected Leonid Kravchuk, the former communist leader of Ukraine, to be president of the republic. Kravchuk then allied with Boris Yeltsin, president of the Russian Republic, to demolish the Soviet regime still headed by Gorbachev. The two leaders, joined by Stanislau Shuskevich, chairman of the Supreme Soviet of Belarus, formed the Commonwealth of Independent States on 8 December, effectively destroying the USSR. On 21 December eight other republics—Armenia, Azerbaijan, Kazakhstan, Kyrgyzstan, Moldova, Tajikistan, Turkmenistan, and Uzbekistan—finalized the abolition of the Soviet Union by joining the CIS as cofounders.

The 21 December meeting named Marshal Evegenii Shaposhnikov, defense minister of the former USSR, as interim commander of the armed forces of the CIS states. Georgia, convulsed by civil turmoil, remained outside the CIS. Estonia, Latvia, and Lithuania welcomed the end of the USSR and the formation of the CIS but also reaffirmed their desire to orient themselves as much as possible toward their northern and western neighbors. On 31 December the CIS leaders met in Minsk, the capital of the commonwealth, and agreed to disagree over the future of the disposition of the armed forces of the former Soviet military. They did create a Council of Defense Ministers and did acknowledge President Yeltsin's central control over strategic nuclear weapons but could not agree on the division of authority between national capitals and the CIS commander-in-chief, Marshal Shaposhnikov.

The Emergence of the Ukrainian Military

The harbingers of a Ukrainian army were proposals for a national army by *Rukh*, the leading Ukrainian nationalist organization before the August coup attempt. The Ukrainian army also has its origins in a "Union of Officers of the Ukraine," whose first "congress" on 28 July 1991 had 6 delegates. The second congress, 2-3 November consisted of 700 delegates, who claimed to represent more than 10,000 members.[6] By November 1991 the Ukrainian declaration of independence of 24 August had completely transformed the hypothetical debate about a Ukrainian army, making the military relationship with Moscow the most critical security issue of the postcoup era.

After the coup attempt, Kravchuk, a Communist serving as chairman of the Ukrainian Supreme Soviet, moved quickly to associate himself with the cause of full Ukrainian independence. On 27 August he announced his intention to appoint a Ukrainian minister of defense and then move to transfer authority over all military forces on Ukrainian soil from Moscow to Kiev, with the eventual creation of a separate Ukrainian armed forces.[7] At this conference he also expressed his concern about Yeltsin's postcoup statement that if a republic such as Ukraine left the Union, it would have to renegotiate its borders with the Russian Republic.[8]

On 30 August Kravchuk met with the commanders of the three Soviet military districts in Ukraine and the commander of the Soviet Black Sea Fleet, along with officials of the Soviet interior ministry and border troops, to discuss jurisdictional relations between Kiev and Moscow in regard to the uniformed personnel on Ukrainian territory.[9] On 4 September the Ukrainian Supreme Soviet appointed a defense minister, Konstantin Morozov, a forty-seven-year-old commander of the Soviet air army stationed in Ukraine. Service members and sometimes whole units responded by seeking to place themselves under the authority of the Ukrainian parliament and its new defense minister.[10]

Morozov told Soviet army newspaper *Krasnaia zvezda* that he had first been approached by a group from the Ukrainian Supreme Soviet and then had met with Kravchuk before assuming the post of defense minister.[11] Morozov (whose mother was a Ukrainian but whose father was Russian), sought to carve Ukrainian ground, naval, and air units out of the Soviet armed forces stationed in Ukraine. Specifically, Morozov wanted to work out arrangements with the Soviet General Staff in Moscow to abolish the three military districts on Ukrainian soil (Kiev, Odessa, and Sub-Carpathia), to transfer jurisdiction over their facilities, equipment, and troops to Morozov's ministry; to acquire Ukrainian control of the Soviet Black Sea Fleet; and to obtain control of Soviet air assets based in the Ukraine.[12] Morozov also wanted to create a system of higher educational institutions for the training of a Ukrainian officer corps, to include a Ukrainian General Staff Academy.[13]

Vitaly Chechilo, chairman of the military collegium of *Rukh*, specified *Rukh's* agenda for the new Ukrainian military: "[O]ur state will be nuclear-weapons free, will maintain neutrality, and will not join any military structures. The Army will be defensive."[14] Chechilo also stated that with the aid of Ukrainian émigrés, *Rukh* had drawn up proposals for a 350,000-member army and a separate national guard.[15] For *Rukh*, the issue of control over the estimated 200 nuclear weapons on Ukrainian soil was a matter of bargaining for full sovereignty. *Rukh*'s presidential candidate, Vyacheslav Chronovil, declared that he was against the removal of Soviet nuclear weapons from Ukrainian soil until Ukraine had its own army.[16]

Rukh's chairman, Ivan Drach, explained that though *Rukh* renounced nuclear weapons for Ukraine, it would not accept Soviet authority over the nuclear forces in the republic: "The strategic missile command is part of a union we no longer want. As long as we have this so-called joint command, we stay within the borders of the Soviet Union."[17] As if to confirm Drach's argument, on 21 October Gorbachev declared that "privatization" of Soviet military facilities and personnel by the governments of Union republics was "unconstitutional."

In response to the highly nationalist mood of the electoral campaign, legislators of the Ukrainian Supreme Soviet voted on 22 October to establish a 400,000-member Ukrainian military, to include the entire Black Sea Fleet of the Soviet navy, but they left open key policy, organizational, and financial questions.[18] Though economic pressures soon forced Ukrainian leaders to scale back their plans to armed forces of about 200,000, they clung to their demand for transfer of the Black Sea Fleet to their control, plus Soviet air forces based in Ukraine.[19] The parliament also voted to establish a separate Ukrainian border guards service and to devote 2.8 percent of the Ukrainian state budget to the Ukrainian military.[20]

On 24 October the Ukrainian Supreme Soviet also declared that Ukraine would be a non-nuclear-weapons state. The parliament acknowledged that the weapons remained under the control of the central Union Defense Ministry but insisted that Ukraine had control over their non-use. The parliament also called for talks with Belarus, Kazakhstan, and Russia on the complete liquidation of nuclear weapons on Ukrainian territory[21] but left unclear what relationship the new Ukrainian military would have to any central defense ministry.[22]

In early November, the Ukrainian parliament voted to create a 30,000-

member "National Guard," to be drawn from forces currently under the USSR Ministry of the Interior, for border guard and internal security duties.[23] In late November Volodymr Kukharets, commander of the newly established National Guard of the Ukraine, demanded transfer of all Soviet internal security personnel to his organization, which he planned to build to a size of between 30,000 and 50,000.[24]

These actions precipitated increasing confrontation with the Soviet Defense Ministry. On 24 October Lieutenant General Valerii Manilov, chief spokesman for the central Defense Ministry, had declared that the Ukraine had the right to form its own army but not the right to appropriate Soviet nuclear weapons on Ukrainian territory or Soviet bases in Ukraine.[25] However, on 4 November the Soviet navy announced plans to build a new Black Sea naval base in the Karnsodar territory of the Russian Republic, rather than directly contest Ukrainian claims of sovereignty over the present base in Sevastopol.[26]

Soviet Defense Minister Evegenii Shaposhnikov reacted to the decisions of the Ukrainian parliament by declaring that it was illegal under Soviet law for Kiev to assume jurisdiction over Soviet units on Ukrainian territory. He also said he had no intention of withdrawing Soviet forces from the Ukraine. Instead, he emphasized the need for a collective defense concept linking Ukraine and the USSR.[27] He maintained this view after the formation of the CIS.[28]

The issue of the Black Sea Fleet intensified after the formation of the CIS. Boris Yeltsin, the Russian president, responded on 8 January by arguing for the placement of the Black Sea Fleet under the central command of the Commonwealth of Independent States. But one day later he demanded that the fleet be placed under the jurisdiction of the Russian Republic.[29] On 13 January Russia and Ukraine agreed to have military specialists negotiate a partitioning of the approximately 300 vessels of the Black Sea Fleet between Ukraine and the CIS.[30]

The Nuclear Question

The second issue affecting Soviet-East European security was indicated by the series of efforts of U.S. President George Bush, Soviet President Mikhail Gorbachev, and Russian President Boris Yeltsin to trade successive unilateral cuts in European theater nuclear weapons and intercontinental strategic weapons. The unstated goal of the competitive reductions in nuclear weapons by Bush, Gorbachev, and Yeltsin was to eliminate those portions of the Soviet 30,000-warhead nuclear arsenal that might be claimed by the independent republics of Belarus, Kazakhstan, and Ukraine.

The significance of the nuclear issue is in defusing tensions between Russia and the three nuclear powers in NATO—the France, the United Kingdom, and the United States. The renunciation of nuclear war fighting postures by these former adversaries (in favor of purely deterrent postures) would constitute an insurance policy against the Europeanization or globalization of local disputes within the former Warsaw Pact zone. It also has the effect of codifying Russian conventional military superiority within this zone. The significance of a Russian monopoly on nuclear weapons will be determined in large part by whether the Russian army is a purely national force or the core of a CIS confederal military.

On 22 October 1991 the Ukrainian foreign minister, Anatoly Zelenko, stated that Ukraine would assume responsibility for destroying strategic nuclear warheads on Ukrainian territory, as called for by existing arms control agreements, and would eliminate the remaining tactical nuclear warheads in the course of future arms control agreements. The Ukrainians agreed to accept central Soviet control over the use of nuclear weapons,[31] a position maintained after the creation of the Commonwealth of Independent States. But the Ukrainian government insisted on control over the destruction of nuclear weapons on Ukrainian territory.

This policy was consistent with the position taken earlier by Leonid Kravchuk during the presidential elections. Kravchuk had simultaneously endorsed Ukrainian sovereignty over the nuclear weapons on Ukrainian territory and the transformation of Ukraine into a nuclear-free state. Though both Belarus and Kazakhstan declared their intention to become nuclear-free states and have not contested central control over the use of nuclear weapons, they have refused transfer of nuclear weapons on their territory to the Russian Federation.[32] They did, however, approve in principle of Gorbachev's program for nuclear arms reduction,[33] and subsequent efforts by Yeltsin.[34]

The Soviet, U.S. and Russian presidents had all wanted to leave Soviet nuclear weapons under the control of whatever central defense ministry Russian President Boris Yeltsin chose to recognize.[35] President Bush's initiative of 27 September required the removal of all ground-based U.S.

tactical nuclear weapons in Europe (artillery and short-range missiles) and all sea-based tactical nuclear weapons as well, but not strategic sea-based missiles on nuclear submarines. Bush left in place U.S. nuclear-capable aircraft in Europe, although the number of air-delivered nuclear weapons was to be reduced.[36] Altogether, the Bush initiative cut the NATO stockpile of substrategic weapons by about 80 percent.[37]

Gorbachev's response of 5 October went even further. After first securing Yeltsin's approval, the Soviet president matched the U.S. unilateral cuts of ground-based tactical nuclear weapons (artillery and short-range missiles), all sea-based tactical missiles and all land-based naval aircraft. In addition, Gorbachev cut the number of strategic warheads to 5,000 from the 6,000 total permitted by the Strategic Arms Reduction Talks treaty of July 1991, canceled the development of a new, mobile Soviet intercontinental ballistic missile, and announced a one-year moratorium on nuclear testing.[38] These measures radically altered the European theater nuclear arsenals of the superpowers, changing policies that had been in place for more than thirty-five years. Poland, Hungary, and the Czech and Slovak Federal Republic collectively welcomed the dramatic cuts in the tactical nuclear weapons of the central Soviet arsenal as a large step toward the denuclearization of their region and of the adjoining republics of Belarus and Ukraine.[39] These unilateral actions brought more change in the European military balance than all European arms control agreements negotiated during the entire span of the cold war.

After the formation of the CIS, President Yeltsin assumed control of Soviet strategic nuclear forces, a transfer of command formally acknowledged by Gorbachev in his resignation of 25 December. At the 21 December meeting in Alma-Ata, which brought in eight additional members of the CIS, the CIS confirmed all previous international agreements concerning nuclear weapons and promised that strategic nuclear weapons would be removed from Belarus by 1 July and from Ukraine at an unspecified date. Both of these states promised to sign the Nuclear Nonproliferation Treaty. The question of the removal of nuclear weapons from Kazakhstan was left unresolved.[40] On 31 December the leaders of the CIS agreed that the president of Russia would have the authority to use strategic nuclear weapons but only with the consent of the leaders of the three other nuclear weapons, republics—Belarus, Kazakhstan, and Ukraine.[41]

The Two "Triangles"

The third issue affecting Soviet-East European security was the attempt of the central European "Triangle"—Poland, Hungary, and the Czech and Slovak Federal Republic—to obtain in one form or another effective NATO security guarantees for the three states against the possible spillover of inter-republican and interethnic conflicts in the former USSR. Following the failure of the August coup attempt in the USSR, Estonia, Latvia, and Lithuania won almost immediate recognition of their independence and soon formed a second "Triangle" which followed the central European orientation toward the NATO/EC group.

The two "Triangles" posed a dilemma for the West. To reject their pleas would be to undermine the most promising emerging models for postcommunist societies in the Soviet empire. But to grant these states special security status would implicitly make the NATO/EC group party to potential military conflicts between the independent national military forces of Eastern Europe and the former Union republics. NATO officials argued (off the record) that to include central Europe in the Western security system was to exclude Russia and risk a reprise of the cold war.

The central European "Triangle" approaches to NATO ran parallel to central European efforts to obtain membership in the European Community, which has proved no more eager than NATO to respond to entreaties from the East.[42] Hungary took the initiative toward Brussels: in the spring of 1990 the last communist foreign minister, Gyula Horn, raised the possibility of Hungary's participation in the political agencies of NATO,[43] a possibility that his successor, Geza Jeszenszky, continued to press.

The eventual orientation of the entire "Triangle" toward NATO was a confirmation of the Hungarian approach to security issues in the region and a rejection of the original Czechoslovak approach. In the spring of 1990, in an address to the Council of Europe in Strasbourg, President Vaclav Havel of the Czech and Slovak Federal Republic had called for the dismantling of both the Warsaw Pact and NATO. He had argued that the CSCE could provide the framework for European security.[44]

But the impotence of the CSCE in responding to the Yugoslav civil war[45] persuaded Havel that the Hungarians had been right about the stabilizing role of NATO in Europe. Twelve months after his speech in Strasbourg, Havel apologized to the North Atlantic Council of Ministers for his previous misunderstanding of NATO's "stabilizing role" in Europe and endorsed the North Atlantic Alliance as the bedrock of a future European security system.[46] Havel also inquired about direct membership in NATO, but was politely rebuffed. The June 1991 NATO Declaration in Copenhagen, however, acknowledged a "direct and material interest" in the processes of democratization and marketization in central Europe. President Lech Walesa of Poland specifically called upon NATO to honor the spirit of the Copenhagen declaration when he addressed the North Atlantic Council in July 1991.[47] Walesa argued that Poland and other East European states could not enjoy the military security necessary for economic and political development if they lacked some sort of security connection to NATO.[48] He called upon NATO and Poland to work together toward their common interest, stability and security in Eastern Europe. He told NATO ministers: "Such working together is not directed against anyone. I repeat, we do not intend to act, and we are not acting, against any state. We wish for one Europe. The Soviet Union has a place in it. At the same time we resolutely reject any ideas of grey or buffer zones; they imply a continued division of the continent."[49]

Walesa did not seek formal membership in NATO. The Polish president limited himself to continuation of the diplomatic relations with NATO established in August 1990.[50] The "troika" states did obtain membership in the North Atlantic Assembly of NATO. The assembly is a body of parliamentarians from NATO states and is completely separate from NATO's military structures.[51] At the October 1991 session of the North Atlantic Assembly in Madrid, Hungary's Jeszenszky persuaded the assembly to hold its 1995 session in Budapest.[52]

In early October 1991 Premier Jozsef Antall of Hungary declared in Washington that NATO should assume responsibility for the security of the entire European area west of the present borders of the USSR. According to the Hungarian prime minister, "What form this security guarantee takes is a secondary question. It might be based on bilateral agreements, full membership in NATO or creation of a satellite security organization in the area adjoining NATO."[53] The "Triangle" states issued a formal appeal in their Krakow declaration of 6 October 1991 for an "institutionalized association" with NATO short of outright membership.[54]

The three states all but ruled out serious national efforts at independent military postures. Severe economic problems in all three "Triangle" states dictated declining defense budgets. In response to deep cuts in

Polish defense spending, which forced the retirement of some 10,000 officers, Defense Minister Vice Admiral Piotr Kolodziejczyk had protested in August 1991, "The Polish Army is going into hibernation."[55] The Triangle states also avoided creation of any kind of formal alliance structures among themselves or with other former East European members of the Warsaw Pact or with Union republics.[56] The logic of this policy was that such structures would impede direct links with NATO and alarm Moscow. But the triangle vigorously pursued overlapping bilateral ties, both formal and informal.[57] Extensive cooperation among the three defense ministries took place on the informal level.[58]

By seeking a security guarantee from NATO, Budapest, Warsaw, and Prague have been demanding a kind of Brezhnev doctrine in reverse: a NATO policy aimed at protecting emerging democratic political systems. The central European Triangle policy sought protection against militant nationalism in the East and the possible renationalization of German defense policy in the West. But most of all, the members of the Triangle were asking for an assurance that if these states endured the pain of transition to Western-style systems, NATO would welcome them as members of the Western community.

One other East European member of the former Warsaw Pact, Bulgaria, also responded to the political-territorial uncertainties in Eastern Europe by seeking a security relationship with NATO short of actual membership.[59] President Zhelyu Zhelev of Bulgaria, a country that during its communist period had frequently been dismissed as a virtual sixteenth republic of the USSR, expressed an explicit desire for a security relationship with NATO[60]—a desire shared by a broad section of Bulgarian society, including even high-ranking military officers and political figures of the communist era.[61] Bulgaria established regular liaison links with NATO through its existing embassy in Brussels and has sought associate membership in the North Atlantic Assembly.[62] NATO's secretary general paid an official visit to Bulgaria in April 1991, and President Zhelev made a reciprocal visit to Brussels in late November. The Bulgarian foreign minister has declared that the new security structure of Europe must be built around NATO, the EC, the WEU, with the CSCE as an all-European institution.[63]

The Baltic States

For the Baltic states, the failure of the August coup attempt meant almost immediate victory for their movements toward independence, which Lithuania had begun when it declared its independence in March 1990. On 20 August, the second day of the coup attempt, Estonia declared its full independence, followed by Latvia the next day. On 23 August shortly after the collapse of the coup attempt, Boris Yeltsin, in the name of the Russian Republic, recognized the independence of all three Baltic states.[64] The three Baltic republics then rapidly obtained international recognition.[65] Formal recognition from Gorbachev's USSR came on 6 September.[66]

Estonia, Latvia, and Lithuania almost immediately began following the central European pattern of negotiating the withdrawal of Soviet troops and seeking a security relationship with NATO. Just as he had initiated the movement for full state independence, President Vytautas Landsbergis of Lithuania vocally demanded the immediate withdrawal of all Soviet forces from the Baltic states.[67] Almost immediately, negotiation with Gorbachev's government began on the withdrawal of nearly 400,000 Soviet military personnel from the Baltic area—army troops, internal security units, and naval forces.[68]

Gorbachev issued a decree on 21 September, freeing all Baltic citizens from the obligation of military service in the Soviet armed forces, internal security troops, and border guards.[69] Officials of the Baltic Council, representing all three republics, obtained a pledge from President Bush to use U.S. influence to speed the Soviet troop withdrawal.[70] On 4 October the Baltic Council issued a demand for the complete withdrawal of all Soviet forces by 1 December 1991.[71] The Soviet government responded by demanding that the Baltic states help pay for relocation of Soviet troops, which the Union Defense Ministry agreed in principle to withdraw by 1994.[72] The chief obstacle to withdrawal was the reluctance of Soviet officers in the Baltic states to leave housing and other amenities that could not be provided them in Russia. This problem remained after the formation of the CIS.

Estonia, Latvia, and Lithuania each sent representatives to the October 1991 Madrid session of the North Atlantic Assembly.[73] The Baltic states had the advantage of coming to the Madrid meeting with the special support of three NATO members, Denmark, Iceland, and Norway—the first states to recognize Baltic independence after the August coup attempt. The three states were admitted as associate members of the North Atlantic Assembly.[74] At the Madrid session of the North Atlantic Assembly NATO Secretary General Manfred Woerner expressed his hope that Estonia, Latvia, and Lithuania would develop "a cooperative security relationship" with NATO modeled on NATO's relationship with the East Europeans.[75] At the first meeting of the North Atlantic Cooperation Council in December 1991 the Baltic states called upon the West to pressure Russia into withdrawing the remaining Soviet troops, and they asked both NATO and CSCE observers to monitor the withdrawal.[76]

All three Baltic states faced not only the question of the withdrawal of predominantly Russian forces left by the Soviet military in the region but also the question of citizenship rights for the ethnic Russian minorities working in the civilian economies of the region. Lithuania had the additional problem of a large Polish minority fearful of losing its cultural autonomy. Furthermore, the Kaliningrad area, administratively part of the Russian Federation, was wedged between Poland and Lithuania and geographically cut off from Russia proper.

NATO and the East

The fourth issue affecting the security of the region is whether NATO will accord special treatment to the emerging democratic/market states of the former Warsaw Pact or whether it will pursue a "no favorites" policy in the hope of preempting the Balkanization of east central Europe. To date, NATO has consistently refused to give either set of "Triangle" states even the hypothetical "associate membership" that some East European political figures had requested in the summer of 1991.[77]

The shape of NATO's policy toward the former Warsaw Pact states first emerged in the North Atlantic Council's London declaration of July 1990, which invited Gorbachev and other Warsaw Treaty Organization (WTO) leaders to address the council in person.[78] The North Atlantic Council had declared in its Copenhagen declaration of 6 June 1991 that the Western alliance had "direct and material interest" in what the council called "the consolidation and preservation throughout the continent of democratic societies and their freedom from any form of coercion or intimidation."[79] This policy had led to the establishment of liaison missions in Brussels between former Warsaw Pact states and NATO.

On 3 October 1991 the U.S. secretary of state and the German foreign minister proposed that NATO establish expanded liaison links with all the former Warsaw Pact states, including the USSR, and move toward the establishment of a North Atlantic Cooperation Council consisting of the NATO states and all of the members of the former WTO.[80] NATO's goal, in late October 1991, as stated by Secretary General Woerner, was to strengthen the CSCE and other institutions, (such as the proposed NACC), as complementary security structures linking the Western alliance with the members of the former Eastern alliance, including the republics of the USSR.[81]

At its November 1991 summit in Rome NATO's North Atlantic Council endorsed the creation of a North Atlantic Cooperation Council incorporated into a strengthened CSCE. NATO invited all the former Warsaw Pact states plus Estonia, Latvia, and Lithuania to participate in regular meetings involving officials at various levels, from that of defense and foreign ministers to specialists on a variety of military, political, and economic issues.[82] The question of participation by other republics of the former USSR was left open. NATO also adopted a document on its new "strategic concept," the essence of which was to abolish the concentration of large national forces on the former central front and to create smaller, multinational NATO force structures for reaction to a variety of possible contingencies.[83]

The thrust of the declaration of the North Atlantic Council in Rome was to avoid a new confrontation with the Russian/Soviet military by making security commitments to Russia's immediate neighbors. Rather, it sought to shape European security issues through ongoing Conventional Forces in Europe (CFE) negotiations, CSCE mechanisms, and economic assistance by its member states. The North Atlantic Council met again on 19 December after the formation of the CIS on 8 December but before the official demise of the USSR.

The main purpose of that meeting was to endorse the EC's decision at Maastricht to designate the WEU as the organization for developing a European defense identity within NATO. Another purpose was to work out a joint NATO position before the 20 December session of the first meeting of the NACC. Before the end of the first NACC session, the Soviet representative announced the end of the Soviet Union and asked for deletion of all references to the USSR in the NACC communiqué.

The communiqué saluted the principles of the Charter of Paris, endorsed an enhanced role for the CSCE and called upon the March 1992 Helsinki session of CSCE to adjust the terms of the CFE treaty to the changed political circumstances in Eastern Europe. It also proposed a series of ongoing meetings of NACC members: annual meetings at the ministerial level; bimonthly meetings at the ambassadorial level between NATO members and non-NATO states; regular meetings of lower-level officials and experts; and a program of greatly expanded contacts in NACC member countries on a wide range of issues related to security.[84] This program drew on NATO's own experience in overcoming barriers that had previously separated the military and security officials of West European countries.

Given the rapid deconstruction of, first, the Warsaw Pact and then of the Soviet military, NATO might reasonably claim that it had reacted quickly and prudently to events that caught all participants and observers by surprise. But it had yet to formulate an active policy designed to shape the emergence of a postcommunist security system in Europe.

The Deconstruction of the Warsaw Pact

In retrospect it appears that the domestic structures and alliance organizations of the entire Soviet bloc rested on the capacity of the Soviet military to honor its constitutional obligation to come to "the joint defense of the gains of socialism" in each national-territorial component of "the socialist commonwealth," a pseudo-superstructure linking the Union republics with the allied "fraternal" states in Eastern Europe. In the circular logic of Brezhnev's empire, the cohesion of the Soviet military in turn depended on the survival of Communist party rule in national communities of the socialist commonwealth.

When Gorbachev tolerated the formation of the Solidarity government in Poland in late August 1989, he unambiguously canceled the security guarantee the Warsaw Pact had previously extended to the ruling parties of Eastern Europe. To his surprise, he also set in motion the cancellation of the Soviet army's security guarantee to the republican branches of the Communist party of the Soviet Union (CPSU) and the Soviet Communist party as a whole. Within two years, the process of communist deconstruction came full circle, when the Soviet military refused to respond to the orders of the leaders of the 19 August coup attempt. The failure of the coup led to the immediate collapse of the CPSU, which in turn led to the accelerated disintegration of the USSR, which in turn touched off the fragmentation of the Soviet military into national-republic military forces.

The entire process of deconstruction constituted an ironic confirmation of the Soviet ideological rhetoric that the fraternal solidarity of the Warsaw Pact was modeled on the fraternal relations within the multi-national Soviet armed forces. In any case, the disintegration of the pact provided a preview of the potential disintegration of what Brezhnev had called "the army of the friendship of peoples." The pattern set by the East Europeans was that of demanding withdrawal of Soviet forces from national territory, rejection of any regional alliance system, and overtures to formal and informal relations with the NATO/EC states. The Baltic states were the first former republics of the USSR to import the East European pattern.

With the disappearance of communist regimes in Eastern Europe, the political logic for Soviet troop deployments also disappeared, not to mention the political prerequisites. In late February 1990 the Soviets agreed to withdraw all forces from Czechoslovakia by July 1991;[85] the Hungarians and Soviets reached an agreement in early March 1990 for a Soviet withdrawal by 1 July 1991.[86] At the March 1990 session of the Political Consultative Committee all the East European members of the WTO endorsed both German unification and the membership of a united Germany in NATO, over Soviet protests.[87]

The Soviets resisted German membership in NATO until July 1990, when Gorbachev and Chancellor Helmut Kohl of the Federal Republic of Germany concluded the agreement for German unification. This agreement also provided for the complete evacuation of all Soviet troops from East Germany by 1994 in exchange for DM 15 billion for the construction of new housing facilities in the USSR for the western group of forces.[88] The Soviet-German agreement paved the way for assurances to Poland on its western border with Germany. These assurances in turn led to the Polish-Soviet agreement of April 1991 for withdrawal of Soviet troops from Poland, a withdrawal now scheduled for 1992.[89] These agreements meant that by 1994 there would be no Soviet or Russian military presence in Eastern Europe.

During the summer of 1990 the East Europeans, who constituted a voting majority in the WTO, had temporarily agreed to use the pact as a device to maximize East European leverage on the negotiations over a CFE treaty, still being conducted on the basis of two opposing alliances, the seven-member WTO and the sixteen-member NATO organization.

During the CFE negotiations of 1990, the Czechs and Hungarians differed on the future of the Warsaw Pact. President Havel of the Czech and Slovak Federal Republic wanted to preserve the alliance as a means of bringing the USSR into a new CSCE security system in which both alliances would dissolve. The irony of Czechoslovak support during the summer of 1990 for the alliance that once invaded Prague had not been lost on Georgi Arbatov, Gorbachev's former adviser, who told Western correspondents at the June 1990 meeting of the pact's Political Consultative Committee, "The Warsaw Pact is ceasing to exist like the Cheshire cat from Alice and Wonderland but there are still some traces of the smile."[90]

Premier Jozsef Antall of Hungary wanted the WTO dissolved as soon as the CFE was concluded so that his country could integrate itself as rapidly as possible with the EC and NATO.[91] In late June 1990 the Hungarian parliament voted to withdraw from the WTO by no later than the end of 1991.[92] On 14 November 1990, just before the signing of the CFE, the six remaining states of the WTO agreed to the complete legal dismantling of the political and military organization of the WTO by 1 July 1991.[93]

The CFE structure, covering the zone from the Atlantic to the Urals, had been based on a 1:1 ratio of forces between NATO and the Warsaw Pact.[94] Despite the colossal cuts required in Soviet conventional forces by the CFE plan, the downsized Soviet arsenal was still without peer in Europe: the treaty awarded the Soviet military one third of all the major conventional weapons systems in the zone from the Atlantic to the Urals (tanks, armored personnel carriers, artillery, fighter-bombers, and helicopters).[95]

During the first eighteen months after the signing of the CFE, it appeared that the Soviet Defense Ministry, then under Marshal Dmitrii Yazov, was trying to circumvent the CFE treaty by transferring some Soviet equipment beyond the Urals and by assigning equipment to naval units within the treaty zone that were not included in the treaty.[96] During this period, Yazov publicly complained that the disintegration of the Warsaw Pact had left the USSR at the short end of the balance of European forces, somewhere between a ratio of 1:2 and 1:1.5,[97] depending on how one counted the forces of the East European states that had once sworn eternal friendship with Moscow.

From the signing of the CFE in November 1990 to the attempted coup of August 1991, Soviet-East European relations were in limbo because the Gorbachev regime demanded bilateral treaties that would prohibit either signatory from joining a military alliance aimed at the other. The Soviet objective was to halt the political, military, and economic reorientation of the East European states toward the NATO/EC system. With the exception of Romania, each of the former WTO states refused to meet Soviet requirements for new bilateral treaties with anti-NATO security clauses.[98]

Romanian willingness to provide the USSR with a pledge not to join NATO reflected Bucharest's eagerness to obtain Moscow's agreement for an eventual unification of Moldavia with Romania. A Soviet-Romanian treaty of April 1991 provided for the opening of consulates in the cities of Kishinev (Moldavia) and Iasi (Romania), the simplification of border crossings between Romania and Moldavia and expanded Romanian-Moldavian cultural ties.[99] Because of domestic opposition to the security pledge to the USSR, however, the Romanian parliament never ratified the treaty,[100] an issue rendered moot by developments after the attempted coup of 19 August.

The Warsaw Pact formally dissolved its military structure on 31 March 1991. In July 1991 the WTO terminated its political structure.[101] By mid-1991 the Hungarian approach had won the support of all the former Warsaw Pact states, including the Czech and Slovak Federal Republic. At the July 1991 ceremony marking the end of the WTO, the Soviet representative of the USSR, Vice President Gennady Yanaev, affirmed the Soviet hard line toward Eastern Europe by calling for the reciprocal disbanding of NATO as a relic of the cold war. Prime Minister Antall of Hungary retorted, "The rejuvenated NATO represents a warranty for European security, and the same holds true for the presence of the United States in Europe."[102] Yanaev returned to Moscow, where he then, as one of the leaders of the seizure of power attempted by the State Committee for the Emergency Situation, laid claim to being Gorbachev's successor.

Following the August coup attempt, the new Soviet foreign minister, Boris Pankin, revised the Soviet position on alliance membership to the satisfaction of Budapest, Prague, and Warsaw, each of which moved quickly to conclude new bilateral treaties with the Union government.[103]

Romania then sought a revision of its treaty with Moscow along the same lines, although not abandoning its goal of eventual unification with Moldova. Finland also sought a revision of its bilateral treaty with the USSR, a treaty that for forty-three years had restricted Finnish security policy along similar lines.[104]

The Deconstruction of the Soviet Military

The Soviet military began to fracture along ethnic-nationality fissures shortly after August 1989, when Gorbachev withheld the Soviet military from defense of the ruling parties of Eastern Europe. Azerbaijan declared sovereignty on 23 September 1989 and soon insisted that at least 50 percent of all Azeri draftees perform their military service in Azerbaijan.[105] Similar declarations of sovereignty (not independence) followed in other republics, often with similar attempts to withhold draftees from service outside their native republics.[106]

During 1990 and 1991, non-Russians increasingly refused draft calls, exacerbating an ethnic crisis within the Soviet military.[107] Draft evasion was not a serious problem in the Russian Republic, which declared sovereignty on 11 June 1990, or in Ukraine, which declared sovereignty on 16 July 1990.[108] But in Russia and Ukraine there were growing protest movements against the *dedovshchina*, or brutal hazing practices, within the Soviet army, practices that often had an ethnic dimension.

Lithuania declared full independence on 11 March 1990, and on 17 July 1990 announced the formation of its own military forces and the termination of the drafting of Lithuanian conscripts for service in the Soviet army.[109] Estonia declared a qualified independence on 30 March 1990 as did Latvia on 4 May 1990; both republics offered their citizens the right of alternative service outside the Soviet army, though Moscow refused to recognize this right.[110]

In January 1991 the Soviet military, probably at the instigation of some of the same officials who attempted the coup of August 1991, attempted to carry out a crackdown on the independence movements in each of the three Baltic states. The apparent goal of the military was to install "national salvation committees" closely linked to the republic Communist parties.

Boris Yeltsin, however, issued an open appeal to Russian soldiers serving in the Baltics not to obey any orders to repress democratically elected governments.[111] In addition, NATO and EC states sharply condemned the use of violence in the Baltics. The Gorbachev regime backed down from the confrontation and then in the spring of 1991 sought to negotiate a new Union treaty with the republics that had declared only sovereignty, not independence.

Yeltsin's appeal to Russian soldiers not to intervene in the Baltics in January 1991 was an implicit attempt to transfer the loyalty of ethnic Russian military personnel from the all-Union Defense Ministry under the CPSU to the increasingly sovereign Russian Republic. This implicit effort made Yeltsin the target of vociferous criticism from the conservative communist apparat and the "national Bolsheviks" in the Soviet officer corps during the spring of 1991. The culmination of this campaign was a 23 July letter to *Sovetskaia Rossiia* signed by several prominent military officers, conservative writers, and two of the leaders of the 19 August coup. The letter declared that the Soviet army would "step forward as the bulwark of all the healthy forces in society."[112]

The scheduled signing of the new Union treaty, to occur on 20 August, appears to have precipitated the attempted coup on 19 August by the "State Committee," which included Marshal Dmitrii Yazov, the Soviet defense minister. Though the loyalties of the components of the Soviet military during the coup attempt are still not clear, the end result was unquestionably to transfer ultimate command of the Soviet armed forces to the president of the Russian Republic.[113] This transfer was marked by a purge of about 80 percent of the former leadership of the collegium of the Defense Ministry,[114] in principle the highest collective body in the ministry.

Yeltsin countermanded Gorbachev's appointment of Evegenii Moiseev as defense minister for a day (22 August) and, with Gorbachev's assent, appointed Evegenii Shaposhnikov, the forty-nine-year-old former air force commander, as the new Soviet defense minister. Yeltsin also named as chief of the Soviet General Staff General Vladimir Lobov, former chief of staff of the WTO (and proponent of cooperative relations with NATO). In addition, Yeltsin appointed Konstantin Kobets, a general who had organized the defense of the Russian parliament building (the Russian White House) during the coup, as state defense adviser of the Russian Republic (RSFSR).

Shaposhnikov then appointed Kobets to head the Union committee charged with investigating the actions of military personnel during the

August coup attempt.[115] Colonel General Pavel Grachev became the semiofficial liaison between the Russian Republic and the Soviet Defense Ministry by virtue of his dual appointments as deputy defense minister of the USSR and chairman of the RSFSR State Committee for Defense and Security.[116] Yeltsin later appointed General Viktor N. Samoilov as the Russian Republic's official military liaison with the Union Defense Ministry.[117]

For a variety of internal and external reasons, neither Yeltsin nor Gorbachev was anxious to clarify the ambiguous relationship of the USSR presidency to the Russian Republic in the chaotic period immediately following the coup attempt. Grachev stated on 18 September that the Russian Republic would establish its own separate defense ministry only if other republics first established such ministries and claimed command of the Soviet troops stationed in different republics.[118]

Both the Union and RSFSR governments accepted the independence of the Baltic states and Moldavia and their right to have their own separate armed forces. Shaposhnikov, however, during his first weeks in office, spoke out vehemently for preservation of a single armed forces for the republics that had not yet decided to secede from the USSR, although he endorsed the creation of small national guards in the republics of the USSR.[119] He declared that "the presence of [Union] armed forces on the territory of the republics on the basis of inter-state agreements is ultimately cheaper, more advantageous and more reliable than for each republic to create and maintain its own army."[120]

His subordinates, such as the commander of Soviet air defense, argued that technological chaos was likely to ensue if the republics claimed air defense responsibilities.[121] Ground forces commander Colonel General Vladimir Semenov argued that financial and security considerations dictated a federal or confederal military force.[122] Chief of Staff Lobov openly raised the prospect of civil war should republican armies replace the Soviet army, and in addition warned that nuclear weapons could not be allowed to fall under the control of republican defense ministries.[123]

Prior to a 10 September meeting of republic spokesmen with Marshal Shaposhnikov, Vladimir Lopatin, a prominent and outspoken military reformer before the coup and after 21 August 1991 the deputy chairman of the RSFSR Defense and Security Committee, told a Japanese newspaper that the Russian Republic hoped to create a Soviet defense community loosely based on the NATO model.[124] Yuri Ryzhov, chair of the Science Committee of the USSR Supreme Soviet and a security adviser to both Gorbachev and Yeltsin, said in mid-September that if republics did create their own armies, Moscow would try to form an "eastern NATO" with independent republic armies loosely controlled by an alliance headquarters in Moscow.[125]

The Soviet representative to the October 1991 Vienna session of the ongoing CSCE seminar on military doctrines stressed that Soviet doctrine was "a new coalition doctrine" of a "rejuvenated union." First Deputy Chief of Staff Colonel General V. Omelichev told the CSCE session that the new coalition doctrine was based on "a synthesis of the principal propositions of the conception of securing the national security of all the sovereign republics which will enter a renewed union."[126] Omelichev could not offer specifics about the new coalition, which had yet to be created.

On 10 September Marshal Shaposhnikov convened a two-day meeting of top officials of the Soviet Defense Ministry and representatives of fifteen republics, including the Baltic states. The session permitted a broad exchange of views but did not produce any joint decision.[127] However, on 12 September Shaposhnikov agreed with the Moldovan prime minister, Valeriu Maravschi, to create a joint commission to work out a plan for the eventual withdrawal of Soviet troops from that republic.[128]

Based on an interview of 20 September, it appears that Marshal Shaposhnikov proposed to the republics a complex system of overlapping military and civilian structures to incorporate both all-Union forces and "republic guards. Shaposhnikov envisaged "national guards" or republican guard" forces of 2,000-3,000 personnel in each republic, plus a federal force of 3 million, initially made up of both conscripts and professionals but eventually moving toward an all-volunteer military.

Shaposhnikov called for the establishment of a civilian defense ministry at the Union level and committees on defense and security at the republic level. The all-Union Defense Ministry, subordinate to the president of the USSR as commander-in-chief, would have a number of committees collectively in charge of all aspects of military affairs. The republic committees on defense and security would have roughly analogous structures.

A military committee of the central Defense Ministry would supervise all service branches and the all-Union forces stationed on the territories of the republics belonging to the Union or allied with it as coalition partners. The commander of all-Union forces in a given republic would be jointly appointed by the Union president and the head of state in the given republic. Each republic's defense and security committee would send a representative with a small staff to serve on the command staff of the all-Union commander in the republic. In addition, the chairs of the republic defense and security committees would have seats on the collegium of the central Defense Ministry.

The new Soviet military would also begin a gradual transition to an all-volunteer force, beginning with a system mixing conscripts and professional personnel.[129] General Grachev later declared that the terms of compulsory service would be shortened from twenty-four to eighteen months as of 1991 and would be further cut to twelve months by 1995. In addition, the total size of the Soviet armed forces would be cut from 4 million to 3 million for 1992 and drop further to a figure under 2.5 million by 1994.[130]

The formation of the CIS transformed the central Soviet Defense Ministry into the Defense Ministry of the Russian Federation, though Marshal Shaposhnikov was recognized as not only chief of the Russian ministry but also interim commander-in-chief of the CIS forces, officially subordinate to a newly created Council of Defense Ministers of the CIS.[131] Shaposhnikov re-emphasized his commitment to a unified, integrated force for the CIS as a whole, but he encountered strong objections from several republics, particularly Azerbaijan, Moldova, and, of course, Ukraine.[132] In Azerbaijan, the principal issue was the ongoing military conflict with Armenia over Nagorno-Karabakh.

For the newly independent state of Moldova, the most immediate security issue was obtaining the negotiated withdrawal of the Soviet garrisons in Moldova as a necessary prerequisite to obtaining international diplomatic recognition. In early November President Mircea Snegur had moved toward the establishment of a draft system to provide personnel for Moldova's Ministry of Internal Affairs and to seek control over Soviet military facilities in Moldova, while continuing to work out plans for a national army of 12,000-15,000 personnel.[133] Although he led Moldova into the CIS, mainly to protect Kishinev from Romanian irredentism, Snegur promised to keep Moldovan forces separate from the forces of the CIS. On 28 December 1991 Snegur told the present CIS military commanders in Moldova that Moldova would be a militarily neutral state with its own independent army.[134]

The Byelorussian approach to defense questions appears to have remained more or less in line with that publicly recommended by Shaposhnikov both before and after the formation of the CIS. On 23 September 1991 the Supreme Soviet in Minsk voted to create a "non-offensive" national military in "national guard" units but also permitted "voluntary service" of Byelorussian recruits in Soviet military units stationed on the territory of Belarus.[135] On 25 October the Security and Defense Commission of the Belarus parliament publicly revealed its plan for a 5,000-8,000-member national guard, to be split off from existing forces of Soviet troop detachments stationed in Belarus. The personnel of the guard were to be trained in "Byelorussian military traditions and rituals"; eventually, the language of the guard was to change from Russian to Byelorussian.[136] After the formation of the CIS, the projected size was later increased to 90,000.[137]

Conclusion: The Deconstruction of the
East European Security System

Europe has witnessed the complete implosion of the East European security structure codified in November 1990 by the Conventional Forces in Europe treaty, an agreement predicated on the existence of both the Warsaw Pact and the Soviet armed forces. The CSCE session scheduled for March 1992 in Helsinki must address the collapse of the CFE framework and perhaps the CSCE system as well. CSCE action—or inaction—may signal the fate of the promise implicit in the CSCE's Charter of Paris—that new democratic regimes in Eastern Europe might set patterns for several of the republics of the USSR in regard to security affairs and domestic policy. This promise was implied by the designation of Prague as the home of a new, permanent secretariat for the CSCE, of Vienna as the CSCE Conflict Resolution Center, and of Warsaw as the home of the office for free elections.[138]

The failure of the CSCE to respond effectively to the Yugoslav crisis suggests that CSCE 1992 will not offer the central Europeans a solution to the security problems generated by the disintegration of the Soviet military, unless the North Atlantic Cooperation Council rapidly becomes an effective new caucus within the CSCE. This would in effect require

NATO to participate directly in East European security affairs. Should the NATO/EC states fail to provide the emerging East European democracies with some sort of security relationship out of fear of provoking hostile responses in Moscow, it may fall to the various defense ministries of the CIS to define postcommunist security relations in the region. In that case, Ukraine and Russia will decide for the CIS as a whole.

Notes

1. "Kravchuk on Ukrainian Independence," RFE/RL Daily Report-USSR, no. 244, 30 December 1991.

2. A public opinion poll taken in Poland in October 1991 caught the uncertainty of the security issues raised by the fragmentation of the Soviet Union. The poll found that a slight majority thought Poland's security would be enhanced if the USSR disintegrated into four adjoining eastern neighbors—Byelorussia, the Kaliningrad oblast of the Russian Republic, Lithuania, and Ukraine. Some 22 percent, however, expressed fears about relations with Lithuania and Ukraine, where there are large Polish communities. Only 27 percent preferred the preservation of the USSR; some 30 percent were undecided. According to the same poll, 52 percent feared that the unrest in the Soviet Union posed a security threat to Poland, and 63 percent thought a civil war likely in the USSR. The last civil war in the USSR (1918/21) witnessed a Polish invasion of Ukraine and a Red Army invasion of Poland. Poll by the Polish CBOS Polling Center as reported in *Gazeta Wyborcza,* carried on PAP News Wire (Poland), 9 October 9, 1991, from Nexis Service.

3. Romanian foreign minister Adrian Nastase declared in a 3 October Reuters interview that his country and the fledgling republic of Moldova would eventually unite. Alan Elsner, "Romanian Foreign Minister Sees Eventual Union with Moldavia," Reuters, 3 October 1991, from Nexis Service. Reuters quoted Nastase as saying that unification of the two Romanian-speaking states would be "the normal course of history.... I don't know if in 20 years, or five years or 50 years. Very much will depend on the processes taking place in Moldavia and Romania, in the Soviet Union...and in Europe in general."

4. "Romanians Tell Ukraine It Must Negotiate Territory," *New York*

Times, 30 November 1991, 5. These areas are southern Bessarabia, northern Bukovina, Herta, and Hotin.

5. "Self-Proclaimed Gagauz Republic Declares Independence," RFE/RL Daily Report-USSR, no. 168, 4 September 1991.

6. "Officers for a Ukrainian Army," RFE/RL Daily Report-USSR, no. 209, 4 November 1991.

7. "Kravchuk Gives Press Conference," Foreign Broadcast Information Service (hereinafter FBIS) SOV-91-170, 3 September 1991, 99, from Radio Kiev 1900 GMT, 27 August 1991.

8. Ibid.

9. "Kravchuk, Military Chiefs Discuss Armed Forces," FBIS-SOV-91-1-70, 3 September 1991, 97, from Radio Kiev 1900 GMT, 30 August 1991.

10. "The Ukraine Creates Its Own Army," *Izvestiia,* 4 September 1991, 1, in *Current Digest of the Soviet Press* 43, no. 36, 9 October 1991, 18.

11. "V krugu slozhneishikh problem," *Krasnaia zvezda,* 2 September 1991, 3.

12. Sergei Balykov, "Interview with Ukrainian Defense Minister," Ukrinform-TASS, 3 October 1991, from Nexis.

13. Ibid.

14. "Ukraine: Rukh Leader Says Republic's Defensive Army will Number 350,000," *Izvestiia,* 5 September 1991, 1, in *Current Digest of the Soviet Press* 43, no. 36, 9 October 1991, 18.

15. *Ibid.*

16. Robert Seely, "Ukraine to Use Nuclear Stock As Bargaining Chip," Times Newspapers Limited, 16 September 1991, from Nexis Service.

17. *Ibid.*

18. Francis X. Clines, "Legislators Back Effort to Create a Ukrainian Army," *New York Times,* 23 October 1991, 1.

19. See Celestine Bohlen, "Yeltsin, in Rebuff to Ukraine, Lays Claim to Black Sea Fleet," *New York Times,* 10 January 1992, 1. See also "Russia and Ukraine Try to Settle Military Dispute," *New York Times,* 12 January 1992, 3.

20. Ibid.

21. "Ukraine Declares Non-Nuclear Status," RFE/RL Daily Report-USSR, no. 204, 25 October 1991.

22. *New York Times,* 23 October 1991, 1.

23. "Kiev Adopts Law on National Guard," RFE/RL Daily Report-USSR, no. 210, 5 November 1991.

24. "MVD Troops Must Be Under Ukrainian Command," RFE/RL Daily Report-USSR, no. 224, 26 November 1991.

25. "Soviet General Agrees to Ukrainian Army," RFE/RL Daily Report-USSR, no. 204, 25 October 1991.

26. "USSR To Build New Black Sea Naval Base," RFE/RL Daily Report-USSR, no. 210, 5 November 1991.

27. "Shaposhnikov on Ukrainian Army," RFE/RL Daily Report-USSR, no. 209, 4 November 1991.

28. "Disagreement on Defense," RFE/RL Research Report, no. 244, 30 December 1991.

29. "Shaposhnikov on Ukrainian Army," RFE/RL Daily Report-USSR, no. 209, 4 November 1991.

30. *Bulletin of the Atlantic Council of the United States,* 24 January 1992, 1.

31. Francis X. Clines, "Soviet Army on Defense, in the Ukraine," *New York Times,* 12 November 1991 (International edition), 5.

32. "Nazarbaev on Future of Union, Nuclear Weapons," RFE/RL Daily Report-USSR, no. 177, 17 September 1991. See also Francis X. Clines, "Soviet Army on Defense, in the Ukraine," *New York Times,* 12 November 1991 (National edition), 5.

33. "Republics Support Disarmament Proposal," RFE/RL Daily Report-USSR, no. 192, 9 October 1991.

34. "Military Commander Supports National Guard," FBIS-SOV-91-170, 3 September 1991, 95, from Moscow INTERFAX in English 1900 GMT, 30 August 1991. According to this report, the current Soviet commander of the Byelorussian military district endorsed in principle the creation of a Byelorussian national guard. See also "Demonstration in Minsk As Supreme Soviet Meets," RFE/RL Daily Report-USSR, no. 176, 18 September 1991; "Toward a Byelorussian National Guard," RFE/RL Daily Report-USSR, no. 208, 31 October 1991; and "Military Service in Kazakhstan," RFE/RL Daily Report-USSR, no. 177, 17 September 1991. See also Fred Hiatt, "Some Soviet Republics Seeking Separate Armies," *Washington Post,* 17 September 1991, from Nexis Service.

35. An American reporter claimed that army officers controlling nuclear

weapons in the Russian Republic had placed themselves under the authority of Yeltsin or at least accorded him the right of consultation. See Clines, "Soviet Army on Defense, in the Ukraine," International edition, 5.

36. "How the Presidents' Plans Compare," *New York Times,* 6 October 1991, from Nexis Service.

37. "NATO Nuclear Planning Group: Final Communique," 18 October 1991, 2, from NATO Press Service.

38. "How the Presidents' Plans Compare."

39. See "Tripartite Meeting in Cracow," CSTK in English 1646 GMT, 16 October 1991, from BBC Summary of World Broadcasts, 9 October 1991, from Nexis Service.

40. "Alma Ata Agreement on Nuclear Weapons," RFE/RL Daily Report-USSR, no. 242, 23 December 1991.

41. "Minsk Agreement on Strategic Forces," RFE/RL Research Report, no. 1, 2 January 1992.

42. In early September 1991 France blocked proposals for the EC to ease trade terms for the "troika." See "France Blocks EC Trade Concession to Eastern Europe," Reuters, 6 September 1991, from Nexis Service.

43. *New York Times,* 24 February 1990, 6.

44. "Havel's 10 May Speech to the Council of Europe," FBIS-EEU-90--096, 17 May 1990, 12.

45. "Czechoslovak President Arrives in Cracow for Summit Meeting," CTK National News Wire (Czechoslovakia), 6 October 1991, from Nexis.

46. See "Documentation: President Havel Visits NATO," *NATO Review,* 39, no. 2, (April 1991): 31-5.

47. See "Documentation: President Lech Walesa Visits NATO Headquarters," *NATO Review* 39, no. 4, (August 1991): 33-34.

48. Ibid.

49. Ibid.

50. See "Walesa in Brussels," *Warsaw Voice,* 14 July 1991, from Nexis Service. "The question of Poland joining NATO is not on the order of the day. Poland intends to be in close touch with the organization but not apply for membership. This was the position President Lech Walesa presented at NATO headquarters in Brussels. In doing so, he managed to avoid the fate that befell President Vaclav Havel, who suggested that Czechoslovakia join NATO and received a categorical, negative reply." See also "Czechoslovakia Would Apply for NATO Membership in Emergency,"

CTK National News Wire, Czechoslovakia, 23 August 1991, from Nexis. Partial text: "Czechoslovak Foreign Minister Jiri Dienstbier said today Czechoslovakia would ask NATO for protection if it felt threatened before new security structures are built in Europe and would even apply for full NATO membership if necessary. Speaking at a press conference of the Civic Movement (OH) of which he is chairman, Dienstbier said that for the time being no negotiations are being held on Czechoslovakia's joining NATO."

51. "The North Atlantic Assembly is the inter-parliamentary organization of the member countries of the Alliance, and as such it provides a forum where North American and European parliamentarians meet to discuss problems of common concern.... Although the Assembly is completely independent of NATO, it constitutes a link between the national parliaments and Alliance officials." *The North Atlantic Treaty Organization* (Brussels: NATO Information Service, 1989), 367.

52. "Hungary Wants Closer Ties to NATO," RFE/RL Daily Report-Eastern Europe, no. 201, 22 October 1991. At the Madrid meeting Jeszenszky told the NATO members that it was of "vital importance" that NATO make a commitment to protect the new democracies in Eastern Europe.

53. Frank T. Csongos, "Hungarian Leader Looking For NATO Shield," UPI, 3 October 1991, from Nexis Service.

54. "Czechoslovak President Arrives in Cracow for Summit Meeting." In an appeal for "an institutionalized association with NATO,"the declaration stated: "It is impossible to have different types and different levels of security in Europe. Security must be equal for everybody."

55. "Defense Spending Cuts Under Fire," *Zycie Warszawy,* no. 202, 29 August 1991, 2, Polish News Bulletin, from Nexis.

56. "Czechoslovak Defense Minister in Poland," *Zycie Warszawy,* 6 September 1991, 2, Polish News Bulletin, from Nexis. Czechoslovakia's defense minister Lubosz Dobrovsky, said in Poland that although the armies of the "troika" should cooperate with each other in response to the possible disintegration of the USSR, they should not form a military alliance or military bloc as such.

57. The three states wanted to cooperate in matters of technical military assistance but to avoid any formal alliances with each other. See coverage of Krakow meeting in FBIS-EEU-91-195, 8 October 1991, 1-7.

The three focused their economic and technical policies on eventual membership in the European Community. See Havel's remarks of 6 October in Ibid., 6: "We are interested in becoming members of all-European bodies, perhaps regional bodies. We agreed to intensify our cooperation, consult on various pressing issues on various levels, and develop coordination of our political actions, but we did not agree on forming some sort of permanent bodies or even less so, some sort of joint bureaucracy. Our three countries still have enough of their own bureaucracies."

58. "Hungarian-Austrian Military Agreement," RFE/RL Daily Report-Eastern Europe, no. 205, 28 October 1991. "On October 25 in Budapest Hungarian Defense Minister Lajos Fur and his Austrian counterpart...concluded a bilateral military agreement...details of which are to be worked out by the two countries' chiefs of staffs. This is the first time that Austria has concluded a military agreement with an East European country." Hungary had earlier signed bilateral military agreements with Romania and Czechoslovakia.

59. "NATO Secretary General Says Visit to Bulgaria was 'Very Successful,'" Bulgarian Telegraph Agency (BTA) in English 1513 GMT, 14 June 1991, from Nexis.

60. See "President Zhelev Reviews Changes in Foreign Policy," BTA in English 1945 GMT, 9 August 1991, from BBC Summary of World Broadcasts, in Nexis On-line Service; "President Zhelev Says Results of His Visit to Germany Exceeded Expectations," DPA in German 1513 GMT, 5 September 1991, from BBC Summary of World Broadcasts, from Nexis.

61. Kjell Engelbrekt, "Bulgaria: Redefining National Security in the New Political Environment," in RFE/RL Research Institute, *Report on Eastern Europe* 2, no. 30, 26 July 1991, 5.

62. Viktor Valkov, Foreign Minister of Bulgaria, "Partnership Between Bulgaria and NATO: A promising development," *NATO Review* 39, no. 5, (October 1991), 13-17.

63. Ibid.

64. Duncan M. Perry, "Regional Topics: Eastern Europe Reacts to Baltic States' Independence," in RFE/RL Research Institute, *Report on Eastern Europe* 2, no. 36, September 6, 1991, 1.

65. "Baltics' Independence Garners Worldwide Support," UPI, 27 August 1991, from Nexis.

66. "B. Pankin on Recognizing the Independence of Latvia, Lithuania, and Estonia," *Izvestiia,* 7 September 1991, in *Current Digest of the Soviet Press,* 43, no. 36, 9 October 1991, 9.

67. "Soviet Military Withdrawal From Baltics," RFE/RL Daily Report-USSR, no. 176, 16 September 1991. See also "Landsbergis on Soviet Troops," RFE/RL Daily Report-USSR, no. 190, 7 October 1991.

68. "They Resigned Themselves to the Disintegration of the Union...," *Izvestiia,* 5 September 1991, 1; "The Soviet Army Prepares to Leave Lithuania," *Izvestiia,* 9 September 1991, 1 in *Current Digest of the Soviet Press,* 43, No. 36, 9 October 1991, 9.

69. "Gorbachev Frees Balts of All Military Obligations," RFE/RL Daily Report-USSR, no, 181, 23 September 1991.

70. "Baltic States," RFE/RL Daily Report-USSR, no. 178, 18 September 1991.

71. "Baltic Council Demands Soviet Troop Withdrawal," RFE/RL Daily Report-USSR, no. 190, 7 October 1991.

72. "Izvestiia: USSR Wants Lithuania to Help Finance Troop Withdrawal," RFE/RL Daily Report-USSR, no. 205, 28 October 1991; "Baltic States: Troop Withdrawal Hostage to Prosperity," RFE/RL Daily Report-USSR no. 206, 29 October 1991.

73. "Baltic States to Take Part in NATO Meeting," RFE/RL Daily Report-USSR, no. 196, 15 October 1991. The planned participation of Baltic representatives in a NATO meeting scheduled for Madrid 17-22 October 1991 had its precedent in East European participation in similar meetings. Echoing the statements of East European leaders, according to the RL report, Talavs Jundziz, Chair of the Latvian Supreme Council Commission on Defense and Internal Affairs, said that "while Latvia does not plan to join NATO in the near future, it looks to NATO to maintain European security."

74. "Baltic States Admitted as Associate Members of the North Atlantic Assembly," RFE/RL Daily Report-USSR, no. 205, 28 October 1991.

75. Speech by Secretary-General Manfred Woerner to the North Atlantic Assembly, 21 October 1991, from NATO Press Service, 8.

76. See RFE/RL Research Report, no. 242, 23 December 1991. "Baltic Foreign Ministers on Soviet Troop Withdrawal," Estonian foreign minister Lennart Meri proposed that NATO and the CSCE jointly monitor the

withdrawal of Soviet/CIS troops.

77. See Speech by Secretary-General Manfred Woerner to the North Atlantic Assembly. In this speech Woerner stressed the intention of NATO to complement, not replace, CSCE and other pan-European security structures. In regard to the countries of central and Eastern Europe, Woerner promised a great expansion of liaison contacts at multiple levels but did not mention any form of "membership" in NATO.

78. "London Declaration on a Transformed North Atlantic Alliance," 5 and 6 July 1990, paragraph 7, in *NATO 2000*, ed. Jamie Shea (London: Brasseys, 1990), 135.

79. "Partnership with the Countries of Central and Eastern Europe," statement issued by the North Atlantic Council meeting in Ministerial Session in Copenhagen, 6 and 7 June 1991, NATO Press Service, 6 June 1991, paragraph 3.

80. Carol Ciacomo, "US, Germany Urge Closer Ties Between NATO and Soviet Union," Reuters, 3 October 1991, from Nexis Service. One NATO official privately justified the alliance's refusal to accord special treatment to the "troika" by arguing that if NATO were to "widen" its membership by drawing in East European states, NATO would either have to include Russia or exclude it. To exclude Russia would create a new military confrontation, which NATO did not want. To include Russia in NATO would be to transform the alliance into a second CSCE, an institution yet to prove itself in the post-cold war era. Including Russia in NATO would also extend NATO to the Pacific and invite applications from U.S. allies in the Asia-Pacific region, a region far beyond NATO's political and military capabilities, Seattle, Washington, 25 October 1991.

81. Speech by Secretary-General Manfred Woerner to the North Atlantic Assembly, 8-9.

82. "Rome Declaration on Peace and Cooperation, November 7-8, 1991, paragraphs 9-12, *NATO Review,* December 1991, 19-22.

83. "The Alliance's New Strategic Concept," *NATO Review,* No. 6, December, 1991, p. 25-32.

84. "North Atlantic Cooperation Council Statement on Dialogue, Partnership and Cooperation, December 20, 1991," NATO Press Service.

85. FBIS-SOV-90-043, 5 March 1990, 34.

86. FBIS-EEU-90-049, 13 March 1990, 38-9.

87. FBIS-EEU-90-053, 19 March 1990.

88. Andrew Michta, "East-Central Europe in Search of Security," *SAIS Review* 11, no. 1 (Winter-Spring 1991): 60.

89. Colonel A. Belyusov, "Troops Leaving Poland," *Krasnaia zvezda,* 9 April 1991, 3. The initial date had been 1994 but was later changed to 1992. See "Compromise on Soviet Troop Evacuation," RFE/RL, Daily Report-Eastern Europe, no. 192, 9 October 1991.

90. Colin McIntrye, "Warsaw Pact Dying or Already Dead, Diplomat Says," Reuters, 4 June 1990, from Nexis Service.

91. *New York Times,* 13 June 1990, 8.

92. FBIS-EEU-90-145, 3 July 1991, 21.

93. FBIS-EEU-90-222, 16 November 1990.

94. Ibid.

95. Randall Forsberg, Rob Leavitt, and Steve Lilly-Weber, "Conventional Forces Treaty Buries Cold War," *Bulletin of the Atomic Scientists,* 47, no. 1, (January-February, 1991): 33.

96. Lambert W. Veenendaal, "Conventional Stability in Europe in 1991: Problems and Solutions," *NATO Review,* 39, no. 4, (August, 1991): 21-22.

97. "We Serve the Soviet Union: conversation with Marshal of the Soviet Union D. Yazov," *Pravda,* 23 February 1991, 1-2. in *Current Digest of the Soviet Press* no. 8, 27 March 1991, 7.

98. A. D. Horne, "Former Satellites Balk at Soviet Treaty Terms: Anti-Alliance Clause a Sticking Point," *Washington Post,* 17 August 1991, A17. See also "Hungarian Foreign Minister on Soviet-Hungarian Treaty," Budapest Home Service 1630 GMT 14 August 1991, from BBC Summary of World Broadcasts from Nexis Service; "Polish-Soviet Treaty Drafted," *Gazeta Wyborcza,* no. 13, 14 July 1991, 2, in Polish News Bulletin, 15 July 1991, from Nexis Service.

99. Cheslav Chobanu, "Viewpoint: On Short-Term Considerations and Good Neighborliness," *Pravda,* 3 June 1991, 6 in *Current Digest of the Soviet Press* 43, no. 22, 20.

100. Horne, "Former Satellites Balk at Soviet Treaty Terms" A17.

101. Stephen Greenhouse, "Death Knell Rings for Warsaw Pact," *New York Times,* 2 July 1991, 7.

102. Ibid.

103. See "Czech and Slovak Republic-USSR Friendship Treaty Initialed," RFE/RL Daily Report-Eastern Europe, no. 189, 4 October 1991.

146 *Christopher Jones*

See also "Polish-Soviet Treaty Ready for Initialing," RFE/RL Daily Report-Eastern Europe, no. 192, 9 October 1991.

104. "Finnish-Soviet Treaty to Be Replaced," RFE/RL Daily Report-USSR, no. 182, 24 September 1991.

105. Susan L. Clark, "Appendix: Sovereignty and Republican Armed Forces," in *Soviet Military Power in a Changing World* ed. Susan L. Clark, (Boulder, Colo.: Westview Press, 1991), 302.

106. Ibid. 301-5.

107. See Stephen Foye, "Statistics Show Low Military Draft Turnout in Republics," *Report on the USSR,*, 2, no. 30, 27 July 1990, 4, and Melanie Newton, "Final Draft Figures Revealed," *Report on the USSR*, 3, no. 17, 26 April 1991, 33.

108. Foye, "Statistics Show Low Military Draft Turnout in Republics." See also Clark, "Appendix," 304.

109. Clark, "Appendix," 303.

110. Ibid., 302-3.

111. "Yeltsin Appeals to RSFSR Soldiers in the Baltics," FBIS-SOV-91-009, 12 January 1992, 94.

112. Quoted in Stephen Carter, "Soviet Military Ideology," *Report on the USSR,* 3, no. 36, 6 September 1991, 16.

113. "Merging of USSR and RSFSR Defense Structures" RFE/RL Daily Report-USSR, no. 176, 16 September 1991.

114. Stephen Foye, "Yeltsin Begins Housecleaning in the Defense Ministry," *Report on the USSR* 3, no. 36, 6 September 1991, 32.

115. "Kobets Named RSFSR Defense Advisor," RFE/RL Daily Report-USSR, no. 167, 16 September 1991.

116. Ibid.

117. Clines, "Soviet Army on Defense, in the Ukraine," A5.

118. "Grachev on RSFSR Defense Ministry," RFE/RL Daily Report-USSR, no. 180, 20 September 1991.

119. See "Defense Minister on Prestige of Army," *Krasnaia zvezda,* 31 August 1991, 1, in FBIS-SOV-91-170, 3 September 1991, 55-58, especially 57. See also N. Bilan, "USSR Defense Minister on Need for All-Union Defense Structure," *Sovetskaia Rossiia,* 20 September 1991, in English from BBC, 23 September 1991, from Nexis Service. In this interview Shaposhnikov declared that "the army must be preserved as one of the attributes of the single system of defense functioning over one-sixth

of the earth's surface. The disorganization of the work of this most complex system, and even more so, its destruction, could objectively become factors which acutely destabilize the political and socio-economic situation in the country, and, indeed, throughout the world."

120. Bilan, "USSR Defense Minister on Need for All-Union Defense Structure," from Nexis.

121. "Unified Air Defense System Urged," RFE/RL Daily Report-USSR, no. 178, 18 September 1991.

122. "Ground Forces Commander on Future," RFE/RL Daily Report-USSR, no. 172, 10 September 1991.

123. Interview with General of the Army Vladimir Lobov, chief of the General Staff of the USSR armed forces, "We Will Not Divide Up the Army," *Pravda,* 9 September 1991, 1-2, in *Current Digest of the Soviet Press,* 43, no. 36, 1991, 9 October 1991, 17.

124. "Lopatin on Union Security Structure," RFE/RL Daily Report-USSR, no. 174, 12 September 1991.

125. Hiatt, "Some Soviet Republics Seeking Separate Armies."

126. V. Nazarenko, "Voennaia doktrina obnovelnnogo soiuza" (The Military Doctrine of a Renewed Union), *Krasnaia zvezda,* 11 October 1991, 3.

127. V. Litovkin, "The Military Council on Arbat Square Has Broken Off: Consultations Will Continue," *Izvestiia,* 13 September 1991, 1, in *Current Digest of the Soviet Press,* 43, no. 36, 9 October 1991, 18.

128. "Moldova in Talks with USSR on Troop Withdrawal," RFE/RL Daily Report-USSR, no. 176, 16 September 1991.

129. Shaposhnikov interview from *Sovetskaia Rossiia,* 20 September 1991.

130. "Further Soviet Military Cuts Discussed," RFE/RL Daily Report-USSR, no. 188, 2 October 1991.

131. "CIS Leaders Stumble Over Unified Army," RFE/RL Daily Report, no. 1, 2 January 1992.

132. "Disagreement on Defense," RFE/RL Daily Report-USSR, no. 244, 30 December 1991.

133. "Moldavia to Introduce Own Military Draft," RFE/RL Daily Report-USSR, no. 210, 5 November 1991.

134. "Moldova Wants 'Neutrality, Independent Military,'" RFE/RL Daily Report-USSR, no. 244, 30 December 1991.

135. "Byelorussia to Form Own Defense System," RFE/RL Daily Report-USSR, no. 183, 24 September 1991.

136. "Toward a Byelorussian National Guard," RFE/RL Daily Report no. 208, 31 October 1991. See also RFE/RL Daily Report-USSR, no. 206, 29 October 1991.

137. RFE/RL Daily Report no. 1, 2 January 1992.

138. "Text of the Charter of Paris for a New Europe," 21 November, 1990 in *Weekly Compilation of Presidential Documents* 26, 26 November 1990, 1880-88.

6

East Meets West: Three Paths to Economic Integration

Katherine W. Owen

T he cold war is over; there is no longer an iron curtain. Yet it is evident that the people of Europe are still separated. Attempts to overcome this separation are being made through a process of democratization and economic reform in Eastern Europe. The extent to which this process has occurred varies from country to country. The transition to a democratic system with a market economy is well under way in Poland, Hungary, and Czechoslovakia, while it remains the spoken desire of Bulgaria and Romania.[1]

While the fall of the communist governments in Eastern Europe overjoyed those in the West, it also presented Western governments and institutions with the opportunity to support and creatively influence these ailing countries as well as the responsibility for doing so. The road to recovery will be long and bumpy. Financial and technical assistance will certainly help smooth the way, but close cooperation with highly developed regions is also needed to pull the countries along. Thus the reform process involves more than a series of domestic economic and political reforms. It also involves integrating these countries into the world economy. Help in integrating the East with the West is occurring on three complementary levels: through cooperative agreements with the European Community (EC), through Western direct investment, and through a network of bilateral and multilateral agreements with Western governments. Each of these levels will now be examined in order to survey the promised economic aid and the merging investment, financial, and structural relations between the Eastern European countries and the West.

The European Community

The European Community is the major player in fostering East-West integration. The EC and its member states form the bulk of the concerted G-24 assistance efforts, which the Community Commission coordinates. The EC also provides the principal capital support for the European Bank for Reconstruction and Development (EBRD), whose main objective is to support private investment in Eastern Europe. The Community's European Investment Bank has ECU 1 billion available for commitment in 1990-92, with a further ECU 200 million being made available under the European Coal and Steel Community Treaty. Moreover, the European Community has extended formal association to the East European countries that have demonstrated a commitment to political and economic reform. It is the intent of the EC that the new associate members become full-fledged members by the end of the decade or early in the next century.[2]

Although the EC has extended its hand to its Eastern neighbors, the issue of association, in particular, is not one that gives rise to unanimity. Germany and Italy, which strongly support bringing the Easterners into the Community, equate greater East-West integration with European stability. East Europeans, because of instability in their countries, have flocked to Germany and Italy in the last few years. Germany and Italy also have significant investments in Eastern Europe and view closer ties with the region as being profitable for both parties. The United Kingdom is also an advocate of East-West integration. It is suspected, however, that London is pushing not only for more cooperative relations but for the eventual membership of Eastern Europe into the EC so as to render the idea of a supranational Europe less likely. The strongest opponent of enlargement has been France. The French initially feared East European association because it was thought this would result in a German-dominated EC; however, it seems the French now see enlargement as a means of diluting Germany's power. The poorer EC countries (Spain, Greece, Portugal, and Ireland) are wary of increased membership because of the potential damage to their economic growth and access to EC funds.[3]

The East, of course, wants to develop a close and complex relationship with the EC as quickly as possible.[4] The Community is obviously attractive because of its geographic proximity and the political and cultural ties it has historically represented. Its importance, however, derives from the fact that it is now the East's link to the world's economy.

The Community's relations with the East European countries have strengthened and developed rapidly since June 1988. At that time the EC established formal links with the Council for Mutual Economic Assistance (COMECON), the Soviet-dominated trade club. The EC-East European relationship was initially a patchwork of individual trade and cooperative agreements. At the heart of the trade pacts was the removal of EC quotas on specific goods. The treaties promised to end all quotas on manufactured imports into the Community by 1995. The EC, however, qualified the agreements with various protective measures to ensure that domestic producers were not threatened with serious injury. The trade agreements were very limited in scope, protecting against imports of Polish steel, for instance. Most favored nation status applied, yet it lacked much practical significance. The aim of the cooperative part of the treaties was to encourage trade and economic relations by means other than traditional trade policy. This effort was to include the organization of various events, such as exhibitions, conferences, and trade fairs. Yet no money was specifically designated to finance cooperation. Thus the cooperative parts of the agreements were of little substance.

Hungary was the first COMECON country to sign an agreement with the EC in 1988, followed by Poland and Czechoslovakia. Czechoslovakia, however, did not obtain the cooperative element until 1990, after free elections had been held. Bulgaria also merited a trade and cooperative treaty in 1990, and Romania was awarded a treaty in 1991. Yugoslavia had been the beneficiary of a similar agreement as early as 1980, an agreement made in recognition of its independence from the Soviet Union. All the agreements were to be in effect for a period of ten years, with the exception of Poland's agreement, which was to last for only five.[5]

These trade and cooperative treaties were really very political in nature. The EC was merely giving a few carrots to the East European countries that were moving fastest toward capitalism and democracy. There were differences in negotiations and in agreements. For instance, Poland and

Hungary enjoyed significantly better access to the Common Market and qualified for help with a training program for bankers, whereas Czechoslovakia had to be content with the removal of a few quotas.

These first steps at building a closer relationship with the East were overtaken by the dramatic events of 1989 and 1990: the political and economic liberalization of Poland and Hungary, the fall of Erich Honecker in October 1989, and Czechoslovakia's swift transition to democracy. The European Community quickly responded. In July 1989, at an economic summit in Paris, the EC accepted the job of coordinating the West's relief efforts. The EC Commission would now coordinate the actions of the Group of 24 countries belonging to the Organization for Economic Cooperation and Development (OECD) through a program known as PHARE (Poland and Hungary Action for Restructuring of the Economy) The aim of the PHARE program is to support the reform process. PHARE was soon enlarged to aid Bulgaria, Czechoslovakia, Romania, and Yugoslavia. The EC's allocations for PHARE increased each year beginning with ECU 500 million in 1990, increasing to ECU 850 million in 1991, and totaling ECU 1 billion for 1992. By January 1991 the EC institutions had also provided ECU 2 billion in loans; member governments had provided ECU 1.6 billion in grants and ECU 4.9 billion in loans, apart from their contributions through such international financial institutions as the World Bank, the International Monetary Fund (IMF), and the EBRD.[6]

Yet all these responses—liberalization of imports through trade agreements, loans, coordination of PHARE aid—were ad hoc. There was a definite need to put the relationship on a more secure footing. The East Europeans were looking beyond normalization toward a more intense relationship. They wanted to go beyond cooperation to association. Serious talk of association within the EC began in early 1990. It was thought that the Community should respond positively to the East Europeans' interest in association as a sign of solidarity with the democratic forces in the neighboring states and because it conformed with the Community's own interests.

It was the United Kingdom's suggestion that the East European countries giving practical evidence of a commitment to economic and political reform be associated with the Community.[7] Practical evidence of economic reform includes liberalization in order to create a market economy. Politically, countries must demonstrate the rule of law, human rights, multiparty systems, and fair elections. In August 1990 the EC Commission sent its proposal for a form of association to the Council and to the European Parliament. In December 1990, negotiations began with the three countries providing evidence of reform: Poland, Hungary, and Czechoslovakia.[8]

The Europe Agreements, as they are known, include provisions establishing political dialogue and cultural cooperation and encouraging the creation of a free trade zone. They are intended to hasten the process of reform and to pave the way for eventual membership within the EC. The new accords significantly broaden the scope of the bilateral trade and cooperative agreements with the EC that took effect by June 1990. A similar accord is to be negotiated with Bulgaria.

The three accords, signed 16 December 1991, are identical in structure but vary in content. They will establish cooperation in the following areas:

•**Political dialogue.** Regular, high-level meetings are to be held on all matters of common interest. The aim is to coordinate foreign policy positions where possible.

•**Free movement of goods.** The agreements are preferential and are designed to create eventual free trade. They include trade concessions in favor of the three central European countries, as well as special protocols on textiles, customs cooperation, and rules of origin. Agriculture and fisheries trade will be based on mutual concessions.

•**Freedom of movement for people.** Cooperation will initially aim at improving conditions for nationals of the three countries already living in an EC member state.

•**Right of establishment.** This is to follow the principle of national treatment, allowing professionals and businesses the same right as citizens of the host country involved. The three central European countries will have a transitional period before according this right; the EC will apply it from the date of entry into force of the agreements.

•**Freedom of movement of capital.** This includes capital earned from business, services, investment, repatriation of profits, or movement of personal funds.

•**Gradual application of EC law.** Notably, this will occur in the area of competition, to enable the three countries to integrate their economies with the economy of the EC.

•**Economic cooperation in all sectors of common interest.** In particular, cooperation will extend to these areas—industrial activities, promotion and protection of investments, standards, science and technology, education and training, statistics, regional development, social policy, transport, telecommunications, money laundering, drug trafficking, and the environment.

•**Financial cooperation.** Poland, Hungary, and Czechoslovakia will be eligible until the end of 1992 for grants from PHARE and for loans from the European Investment Bank. The EC will also examine the possibility of giving macroeconomic assistance, such as balance of payments support.

•**Cultural cooperation.**[9]

The implementation of these accords is to be overseen by a ministerial-level Association Council. Additionally, a parliamentary level Association Committee will be set up to have a consultative role. The Europe Agreements are to be of indefinite duration after an initial transitory term of a ten-year period of two five-year phases. The associate, before entering the second phase, must have made sufficient progress in establishing a market economy and in consolidating democracy. The Europe Agreements can be renounced by either side if the conditions on which they are based have not been met.

During the negotiation of these agreements, the greatest difficulties arose over the four freedoms of movement—goods, services, capital, and people. With regard to the movement of goods, the East Europeans hoped for a more generous agreement with a shorter timetable for the removal of tariffs and quotas. Under the Europe Agreements, tariffs and quotas on industrial products are to be eventually phased out by both parties within a ten-year period. The EC has already moved toward free trade by applying the Generalized System of Preferences and removing or suspending most of its quotas on imports of industrial products, with the exception of textiles. Although it has recently been conceded that textile quotas should rise, tariffs will be eliminated by the end of the first five-year period.

The agreements aim at establishing a free trade area between the three East European countries and the EC. Concessions granted for liberalized trade in industrial products are reciprocal but weighted in favor of Hungary, Poland, and Czechoslovakia, which generally have a longer period than the EC for liberalizing their markets.

The EC, however, still has recourse to protectionist measures. For example, it has the ability to implement anti-dumping duties and Voluntary Restraint Arrangements. There are also trade restrictions on strategic goods. These apply particularly to new technologies and affect such things as the export of certain telecommunications equipment. The Community is negotiating separately the export of strategic materials to the East, attempting to safeguard against onward transmission of these items to potentially adversarial powers.

Farm trade is a separate and hotly contested issue. Approximately one fourth of Eastern Europe's exports to the EC consist of farm products. Yet the EC clings to protectionist barriers here. The fear is that the EC will only add to its food mountains by allowing Hungarian and Polish agricultural products into the Community, thus contributing to the cost of the Common Agricultural Policy. The EC has granted some concessions, but mostly for less threatening items, such as soft fruit and mushrooms. The Hungarians and the Poles in particular want greater access for their other products, especially for beef, lamb, dairy products, and cereals. The East Europeans say the EC is keeping trade barriers in the areas where their exports are most competitive. They are asking that the Community practice what it preaches about free market economics. Access for these agricultural exports would be an easy means of earning hard currency in the short term.

Without liberalized trading with the West, Eastern Europe is doomed. The collapse of COMECON plunged the East European countries into a severe recession. Companies saw their main market, the Soviet Union, vanish. Bulgaria was the country most affected. More than 80 percent of its trade was with the other COMECON countries.[10] East European officials believe that free trade is a most important part of the solution. As one Polish official put it, "It's not credible to give assistance on the one hand and close the door to [trade] on the other."[11] Free trade is very desirable in the long run, but the truth is that the East Europeans will be loath rather than eager to want it in the short run. They will probably desire that Western markets open up to their exports without a quid pro quo from their side necessarily, lest Western goods flood their markets. Free trade or liberalization will surely cause a sharp decline in industrial production, high unemployment, and the closing down of the bulk of industrialized units.

The opening of trade in services and capital is analogous to the rules and regulations relating to the trade of goods. The East Europeans are currently very weak in this area, and the free flow of capital and services into their countries will be very important. As the associates' financial institutions become more sophisticated, their capital markets should begin to integrate with the international capital markets. Progress toward freedom of capital exports and the linkage of financial markets should then occur in the second phase of the transitional period. With convertible currencies the associates could peg their currencies to the ECU. This would help them prepare to become members of the EC.

As for the freedom of movement of peoples, the agreements are aimed primarily at improving the lot of those Easterners already legally established in the Community. Furthermore, the agreements provide for "full application of national treatment for the establishment and operations of all firms and all professions throughout the Community and Czechoslovakia, Hungary and Poland."[12] The fear of mass migration of peoples is the reason this "freedom" is so limited. Westerners are increasingly becoming xenophobic. In reality there are grounds to fear the impact of migrant workers. In 1990 alone, West Germans received nearly a million Germans into their country from the East. East Europeans now have visa free travel to most EC countries. Yet they still will not have the freedom to come and work.

The subjects included in the cooperative part of the accords are similar to the subjects listed in the bilateral agreements. Some subjects concern microeconomic policies, vocational training, tourism, the environment, and culture. Cooperation, however, is not significant without the means to finance it. The countries are now able to receive grants (under PHARE until the end of 1992, and under continuation of PHARE or some other multiannual structure beginning 1993) and loans from the European Investment Bank for these sorts of projects.

There is no single deal to help Eastern Europe today as there was with the post-1945 Marshall Plan. Assistance is coming from more than several sources. The main purpose of aid must be to get the East European countries on the track to self-sustaining growth. The old saying applies: Give a man a fish and he eats for a day; teach a man to fish and he can eat for a lifetime. Therefore, the amount of aid should be enough not only to sustain the reforms but also to "create the momentum that will draw the necessary private capital along with it."[13]

This is not as easy as it sounds. There are difficulties in providing assistance, some of which are self-inflicted. Most of the aid has taken the form of technical assistance in such areas as economic restructuring and privatization of state-owned companies. But many Polish and Hungarian officials have concluded that their countries are "technically over-assisted" in most areas, to the point that assistance is doing more harm than good in some instances.[14] Most of the technical assistance goes to consultants who are unfamiliar with institutions peculiar to postcommunist economies. East European officials are overburdened, working very often with untrained staffs. They complain that they cannot do their jobs because so much time is spent with consultants. Moreover, some of these consultants look for profitable assignments, which may be completely unnecessary.

Other problems include the time limits imposed by budgetary controls that have inhibited the support of projects or programs possibly requiring expenditures beyond one or two years. Thus, money approved by the EC budget for 1990 had to be allocated in that year and spent no later than 1991. This rule has since been relaxed so that disbursement may go beyond 1992.

Despite the coordination efforts of the European Community Commission, it is difficult to determine exactly how much aid has been given. The G-24 allocated for the PHARE program ECU 5.7 billion in grants, as well as ECU 9.9 billion in loans and credits from governments and the EC, together with ECU 3.9 billion from the World Bank. The EC has been the single biggest contributor to the program, with ECU 2.5 billion in grants. With the member states, this amounts to ECU 4.1 billion, or 72 percent of the grants awarded. The EC and its member states have also given ECU 7.0 billion in loans and credits, or one half of the loans and credits awarded. This compares with the U.S. contribution of ECU 763 million for grants and of ECU 179 million for loans and credits. Japan has contributed ECU 42 million worth of grants and ECU 1.5 billion worth of loans.[15]

PHARE is not a macroeconomic stabilization fund; its grants are not to support the economies of the beneficiary states as a whole or to cover their general financing or investment needs. These sorts of operations are the responsibility of other institutions—such as the IMF, the World Bank, the European Investment Bank, and the EBRD—to which the EC contributes.[16]

PHARE funds must be used to finance projects aimed at economic restructuring in certain priority areas: agriculture, industry, investment, energy, training, environmental protection, trade, and services. This implies the transformation of the production and distribution system, with an emphasis on private ownership and investment as well as the establishment of a broader regulatory, commercial, and organizational infrastructure. The PHARE program money will be used to assist in framing new laws, regulations, and institutions and to reform accounting procedures, company laws, and banking and insurance practices.

The other main source of financial aid is the EBRD. Its charter stipulates that its purpose is to support transition to market economies, and in doing so it will be the first international institution to act as a merchant bank. The bank's total capital amounts to ECU 10 billion, 51 percent of which is subscribed by the EC member states together with the Commission and the European Investment Bank. The EBRD expects to lend at a rate of about ECU 1 billion a year for the first five years. At least 60 percent of its loans and equity investments will go to the private sector, to financial intermediaries that will on-lend to the private sector, or to public companies to help make them more competitive and ready for privatization. The public sector is entitled to loans and equity investments (up to 40 percent) in particular areas, such as physical and financial infrastructure and the environment, essential to economic development and to the transition to a market economy.[17] The bank will try to create favorable conditions so that private banks and companies may more easily enter the East European markets. Toward this end the EBRD will focus on infrastructure projects; help establish and strengthen financial institutions, capital markets, and regulatory bodies; and participate in industrial restructuring and privatization by participating in both debt and equity financing. The EBRD will also be involved in mutual funds to help manage the shift from public to private ownership.

Aid, however, is not the total solution. Through the EC's efforts the nations of Eastern Europe have found support in reviving their shattered economies. But those governments will have to assist in this reconstruction. "While these governments are looking to the West, and the EBRD, for aid to curb unemployment, maintain stability and get their economies back on their feet, it is only through a large inflow of foreign investment that the basis can be created of sustained economic growth."[18]

Foreign Investment

Foreign investment will play a very useful role in resurrecting the region's economies. To catch up with the average incomes in Western Europe in the next decade, however, the East European countries will need $420 billion per year in investment.[19] This scale of investment has not been forthcoming, even though the amount of foreign investment has been steadily increasing. The number of foreign registrations in Eastern Europe and the Soviet Union soared during 1990, from about 5,000 at the beginning of the year to over 16,000 at the end of the year; the amount of statutory capital (planned investment) rose from less than $5 billion to over $8 billion.[20] United Nations estimates and national government data for a few of the countries, however, indicate that only a small proportion of these proposed projects are operational and that relatively little foreign capital has actually been invested. Of those projects proposed, European companies made up 60 percent of the total; U.S. companies accounted for 12 percent of the total number of registrations as of January 1991.[21]

As of spring 1991, Hungary had attracted the largest amount of investment which totaled $1 billion.[22] Poland, coming in second, had attracted a total of $350 million in foreign investment, mainly in joint ventures. There have been big single deals, such as that involving the Skoda car works in Czechoslovakia, in which a 70 percent share was bought by Volkswagen of Germany; the Tungsram electric bulb group in Hungary, which was bought by General Electric of the United States; and the Polish Zamech turbine manufacturer, which was bought by ABB of Switzerland. The overall flow of investment, however, has been a disappointment for several reasons. Forty years of communist rule took its toll; a lack of competition and investment led to industrial obsolescence. The East European countries have been advised to privatize as quickly as possible. It is hoped that selling state assets will attract foreign investment, build their budding market economies, and break the stranglehold of the state bureaucracy. (See Table 1.)

Table 1: Big Deals

Investors	Partner	Industry	Amount Committed in Millions of Dollars
Volkswagen (Germany)	**SKODA , BAZ** Czech.	cars	6,630
CBS France	**Tourinvest** Czech.	hotels	175
GE U.S.	**Tungsram** Hungary	lighting	150
GM U.S.	**Raba** Hungary	engines, cars	150
Pilkingtom Britain	**HSO Sandomierz** Poland	glass	140
Guardian U.S.	**Hungarian Glass** Hungary	glass	120
Suzuki Japan (partnership w/ C. Itoh and International Finance Corp.)	**Autokonzern** Hungary	cars	110
Linde Germany	**Technoplyn** Czech.	gases	106
Electrolux Sweden	**Lehel** Hungary	appliances	83
Hamburger Austria	**Dunapack** Hungary	packaging	82
Ford U.S.	**New Plant** Hungary	car components	80
Sanofi France	**Chinoin** Hungary	pharmaceuticals	80
Oberoi India	**Hungarhotels** Hungary	hotels	80
US West U.S. (partnership w/ Bell Atlantic)	**Government** Czech.	telephones, switches	80
Sara Lee U.S.	**Compack** Hungary	food processing	60
ABB Switzerland	**Zamech** Poland	turbines	50
Siemens Germany	**Electromagnetica and Rom Post Telecom** Romania	telecommunications	35
Ilwa Italy	**Salgotarjau Iron** Hungary	steel	25
Siemens Germany	**Tesla Karin** Czech.	telecommunications	15
Bau Holding Austria	**Nyiregyhaza** Hungary	construction	11
Watmoughs Britain	**Revai Printing** Hungary	publishing house	7

Source: *Business International*, cited in *The Economist,* 21 September 1991.

Privatization, however, is frustrating, expensive, and time-consuming. In the mid-1980s state-owned companies accounted for more than 80 percent of total value-added, a measure of an economy's wealth creation, compared with 17 percent or less in the EC and the U.S.[23] Romania topped the list with about 40,000 state-owned firms, followed by Poland, with 7,500; Bulgaria, with 5,000; Czechoslovakia, with 4,800; and Hungary, with 2,300.[24] These countries hope to privatize half of the state-owned firms by 1994.

To begin the process of selling a state-owned company, the government first must seize control from its managers and workers, who own it in all but legal name. Under East European socialism, many investment decisions were made by managers. As regimes began to crumble in 1989, states effectively abrogated their role as the owners of state-owned companies. Little or no state oversight gave workers and managers the opportunity to take value out of their firms through high wages, excess employment, or outright theft. Given this amount of control, cooperation of the work force is essential in order to sell these companies.

Yet even with cooperation, privatization is fraught with problems. There is no real estate valuation, cash-flow analysis, or marketing plan. East European companies are now trying to identify assets, draw up business-like balance sheets, and reorganize into coherent operating structures. Trying to calculate the value of state-owned firms in Eastern Europe is an uncertain process at best. And many of these firms are actually "value-subtractors." This means that at world prices the value of the resources they consume is worth more than what they produce. This situation came about owing, in part, to cheap Soviet energy prices and to the fact that there were captive consumers. According to one recent study, 20-25 percent of manufacturing industries in Poland, Czechoslovakia, and Hungary could be value-subtractors.[25] In Czechoslovakia this includes the food industry and the leather and tobacco companies. In Hungary iron and steel companies are listed. Basic chemical, cement, and nonferrous metallurgy industries are included as value-subtractors in Poland.

Another problem is the near total confusion about who owns what. It is very difficult to define property and ownership rights in Eastern Europe. Investors need to know if the property they desire is indeed buyable. Often, no one person has the authority to sell a property. Central and local authorities and current occupiers and former owners make competing claims.[26] Once things get to the negotiation stage, the numerous participants make making a deal painful. Foreign buyers, state company managers, State Property Agency officials, accountants, and legal counsels are all involved. Moreover, the formalities involved in setting up the business can take an inordinately long time. There can be an additional three months simply to process an application for a new business in the company registration court.

Considerable strides have been made in setting up a legal framework for privatization. Hungary and Poland are currently the easiest countries in Eastern Europe for a foreign investor to enter. Government approval, however, is required to make investments in certain industry sectors in Poland and in Bulgaria. In Czechoslovakia and in Hungary approval is required if a joint venture is to be formed with a government entity. Albania, Romania, and Yugoslavia still require approval of all foreign investments. Wholly owned foreign investments are allowed in all Eastern European countries except Albania. Full repatriation of profits is generally permitted in Bulgaria, Hungary, Poland, and Yugoslavia. Other East European countries have specific restrictions.

There are deals being made. According to Bela Kadar, Hungary's minister of international economic relations, half of all foreign investment in Eastern Europe (excluding Germany) went to Hungary in 1991. This amounted to somewhere between $750 million and $1 billion.[27] This amount is but a fraction of that enjoyed by the southern European or southeast Asian countries that compete with Eastern Europe for foreign investment. Investors are attracted to Hungary because it has the most liberal investment regime in the world. Foreign investors have the right to set up in the service sector, acquire major control without special permission, and repatriate profits fully. Investors encounter difficulties in Hungary as well, however. For example, one of the largest and soundest of the twenty companies included in Hungary's privatization program is the Danubius Hotel chain. It should therefore be one of the easiest to sell. The company has eighteen first-class hotels, each of which lies on land owned by the local authority, which is entitled to shares in the new private sector entity. This requires, then, eighteen separate and difficult negotiations.

The problems involved in selling state-owned companies one-by-one have prompted schemes of mass privatization. After a year of heated debate, Poland and Czechoslovakia have launched mass privatization programs. Poland's approach involves the free distribution of shares in large investment funds, which in turn are given ownership in hundreds of state-owned companies. The funds will actively exercise their ownership rights by trading shares with each other and by restructuring, merging, expanding, or closing companies. Ultimately, citizens will become owners of the companies through the funds. Plans are for between five and twenty funds to be created, officially controlled by Polish boards of directors, and managed by Western fund managers. All adult Polish citizens will receive an equal number of shares in all the investment groups. Approximately 400 large companies representing a quarter of Poland's industrial output are to be given to the funds.[28]

Czechoslovakia's plan is somewhat different. It is based on investment vouchers. All adult citizens can buy vouchers for a nominal sum. Shares of all the companies participating in the plan will be sold for the vouchers at auction. Voucher holders will use them to bid for as many shares of any company as they want. This process will be repeated so that several thousand companies will eventually be "given away." Citizens may also become shareholders in private investment funds approved by the government. The funds can solicit vouchers, which will be used to bid for shares on behalf of the shareholders.[29]

The details are yet to be worked out for these programs. They are risky and no one knows whether or not they will work. The region's economies, however, will not recover if companies remain in the hands of the states. Even if these privatization schemes are succesful, a genuine market economy will still be a dream and not a reality. Western governments will increasingly have to help finance reform projects.

Western Government Assistance

Western government intervention in the region is a third component facilitating East-West integration. A study undertaken by The Institute of International Finance urged that "because of the nature of the task and the political implications, Western governments will need to take the lead in organizing assistance through their own national agencies and international institutions."[30] The IMF, the World Bank, and the EBRD are examples of international institutions to which the report referred; official export credit agencies (ECAs) are the national agencies mentioned in the study.

East European countries have encountered a sharp decline in their creditworthiness, owing to the economic and political turmoil they have experienced. It has, therefore, been increasingly difficult for them to attract financing from Western commercial banks or other private lenders unless these lenders have had repayment guarantees from Western governments.[31] According to an OECD report, "The willingness of private banks to lend to these countries on a sovereign risk basis [has] declined to nearly the vanishing point."[32] As a consequence, official creditors have stepped in to offset the decline in lending of private creditors. This is being done in three main ways. East European countries can seek increased financial support for their economic reform programs through international financial institutions such as the EBRD. Additionally, Western governments can provide repayment guarantees to private creditors investing in Eastern Europe. Finally, official creditors are becoming involved through bilateral assistance programs.

Official creditors then fall into two camps: multilateral and bilateral. The major multilateral creditors are those previously mentioned—the IMF, the World Bank, and the EBRD. The bilateral creditors include the ECAs, official aid agencies, and special bilateral programs, such as the national treasury bridging loans and the American/Polish and American/Hungarian Enterprise Fund.[33]

The European Community Commission has been made the clearinghouse for bilateral assistance to Eastern Europe through the PHARE program. Figures on this assistance, however, can only be rough estimates, given the vagueness of the categories and promises. The best guess is that the G-24 has promised about ECU 33 billion ($38 billion) of aid to Eastern Europe.[34] What is indisputable is that Germany takes the lead of all aid given, despite the strain of its $100 billion outlay for eastern Germany's economic restructuring. Germany's grant contribution is ECU 766 million (of which ECU 665 million constituted a cancellation of Polish debt in advance of the general writing down in March 1991). The United Kingdom ranks second among the EC members, with ECU 230 million, followed by Denmark and Italy, with ECU 202 million each. France and the Netherlands trail with ECU 120 million and ECU 41 million, respectively.[35]

The single largest component of Western official financing to Eastern Europe is trade financing provided by ECAs.

> [A]n export credit arises whenever a foreign buyer of exported goods or services is allowed to defer payment. Export credits are generally divided into short term (usually below two years), medium term (usually two to five years), and long term (usually over five years).... official support may be limited to "pure cover," by which is meant insurance or guarantees given to exporters or lending institutions without financing support.

Alternatively, it may be given in the form of "financing support," which is defined as including direct credits, refinancing and all forms of interest subsidies.[36]

Germany comes in first in this category as well. About one-half of the Community's ECU 7.0 billion loans constituted export credits allocated by member states. Germany was the biggest provider of export credits, with ECU 1.7 billion allocated.[37] Italy and Austria are also very active in the region, together with Germany accounting for almost two thirds of the business. The ECAs of France, Japan, the United Kingdom and the United States share about one fourth of the region's business. During 1990, the ECAs made an estimated $6-8 billion in new commitments to the region.[38]

Almost all industrial countries have ECAs. Their structures, operations, and relationships to their governments vary widely, however. For example, MITI (the Ministry of International Trade and Industry), Japan's ECA, is part of the government ministry, whereas the U.S. Eximbank is an independent government agency. Germany's Hermes is a private firm operating on behalf of the government. ECA business involves high-risk transactions. As of spring 1991, total ECA exposure in Eastern Europe and the then Soviet Union represented approximately two thirds of the region's estimated $65 billion of official bilateral debt.[39]

Since the debt crisis began in the early 1980s ECAs and commercial banks have had to devise policies for countries with severe balance of payments problems. East European net debt was nearly $100 billion at the end of 1990. Poland's debt stood at $43 billion, followed by Hungary at $20 billion, Yugoslavia at $16 billion, Bulgaria at $10 billion, Czechoslovakia at $7 billion, and Romania at $1 billion.[40] Working multilaterally through the Paris Club, ECAs and other official creditors have provided debt relief. At a January 1991 meeting of the G-7 finance ministers, agreement was reached on a 50 percent write-off of Poland's bilateral debt of $33 billion. This was done because Poland had suspended the servicing of its debt and the interest due was accumulating as new debt. The Hungarians also have a very heavy debt, but they continue to service in full. No one is seriously considering a write-off here, but something has to be done, otherwise the success of their economic reforms will be in jeopardy. A loan of one half of their debt with very low interest rates for an initial short term, rising thereafter in stages, has been proposed.

Again the main aim of the aid is to help these countries achieve sustained economic growth. The EC Commission estimated the external financing needs of the East Europeans at ECU 14 billion for 1991.[41] Until private investment really takes off, the problem is one for the public authorities.

Conclusion

The task of building market economies and installing democratic institutions in Eastern Europe is enormous. Not only must the Easterners build from scratch a reasonable facsimile of Western market economies and political institutions, but they have to do it as they are tearing down equally complex economic and political structures. East and West must act together quickly. Analysts agree that gradualism is no answer to the problems plaguing the region.[42] Yet this rapid transition brings additional problems, such as rapid growth in unemployment. If reforms falter, Eastern Europe's course is likely to be that of many developing countries: inflation, political instability, and corruption.

The countries of Eastern Europe, however, have a huge advantage over other poor, developing countries. They have the West's attention. The EC is just next door, foreign investment is beginning to flow, and Western governments together with international financial institutions are offering technical help as well as some kinds of monetary assistance.

There is no painless route or one-shot solution. If these countries' reforms succeed, the effects on them and the West will be tremendous, and some of them will not be pleasant. For example, trade expansion will likely cause friction because the more the East European countries succeed as exporters, the more apt they will be to encounter protectionism. The effects of net flows of capital to Eastern Europe will mean either diminished flows to the rest of the developing world or an increase in global interest rates. The most dramatic effects of East-West integration, however, will be on the EC. The Community will have to devise a structure that will allow the East European economies to be integrated progressively given their much lower levels of competitiveness. An increase in membership will also place an administrative burden on the Community.[43]

Whatever the consequences, the West is charging toward closer and more substantive relations with the East based upon increased cooperation in all areas. All in the West are aware of their common responsibility to bring the peoples of Europe together in a secure and peaceful environment in this new, post-cold war era.

Notes

1. "Jam Tomorrow," *The Economist* Survey, 21 September 1991, 4.

2. European Community, *Europe Agreements with Czechoslovakia, Hungary, and Poland,* Brussels, EC, Commission, November 1991 (DOC. IP [91] 1033).

3. "EC Girds Itself for Invisible Expansion," *Christian Science Monitor,* 24 December 1991, 5.

4. European Community, "Despite Economic Hardships, Most Central and Eastern Europeans back the Free Market: Eurobarometer/Gallup Poll also shows widespread dissatisfaction with current democracies and big support for EC Association and Even Membership," Brussels, EC Commission, 27 January 1992 (DOC. IP [92] 47).

5. European Community, *The European Community and Its Neighbors* (Luxembourg: EC Official Publications Office, 1990).

6. European Community, *PHARE SCOREBOARD,* G-24 Coordination Unit, Directorate General for External Affairs, Brussels, EC, Commission, 30 January 1991. See also John Pinder, *The European Community and Eastern Europe* (New York: Council on Foreign Relations Press, 1991), chaps 3 and 7.

7. European Community, *The Development of the Community's Relations with the Countries of Central and Eastern Europe,* Brussels, EC, Commission, February 1990 (DOC. SEC [90] 196 Final).

8. European Community, *Europe Agreements with Czechoslovakia, Hungary, and Poland.*

9. European Community, *EC and Central European Countries to Sign Major New Accords,* Washington, D.C. EC Office of Press and Public Affairs, November 1991 (No. 28/91).

10. "Jam Tomorrow," 4.

11. Janine R. Wedel, "Polish Officials Sour on US Aid Approach," *Christian Science Monitor,* 2 March 1992, 18.

12. European Community, *Europe Agreements with Czechoslovakia, Hungary, and Poland.*

13. Pinder, *The European Community and Eastern Europe,* 96.

14. Wedel, "Polish Officials Sour on US Aid Approach," 18.

15. European Community, *PHARE SCOREBOARD.*

16. European Community, *PHARE: Assistance for Economic Restructuring in the Countries of Central and Eastern Europe,* Brussels, EC, Commission of the European Community, 1992, 7.

17. "An International Institution of the Third Kind," *Europe,* May 1991, 18-20.

18. Judy Dempsey, "Time to Sort Out Who Owns What," *Financial Times* 16 April 1991.

19. Susan Colias and Dani Rodrick, *Eastern Europe and the Soviet Union in the World Economy* (Washington, D.C.: Institute for International Economics, May 1991), 76-80.

20. U.S. Dept of Commerce, International Trade Administration, Office of Trade and Investment Analysis,"Facts on U.S. and World Direct Investment in Eastern Europe and the Soviet Union," (Washington, October 1991).

21. Ibid.

22. Nicholas Denton, "Hungary Takes the Lead on Foreign Investment," *Financial Times,* 14 May 1991.

23. "Owners Are the Only Answer," *The Economist* Survey, 21 September 1991, 10.

24. Ibid.

25. Ibid. See also Paul Hare and Gordon Huges, Discussion Paper no. 543 (London: Centre for Economic Policy Research, 1991).

26. Denton, "Hungary Takes the Lead on Foreign Investment."

27. Ibid.

28. "Voucher Power," *The Economist* Survey, 21 September 1991, 18-20.

29. Ibid.

30. "Building Free Market Economies in Central and Eastern Europe: Challenges and Realities" (Washington, D.C.: The Institute of International Finance, 1990).

31. Daniel L. Bond, "Trade or Aid?: Official Export Credit Agencies and the Economic Development of Eastern Europe and the Soviet Union," Public Policy Paper no. 4 (New York: Institute for East-West Security Studies, 1991).

32. Organization for Economic Cooperation and Development, *OECD Financial Market Trends,* (Paris, OECD, 1990).

33. Bond, "Trade or Aid?" 3.

34. "Aid to Eastern Europe: The Scorecard," *The Economist,* 29 June 1991, p. 43. See also European Community, *PHARE SCORECARD.*

35. European Community, *PHARE SCORECARD.* See also Pinder, *The European Community and Eastern Europe,* chap. 7.

36. Organization for Economic Cooperation and Development, *The Export Credit Financing Systems in OECD Member Countries,* 4th ed.

(Paris, OECD 1990), 7.

37. European Community, *PHARE SCORECARD.* See also Pinder, *The European Community and Eastern Europe,* chap. 7.

38. Bond, "Trade or Aid?" 7-8.

39. Ibid.

40. Pinder, *The European Community and Eastern Europe,* 93.

41. Ibid.

42. "Gradualism is 'No Answer for Eastern Europe,'" *Financial Times* 30 April 1991.

43. "New Kids on the Bloc," *International Management* January 1992: 46-49.

7
Analyzing the Changing Foreign and Domestic Politics of the Former USSR

Mark N. Katz

For the past few years, history seems to have been switched from "normal" speed to "fast forward." Vast transformations have been occurring in what once appeared to be immutable aspects of Soviet foreign and domestic politics as well as international relations generally. Nor have these transformations necessarily come to an end. Others may yet be in store.

How should questions about the foreign and domestic politics of the former Soviet Union be analyzed during this period of rapid change? The question is an important one, since the methodology or approach scholars employ can in large measure determine the answers to the questions they ask.

This chapter argues that traditional Sovietology, or analyzing domestic and foreign policy issues from the perspective of Russian and Soviet history, is not the most fruitful method for studying the current situation in which rapid change is occurring. A more productive approach, in this author's view, is what will be called here comparative historical analysis—an approach that seeks to relate questions regarding the foreign and domestic politics of the former USSR to similar situations that have occurred elsewhere. No claim is being made that this method will yield definitive answers. What it can do, though, is bring to light a range of answers or possibilities that traditional Sovietology, or the examination of questions solely in terms of the Russian/Soviet historical experience, does not.

This chapter first examines what traditional Sovietology is and why it is no longer as useful a methodology as it once was. It then outlines what comparative historical analysis is and discusses why it might be a more appropriate methodology for analyzing the current situation. Finally, the chapter presents two examples of how the different methodologies might yield very different results when applied to the same question.

Sovietology

The Soviet Union was a country whose domestic and foreign policies could not be analyzed with the social science and historiographical methodologies that could be applied to more open societies. The highly limited access that Western scholars had to the Soviet Union from the 1917 revolution until well into the Gorbachev era prevented this. The importance of the Soviet Union and the threatening nature of its policies, however, especially after World War II, made studying this country imperative.

What Sovietology set out to accomplish was to analyze the domestic and foreign policies of this enigmatic but extraordinarily important country on the basis of what little evidence was available. The most abundant sources of information about the USSR were (1) statements appearing in the official Soviet media and (2) Soviet actions—about which detailed information often came from Western governments rather than from Moscow.

The analytical method employed by Sovietology was clear and simple: previous Soviet statements and actions were the best (really, the only) guide to future Soviet behavior. There was, of course, frequent debate among scholars and policy analysts concerning how the Soviets might behave under various sets of circumstances. What these debates often centered on was the determination of what set of previous Soviet statements and actions was most relevant to understanding how the Soviets would behave in an ongoing or anticipated situation.

Such a debate about the analysis of past Soviet behavior was evident during the 1991 Senate confirmation hearings of Robert Gates as director of the Central Intelligence Agency (CIA). The sharply differing statements made by Melvin Goodman and Graham Fuller were as much about how to undertake Sovietological analysis as they were about the nominee.

One of their disagreements centered around the CIA's analysis of Soviet relations with Iran in the mid-1980s. At the time, Fuller argued that the USSR might invade Iran. Part of his argument was based on the precedent Moscow had already set by invading another non-Warsaw Pact member state neighboring Iran—Afghanistan. At the same time, Goodman argued that the Soviets were not likely to invade Iran, since nothing in Soviet statements or actions indicated that they would.

At the hearings Fuller acknowledged that his analysis had been mistaken. But he offered an insightful criticism of the methodology employed by Goodman and his colleagues in the CIA's Office of Soviet Analysis (SOVA) when he said, "No SOVA analysts would have been likely to tell you, until the troops were lined up and ready to go, that the USSR would ever send the Red Army into Afghanistan, because the Soviet Union had no history and no background of doing that."[1]

Both men were accusing each other of practicing straight-line analysis that refused to account for other possibilities. In fact, both of them were engaging in straight-line analysis (Soviet actions could be predicted on the basis of previous Soviet actions and statements), but they were employing, and basing their analysis on, different data sets. This was only one of many possible examples of debates within Sovietology concerning the possible future behavior of the USSR. Thus, even when the USSR was generally regarded as an ideologically inspired imperial state, Sovietology could not predict its behavior with any certainty.

Of course, Sovietology has not always sought to predict Soviet behavior. Sovietologists have often focused their efforts on describing and explaining past Soviet behavior. According to Alexander Motyl, such Sovietology is characterized by "the vigorous pursuit of data on the faulty rationale that, as only data can generate knowledge, more data must translate into more knowledge."[2] This data was often analyzed without employing an explicitly articulated theory or concept. It was this type of Sovietology that Motyl dismissed as "an awkward amalgam of data collection, policy analysis, and journalism that is as divorced from scholarship as sense impressions are from theory."[3]

Motyl's description may be somewhat unfair. Although an explicit theory for understanding Moscow's behavior was usually absent in Sovietological analysis, an implicit theory was necessarily present, as Motyl acknowledges. And for the period of the cold war, Sovietologists could reasonably analyze Soviet domestic and foreign policies in light of what was a generally accepted and often unstated set of theories about the general thrust of Soviet behavior.

There was little debate, for example, about the proposition that the Communist party of the Soviet Union sought to maintain itself in power domestically through dictatorial means. Nor was there much debate about the proposition that the Soviet Union sought to retain control of Eastern Europe and to expand its influence over other countries. For most of the Soviet period, Sovietology did not challenge these and other seemingly immutable basic propositions about Soviet foreign and domestic policy, but devoted itself to analyzing and debating more detailed issues. Furthermore, Sovietology could approach these more detailed issues about Soviet domestic and foreign policies, even though the data at its disposal was of relatively low quality, with some degree of confidence precisely because there was relatively little debate about the general issues.

This intellectually comfortable situation no longer exists. The domestic and foreign politics of the former Soviet Union can no longer be understood in light of what once seemed to be permanently valid theories about continuing Communist party rule and Soviet expansionism, theories that underpinned Sovietology. Yet while the old principles on which Soviet domestic and foreign policies were based have disappeared, what they will be replaced by in the former Soviet Union is far from certain, and may not be clear for a considerable period of time.

In addition, there has been a fundamental change in the quantity and quality of research data available from as well as Western access to, the former Soviet Union. The media in the former Soviet Union, instead of being the voice of the governing authorities, now represents a wide spectrum of viewpoints. Indeed, the spectrum of influential political movements is in many ways broader than that existing in most Western countries. Furthermore, it is now possible for Western scholars to visit the former USSR much more easily than before and to talk freely with virtually anyone.

While this greater availability of data is welcome to Western scholars, it also makes more difficult the task of understanding the former USSR. Before, the Soviet press usually made extremely dull reading, but since all statements on policy issues were official, the Western scholar could be reasonably confident that they represented official policy, or at least a leadership point of view. By contrast, the press in the former Soviet Union is now far more interesting to read, but it does not represent, just as the Western press does not, official policy. Especially at a time when government leaders of the various republics often issue statements contradicting ones made by other leaders or even themselves, it is far more difficult now to determine what government policy is than it was during the Soviet period.

Since the fundamental premises that Sovietology used to rely on have been swept away, and since the nature of the research data now emanating from the former USSR is qualitatively and quantitatively much richer than what was previously available, Sovietology simply cannot proceed in the same manner as it has. There is no longer a firmly established political setting consisting of a small number of relatively like-minded decision makers in the Kremlin. The decision-making process in Russia and the other republics now involves far more actors and is far more complicated. Understanding this more complex phenomenon requires a more complex methodology.

What Is To Be Done?

Concluding that traditional Sovietology is no longer the most appropriate methodology for understanding the domestic and foreign policies of the former USSR is one thing. Identifying what is an appropriate methodology for understanding this phenomenon is another. There is a wide variety of social science and historiographical methodologies to choose from. Of the existing methodologies, it may turn out that different ones will be appropriate for understanding different questions. New methodologies altogether, or variations on the existing ones, may have to be developed.

In addition to choosing what issues to study, scholars will have to choose what methodology to study them with. Where the choice of methodology is not obvious (and this author would argue that during this time of rapid and fundamental change both in the former USSR and world politics generally, the choice of methodology is far from obvious), how should the scholar decide which methodology or methodologies to apply to a particular problem? This is a crucial issue, since, as stated earlier, the method used to address a question may in large part determine the answer or conclusion that is reached.

What type of methodology would be useful for analyzing the complexity of the internal and external politics of the former Soviet republics in an era when even the basic nature of what their political systems are evolving into is uncertain? What must such a methodology explain?

An analogy from mathematics may be useful in addressing these questions. Algebra can be used to analyze straight lines. But not all lines are straight; some are curved. To analyze curved lines, a more complex form of mathematics is required: calculus. This analogy is particularly apt with respect to traditional Sovietology and what might replace it. Although algebra cannot explain the more complex problems that calculus addresses, calculus does not reject algebra as a false science. Similarly, just because traditional Sovietology does not explain the present, more complex situation (just as algebra cannot analyze curved lines), the methodology that can explain it need not—indeed, should not—reject what has previously been learned through traditional Sovietology but incorporate it when appropriate.

What sort of methodology does this? It is possible that several may; this is an issue that needs to be explored. It is also possible, of course, that certain methodologies, even sophisticated ones that can be successfully applied to the study of politics in the United States or other Western states, may not transplant easily to the study of the politics of the former Soviet Union. Although this is a subject that deserves fuller treatment, it appears that many quantitatively oriented social science methodologies might not be useful for analyzing the former Soviet Union, at least at present. As with traditional Sovietology, many of these quantitative methodologies are applied to the study of politics in countries where the basic foundations of the political system are well established. The related analyses and predictions are made about detailed issues within a firmly established political structure. Since the political structure of the former Soviet republics as well as the relations of these republics with one another and third countries have not yet been firmly established, and may not be established for some time, these quantitative methodologies would suffer from some of the same problems that traditional Sovietology does in attempting to analyze the current situation.

As does traditional Sovietology, many quantitative social science methodologies draw upon past experience to predict behavior—a form of straight-line analysis. But this is an era when any form of straight-line analysis about the former USSR, whether it is traditional Sovietology or quantitative social science, will probably not be useful. There can be no assurance that past trends will be a useful guide to the region's future.

This may change in time. If Russia and the other republics establish a track record of holding regular elections, then quantitative analyses can be made of voting patterns, among other issues. Repeated elections under relatively stable conditions, though, need to occur before such analyses will have the necessary data to draw confident conclusions—and this, of course, has not yet happened.

One form of quantitative social science, though, has sprung up and flourished in many of the former Soviet republics during the past few years: public opinion polling. This, however, is still an inexact science even in the West, where it has been practiced for many years. Since its practitioners in Moscow and elsewhere do not always seem to employ it in a scientifically rigorous fashion, conclusions based upon polling results cannot be accepted with full confidence.[4] And in rapidly changing circumstances, public opinion can also change rapidly: what the public thinks today is not necessarily a useful guide to what it will think next year, next month, or even next week. Therefore, what the polls reveal about public opinion at present cannot necessarily be accepted as possessing much validity for the future.

What is needed is a methodology that specifically provides a framework of analysis for understanding grand historical transitions such as the one occurring now in the former Soviet Union—a calculus that explains the curving lines of politics and international relations. Does such a methodology exist?

Comparative Historical Analysis

Such an approach does exist, though it needs to be further developed. The fundamental premise of this approach, which can be called comparative historical analysis, is that although each nation's history is distinctive, there are also similarities in the histories of nations. This approach differs from Sovietology, which emphasizes the unique nature of Russia/the (former) Soviet Union.

Nations sometimes go through similar experiences, such as war, revolution, civil war, expansion, retrenchment, dictatorship, democratization, prosperity, and depression. There is no inevitable law that says all nations will experience all these events, or in any particular order even if they do. But since these events do occur in different nations at different times, knowledge of how such events or trends unfolded in other countries in the past can inform the analysis of similar events or trends occurring later in others. Indeed, where particularly traumatic events are occurring in one country, an understanding of similar events in another country may provide a better framework for understanding these events than the history of the country where they are occurring.

The task of the analyst using this methodology is to select what he or she thinks is an appropriate historical analogy to explain current developments, to justify the choice of one or more analogies as opposed to others, to compare the elements of the two (or more) situations in order to get a sense of whether a similar or different outcome may occur at present, and to discuss how the outcome may or may not vary if there are important changes in the elements of the current situation. In other words, the task of the analyst is to find one or more curved lines from the past that can help explain the curving line of the present.

Comparative historical analysis is a more useful tool than Sovietology, or attempting to understand the Russian present solely on the basis of Russia's past, because it acknowledges that the Russian and Soviet historical experiences may not serve as the best guide to understanding how the foreign and domestic politics of the former Soviet Union are evolving.

Another advantage of comparative historical analysis is that it focuses the debate on the larger questions about foreign and domestic politics, not the details. This is especially important at a time when the larger questions are unsettled and may remain so for some time. One analyst may interpret current events in Russian politics as being analogous to events in Portugal in the mid-1970s, when a poor country shed its empire and successfully democratized. Another analyst may interpret them as being analogous to events in Germany in the 1920s and early 1930s, when an attempted transition to democracy in the midst of economic depression failed. In the debate between them, each is forced to argue why current developments in Russia resemble the paradigm each analyst chose, and why they do not resemble the paradigm the other one chose. History never repeats itself exactly, but this form of analysis can help clarify whether current developments may be moving in one direction or another. More important, comparative historical analysis may help elucidate what needs to be done to prevent undesirable forms of political evolution, such as the demise of democracy.

Comparative historical analysis is not an unknown methodology. A particularly fine example of it is Graham Fuller's recent book on Iranian foreign policy.[5] Fuller set out to analyze the evolution of Iranian foreign policy interests in the post-Khomeini era. To do this, he examined Iran's relations with each of its neighbors and other important countries in different eras. He then attempted to define an Iranian foreign policy "norm" toward other countries, noting how this norm might vary depending on possible changes both in Iran and in other countries. Some of these changes, including democratization, were ones that Iran and some of the neighboring countries had not fully experienced (or even partially in some cases) but that, given the expansion of democracy in other regions of the world, cannot be ruled out in the Middle East. Fuller did not conclude with just one prediction about the future thrust of Iranian foreign policy but with a range of predictions about what might occur under certain circumstances.

Some scholars will dismiss this approach as being policy-oriented, future-oriented, speculative, and hence, unscholarly. It is true, of course, that statements about the present and future course of politics cannot be analyzed with the same degree of certainty that hindsight allows one in examining the past. Yet valuable lessons can be learned from failed predictions. At the very least, failed predictions invite—perhaps force—scholars to reformulate their conceptual framework to account for why what they thought would happen did not, or for why what they thought would not happen did.

Further, while scholars can avoid making statements about the future, either owing to the conviction that it is impossible to do so or to the fear of being proved wrong, policymakers cannot. They need to operate on the basis of some idea both about the future course of politics in other nations in order to fashion their own foreign policy, and about how the foreign policy they formulate will affect politics in other nations as well as international relations generally. If those who know the most about the domestic and foreign politics of the former USSR are unwilling to engage in future-oriented analysis, then policymakers will rely on those who may be more willing but less knowing.

Finally, Sovietologists should not decry the attempt to make predictions through comparative historical analysis since Sovietology also tried to make predictions. By adopting the broader approach of comparative historical analysis, scholars will acknowledge that the narrower basis upon which Sovietology made predictions (past Soviet statements and actions being a guide to future Soviet behavior) is no longer adequate.

APPLYING COMPARATIVE HISTORICAL ANALYSIS

The following are outlines of how comparative historical analysis might be used to conceptualize two aspects of the current politics of the former USSR.

Nationalism vs. Economic Rationalism.

Comparative historical analysis may shed light on which of two competing explanations about the strength of non-Russian nationalism is more accurate.

During the Gorbachev era, many Western analysts argued that although non-Russian nationalism was rising, the non-Russian republics would not secede from the USSR, or remain outside of it for long, because independence was economically irrational. For better or worse, more than seven decades of Soviet central planning had closely tied together the economies of all the Union republics; economically rational people would not seek independence or want to keep it long, given the economic disruption independence would cause. "Even if the choice were freely offered," wrote Martha Brill Olcott in 1990, "the economic burdens of independence would lead few republics to choose this option."[6]

This view was also reflected in U.S. government policy. In President George Bush, in his August 1991 speech to the Ukrainian parliament in Kiev, U.S. stated, "The vast majority of trade conducted by Soviet companies, imports and exports, involves, as you know better than I, trade between republics. The Nine Plus One Agreement holds forth the hope that republics will combine greater autonomy with greater voluntary interaction—political, social, cultural, economic—rather than pursuing the hopeless course of isolation."[7] At the time, President Bush evidently believed that the future economic prosperity of the non-Russian republics was clearly linked to the continued political integration of the USSR.

On the other hand, the argument that non-Russian nationalism would insist upon independence appeared dubious. Most of the non-Russians within the Russian empire had been unable to sustain an independence movement in the past. This was owing not only to Russian opposition to their independence but also to the fact that many non-Russian nationalities themselves were divided over the issue. The established pattern in Russian and Soviet history was that non-Russian nationalism was usually not strong enough to assert itself, and usually not for long when it did. Non-Russians who asserted that the present situation was different appeared to many to be partisan advocates instead of objective analysts.

The strength of the economic rationalist argument against independence and the weakness of the nationalist argument in favor of it seemed clear to many Soviet specialists as well as the Gorbachev leadership. The merits of the two arguments, however, appear quite different when compared to the experience of nationalism in other parts of the world.

Russia is, in many ways, the last great European colonial empire. During the twentieth century, all the other European colonial empires—the British, French, Dutch, Belgian, Spanish, and Portuguese—were virtually liquidated. These, of course, were all overseas empires. But two other empires that had expanded over geographically contiguous areas—the Austrian and the Ottoman—had also been liquidated early on in the century.

Some of these empires were liquidated more as a result of the imperial power's being defeated in war with another Great Power. But nationalist forces demanding independence also sprang up when they sensed that the imperial power's grip was weakening, or even before that was evident. With very few exceptions—usually islands with very small populations—colonized and occupied nations overwhelmingly opted for independence as opposed to continued rule by the occupying power. And with only one exception—Newfoundland—no country that became independent has voluntarily accepted being ruled by the metropole once again.[8]

What this shows is that the economic rationalist argument that a country is better off remaining a colony than becoming independent seems mainly to be accepted in countries with very small populations. The fear of economic hardship did not deter the overwhelming majority of colonies from becoming independent. In many of these former colonies, especially those in Africa, the population became and remains economically worse off than it was under colonial rule. Deteriorating economic conditions, though, have not induced these countries to offer to surrender their independence to the former colonial power.

If nationalism has been undeterred from seeking independence by economic rationalism in all but the very smallest countries in the Third World, why should anyone expect that nationalism would demand anything less in the non-Russian republics of the former USSR? Far from seeing continued rule by Moscow as beneficial economically, the non-Russians regard the Soviet experience as having damaged their economies.

If the experience of nationalism in the Third World is a guide, the strength of non-Russian nationalism is not likely to be a short-term phenomenon but a long-term, permanent one, despite the near certainty that the non-Russian republics will all endure economic hardship for many years.

Finally, the experience of other nations also shows that the economic rationalist argument against independence is inaccurate in another sense. The argument assumes that independent nations cannot cooperate effectively in the economic sphere. Yet despite many disagreements about economic matters, there is considerable economic cooperation among nations. Many regional economic groupings, including ones in the developing world, have come into existence. The experience of other nations, then, indicates that the former Soviet republics can cooperate economically through the Commonwealth of Independent States if they want to.

Russia: Nation or Empire?

Whether the non-Russians gain or retain independence, of course, is not a matter for them alone to decide. Whether Russia is willing to permit them to become or remain independent is and will be a crucial determinant in the ability of the non-Russians to do so. What will the Russian attitude be?

As late as September 1991 the eminent Soviet specialist Stephen F. Cohen expressed extreme doubt that the USSR would break up into its constituent republics. He noted that "Russia has always been the 'center' of the empire and the union," and that one of the many factors operating to preserve the Union was "historical tradition." Cohen envisioned Moscow's working to preserve the Slavic core of the USSR as being particularly likely: "It is hard to imagine, for example, the other Slav republics, the Ukraine and Byelorussia, as states apart from Russia, or that Moscow would actually let them go."[9]

Cohen's analysis is noteworthy for two reasons. First, Cohen is not known for being a conservative inclined to see Moscow's behavior as threatening. Instead, he is known for being a liberal who has described past Soviet behavior as defensive. He has criticized U.S. foreign policy for taking what he considered to be a counterproductively harsh approach toward the USSR. Cohen's portrayal of a Russia determined to preserve the Union, then, would appear highly credible, since he is not someone given always to seeing Russian policy as expansionist or imperial.

But the second reason why Cohen's analysis is noteworthy, of course, is that it was wrong. By the end of 1991, Russia had recognized not only the independence of the three Baltic states, which the West especially supported, but also the independence of all the other Union republics. Furthermore, the Russian parliament appeared unwilling to use force to prevent secession from Russia by the autonomous non-Russian republics within it.[10]

The point being made here is not to criticize Cohen for having made a forecast that was proved wrong so quickly after it was made. Indeed, his analysis as well as those of many others who made a similar one was highly sensible from the context of Russian history. The Russians have historically sought to control the borderlands around Russia. They have not ceded this territory voluntarily in the past. They have done so only under extreme duress (owing to invasion or loss of control resulting from internal upheaval), and they have exerted themselves to recapture lost territory at the earliest opportunity. As a result of this legacy, it would seem only prudent to expect that Russia would act to retain control of the borderlands now, or to regain control over them in the near future.

Comparative historical analysis, however, allows one to question whether the Russian historical legacy is the best guide to Russia's behavior toward the non-Russians of the former Soviet Union. Instead of regarding Russia as a completely unique nation, unlike any other, Russia can be seen as an example of a European nation with a colonial empire. If all the other European powers gave up their colonial empires in the twentieth century, it should not be seen as surprising that Russia would do so too.

There is, of course, no necessity for Russia to divest itself of its colonial empire just because other European nations did so. It is, however, instructive to note the circumstances under which other European powers gained and lost their colonial empires. Before the twentieth century, these empires were acquired either by nondemocratic societies or by democratizing countries for which the acquisition process was relatively inexpensive in terms of lives and money. Imperialism was often fairly popular when it was perceived to be fairly cheap.

Some European powers lost all or part of their empires as a result of defeat by other Great Powers (Spain in 1898; Germany and Italy in 1918). In the twentieth century, however, the bulk of decolonization occurred because democratic societies became unwilling to pay a large cost in terms of blood and treasure to keep other nations as colonies when the latter asserted their desire for independence. For the most part, the decolonization process proceeded fairly peacefully. In those cases where the European government attempted to prevent decolonization by force, domestic politics in the colonizing country eventually forced it to withdraw. Indeed, it was the increasingly burdensome military effort undertaken by a dictatorial regime in Portugal in order to retain its African colonies that contributed to the popular uprising in that country, which led to both democratization and decolonization.

The way in which Russia has now begun to resemble other European nations is that it has embarked on the path of democratization. There may be many Russians like Mikhail Gorbachev, who would have preferred to keep the USSR whole as a state dominated by the Russians. The government of Boris Yeltsin, however, recognized that this could not be done unless the Russians were prepared to keep the Union together by force—a task that could not be accomplished cheaply or easily. Since it was impossible for Russia to hold the Union together without force, and since Russia was unwilling to do so by force, the only alternative for Russia was to recognize the independence of the non-Russian republics.

While Moscow's acquiescence to the loss of its empire appears to be an aberration in terms of Russian history, it appears to be very much in keeping with the established pattern of twentieth-century European decolonization. An end to Russian democratization, though, may bring about decreased tolerance in Moscow for decolonization.

Conclusion

These are just two examples of how comparative historical analysis might lead to different conclusions about current politics in the former USSR than traditional Sovietology or analysis of the current situation based solely on the Russian/Soviet historical experience. There is a vast array of other questions that this method can be applied to.

It must be emphasized that this method of analysis will not necessarily yield definitive results. But then, traditional straight-line Sovietology cannot do so either, when the Soviet past is not necessarily a reliable guide to the future. What comparative historical analysis can do more effectively than traditional Sovietology is yield a wider range of possibilities about the direction of the foreign and domestic politics of the former USSR.

Analyses using this comparative historical methodology, though, will be successful or unsuccessful depending on how accurate the historical analogies are that analysts select to explain the present. Deciding upon what historical analogies are appropriate for analyzing the present will not be easy. Russia alone resembles a disintegrating colonial empire, a Third World country, and a Western democracy in certain respects. Arguments about which historical analogy is most appropriate for explaining the present situation, however, are extremely important, since they force scholars to state and defend explicitly their theories and assumptions about the fundamental elements of the former USSR's domestic and foreign politics. An examination of the details of, for example, Moscow's domestic or foreign policy in which the analyst avoids discussing his or her views of the basic nature of Russia's political evolution will inadequately account for how contingent a particular policy may be on more fundamental trends.

Finally, it must be recognized that just as with traditional Sovietology, there are probably limits to how useful comparative historical analysis will be for understanding the former Soviet Union. If, for example, Russia and/or the other republics develop into established, stable democracies, a methodology seeking to understand societies in the midst of fundamental political change will no longer be appropriate. Some of the sophisticated social science methodologies that are suitable for understanding the Western democracies may then be more useful for understanding the former USSR. At present, though, it does not seem likely that a stable pattern of politics in this area will emerge anytime soon.

Fundamental transformations are occurring in the domestic and foreign politics of the former USSR. If Western scholars are to understand these phenomena adequately, a fundamental transformation is needed in the methodology they employ in their analyses.

Notes

1. "Excerpts from Senate Hearing on Nomination of CIA Chief," *New York Times,* 2 October 1991, A16.

2. Alexander J. Motyl, *Sovietology, Rationality, Nationality: Coming to Grips with Nationalism in the USSR* (New York: Columbia University Press, 1990), 3.

3. Ibid., 1.

4. To obtain an accurate portrayal of public opinion, a poll should give the person being surveyed the entire spectrum of possible responses, and the responses available should be mutually exclusive. In a 1990 poll conducted by the All-Union Center for the Study of Public Opinion about Soviet citizens' preferences for a future social system, however, communism was not offered as a choice. The three choices offered besides "uncertain" were "democratic socialism," "'Swedish' socialism," and "capitalism." Swedish socialism, of course, is democratic socialism. (Lev Gudkov, "Russians Outside Russia," *Moscow News,* no. 41, 21-28 October 1990, 7.)

Further, it is unclear what steps, if any, pollsters in the former USSR take to ensure that their survey sample is representative of the larger society.

5. Graham E. Fuller, *The "Center of the Universe": The Geopolitics of Iran* (Boulder, Colo: Westview Press, 1991).

6. Martha Brill Olcott, "A New, Improved USSR: Encouraging Regional Freedoms Can Make a Stronger Union," *Washington Post (Outlook),* 20 May 1990.

7. "Excerpts from Bush's Ukraine Speech: Working 'For the Good of Both of Us,'" *New York Times*, 2 August 1991.

8. Brian Hunter, ed., *The Statesman's Year-Book, 1991-1992* (New York: St. Martin's Press, 1991), 312; and John F. Burns, "Joseph R. Smallwood Dies at 90; Led Newfoundland into Canada," *New York Times*, 19 December 1991.

9. Stephen F. Cohen, "Cold Dawn in Moscow," *New York Times*, 4 September 1991.

10. The Russian parliament overruled Boris Yeltsin's declaration of a state of emergency in the Chechen-Ingush Autonomous Republic, which had declared its independence. Eleanor Randolph, "Yeltsin Eases Stand on Enclave," *Washington Post*, 13 November 1991.

8

Conclusion

Beyond Postcommunism: Eastern Europe or Europe?

Andrew A. Michta and Ilya Prizel

The collapse of communism and the consequent disintegration of the Soviet Union has revolutionized Europe's geopolitics. The region's diversity, which for half a century disappeared under the facade of the Soviet-imposed unity and the ideological straight jacket of communism, has once again resurfaced. The postcommunist transformation of the former Soviet clients has been traumatic and will no doubt impose additional strain on intra-European relations for years to come. Moreover, it will take at least until the end of this decade for the fragile markets and nascent democratic institutions to become solidified and stabilized sufficiently to make the promise of the region's integration in Europe a realistic option. It may take considerably longer for the volatile nationalism of postcommunist Eastern Europe to settle into a pattern of political compromise and collaboration that the West will find acceptable. Yet, it is clear that it is the former Soviet satellites that will have to carry most of the burden of readjustment.

The newly evolving geostrategic balance in Europe has simultaneously improved and complicated the prospects of postcommunist Europe's joining the West European mainstream. Clearly, the disintegration of the USSR and the creation of a belt of new states, stretching from the Baltic to the Black Sea, have effectively separated Russia, with its military might and plethora of political and economic problems from north central Europe, thus enhancing the prospect of the ultimate admission of Czechoslovakia, Hungary, and Poland into the European Community (EC). Few in either the North Atlantic Treaty Organization (NATO) or the EC wanted to expand either organization to the borders of Russia. Now that Russia's European profile has receded to its pre-Petrine period of the early eighteenth century, however, Chancellor Helmut Kohl has stated that the EC will expand to the banks of the river Bug, making Ukraine and Belarus a substitute cordon sanitaire separating Russia from the rest of Europe, a role that in the past was "performed" by Czechoslovakia, Hungary, and Poland.

While, on the one hand, the disintegration of the USSR has enhanced the prospect of the east central Europeans' "return to Europe," the changed balance of power within Western Europe may well have a countervailing effect. The emergence of Germany as by far the predominant power in the heart of Europe is complicating both the "deepening" as well as the "widening" of the EC. The rejection of the Maastricht accord by Danish voters is a symptom of the continent-wide anxiety of a surrender of sovereignty to Brussels and by implication, to the European bloc's senior partner—Germany. Similarly, the fear of German hegemony may well slow the integration of the Visegrad Three into Europe. French officials do not hide their concern that the admission of the European Free Trade Association (EFTA) states of Austria, Iceland, Norway, Sweden, and Switzerland into the EC will tilt the balance of power within the EC in Germany's favor and weaken France's relative weight. Given the overwhelming German presence in Czechoslovakia, Hungary, and Poland, the French government has made little effort to disguise its determination to slow, if not resist outrightly, the admission of these three countries into the EC.

Three years into the postcommunist reconstitution of Eastern Europe it is time to take stock of the change and to judge the scope of the task ahead. As the initial euphoria after the decomposition of the Soviet empire wanes, the newly independent postcommunist states in the region are only beginning to appreciate the extent of economic and social ruin bequeathed to them by the half century of communism. They must play catch-up in a complex, highly competitive global economic system, with little of value in their industrial plant to draw upon. They must develop a working parliamentary system in societies where parliamentary tradition is weak or nonexistent. They must bridge the national and ethnic divides in a part of the world quintessentially defined by national and ethnic hatreds. Finally—in the face of the West's growing impatience and disillusionment, caused by the persistent confusion, the inadequacies of their domestic politics, and the flare-ups of ethnic violence—they must convince the West that they are capable of earning their place in Western Europe's economic and security systems. All of these imperative goals must be achieved within the arguably unrealistic timetable of the remainder of the decade. (The issues facing the postcommunist countries of Eastern Europe have been reviewed in some detail in the preceding chapters of this book).

The prospects for the region's successful transformation to stable democracies have been judged to be uneven, ranging from the relatively good ones for the individual Triangle states, to the discouraging ones for the war-torn Balkans, with increasingly violent confrontation in the corners of the former Soviet Union. Even in historically peaceful and democratic Czechoslovakia, the elections of the summer of 1992 raise the prospect of the disintegration of the seventy-four-year old Czech and Slovak union and with it, new tensions between Slovakia and Hungary along with the danger of Magyar separatism with Slovakia itself.

The spectacle of East European nationalism at its worse has become particularly odious as the Serbian-controlled Yugoslav federal army and Serbian irregulars wage war against Serbia's historical ethnic foes within the former federation. In fact, among the postcommunist successor states in Eastern Europe, only Hungary, a country surrounded by a large Magyar diaspora in all of its neighboring countries and having no substantial minorities on its territory, has been a vocal proponent of the collective rights of minorities, while even such ethnically homogenous countries as Poland seem to be grappling once again with the vestiges of past ethnic tensions.

The future of the postcommunist states depends largely on whether various regional aggregations of states—such as that described in the Baltic region cooperation agreements, such as the Visegrad trilateral cooperation pattern for Czechoslovakia, Hungary, and Poland, or even such as may be envisioned for Slovenian-Croatian cooperation—can function within the larger context of post-cold war Europe. The Pentagonal/Hexagonal regional cooperation initiative for the Danubian basin, which has brought together postcommunist states as well as developed European democracies, offers hope. If anything, it shows that the old structure of intra-European politics, that is, state-to-state relations built around the great, medium, and small powers, can become flexible enough (now that the superpower rivalry is gone) to accommodate a nascent pan-European federalism and a cooperative national security system reinsured by a transatlantic connection. Unfortunately, in 1992 Pentagonal/Hexagonal projects were stymied by war in the Balkans.

A return to the traditional paradigm of international relations in Europe does not have to mean that a self-contained pattern of European national animosities will be inevitably and fully restored. The fundamental difference in the intra-European relations after the cold war is the absence of revisionist Great Powers, or to put it simply, the presence of a democratic Germany and an inward-looking Russia. The transformation that Western Europe has undergone during the postwar period has already remade the Franco-German relationship, which historically was one of Europe's most intractable national problems. There is no reason why over time a similar transformation cannot attend the Polish-German relationship. As much as it is no longer possible to entertain the idea that the youth of France and Germany would be willing to fight over Alsace-Lorraine, so it can become equally unthinkable for young Poles and young Germans to confront one another over the Oder-Neisse Line or the rights to control of Silesia.

Yet even here a note of caution is warranted: while Russia under Yeltsin's cautious leadership has eschewed a return to its traditional xenophobic conduct of foreign policy, there is a growing number of Russian politicians who call for a return of an "assertive" foreign policy. Similarly, in Ukraine the cautious posture of President Leonid Kravchuk is coming under increased pressure from ever-growing nationalist sentiments that are insisting on Ukraine's exit from the Commonwealth of Independent States (CIS), regardless of the ultimate impact of such a move on the relationship with Russia. Yet perhaps the most serious threat to the stability of Europe emanating from the former Soviet Union is the emergence of splinter polities, such as the Dniester Republic or Crimea, whose convoluted nationalist politics can draw larger players, such as Russia, Ukraine, and Romania, into a confrontation that they would rather avoid. The presence of former Soviet troops in parts of the former Soviet Union, troops over which no government exercises effective control, makes the volatile situation in these regions outrightly dangerous.

Postcommunist Eastern Europe is facing its historic opportunity to build a new relationship with Russia and Germany. This relationship, especially Germany's role in the new Europe, will ultimately determine whether the region will move in the direction of full integration with the developed northwestern core of Europe, or whether it will retain its peripheral status for the foreseeable future. The question of Germany's new role is today pivotal to the transformation of the former Soviet clients into viable members of the European Community. More than any other country in Europe, Germany has both the national interest and the resources needed to stabilize the region. Yet Germany's future role in Europe remains somewhat murky.

The extraordinary costs of reunification have dampened German enthusiasm for new commitments in either the EC or east central Europe. Furthermore, the growing frustration among German citizens in the new Länder, a part of the country where the commitment to both democracy and pan-European ideals is far more superficial than in the old West Germany, has the potential of creating a prolonged unstable political situation. It should be borne in mind that many East Germans voted for the party that had promised rapid transformation to West German standards of living. As the promise of quick prosperity recedes further and further into the future, the prospect of major electorial shifts away from the traditional parties and toward fringe movements on either the Left or Right may destabilize the edifice of German politics and thus constrain Germany from playing a role in Eastern Europe that its geography and economic power might indicate.

Much will also depend on the final outcome of the imperial succession in the former Soviet Union. So far the Russians have demonstrated a remarkable willingness to accept the disintegration of the empire and the attendant loss of control over non-Russian nationalities. The process through which the CIS will ultimately either completely dissolve or, conversely, be replaced with a nationalist Russia seeking to reassert control over the region will have an impact on the direction of postcommunist change in Eastern Europe on par with the importance of changes in Germany's eastern policy. If the fragmentation of the CIS continues to take place with a minimum amount of violence, as it has so far, the overall security situation of eastern and central Europe will continue to improve—for the threat of overall regional instability as well as domestic political and economic problems in individual postcommunist states are minor issues compared with the impact that a reconstituted Russian empire would have on the relative security position of its western neighbors. The outcome of the ongoing Russian-Ukrainian squabble over sovereignty in the Crimea is likely to chart the course of events on Europe's eastern periphery.

Another set of issues that will remain in the forefront of intra-European politics for the foreseeable future is the question of how best to dispose of the residual Soviet military power and, accordingly, how to bring about a successful conversion of Soviet industry from military to civilian purposes. If the problems encountered by the former Soviet clients in Eastern Europe are any indication (for example, the problems of converting military plants to civilian production in Czechoslovakia or in Poland), Russia and Ukraine are facing a truly herculean task. The protracted economic crisis, inherited by the Soviet successor states from seventy-five years of communism, combined with the vast amounts of weapons available and the long-suppressed national grievances constitute an explosive mixture. In the end it may be small comfort that so far violence has been limited to intrastate conflict; after all, taken in international legal terms, the ongoing fighting between Serbia and Croatia or Serbia and Bosnia-Herzegovina is as much a civil war as it is an international conflict now that both Croatia and Bosnia-Herzegovina have gained diplomatic recognition in the West.

It is more than likely that postcommunist Europe will see additional border changes to those already affecting the former Yugoslav federation and the members of the Commonwealth of Independent States. Now that the sanction of Soviet power has been removed, the primary rationale for maintaining the often poorly drawn borders is no longer present. The issue is not so much whether but to what extent and, even more important, in what fashion future border adjustment will take place on Europe's eastern and southeastern periphery. As long as border revisions occur without use of military force, postcommunist frontier adjustments need not spell international disaster. Here the existing Western institutions have much to offer to smooth the transition process.

The least effective among the existing pan-European structures has been the Conference on Security and Cooperation in Europe (CSCE). The CSCE is not likely to live up to the expectations vested in it in 1990 and 1991, as seen in the organization's failure to deal effectively with the Yugoslav crisis; nevertheless, it has contributed to Europe's security. Although the 1992 broadening of the CSCE to include the Soviet successor states has further weakened its already questionable ability to act effectively in a crisis, the general acceptance of CSCE principles by all the postcommunist successor states is a reassuring phenomenon in that these rules explicitly commit each CSCE member to renounce war as a means toward border adjustment. In addition, the CSCE has given the post-communist states a useful forum for discussion, consultations, and the expression of grievances, thus constituting yet another layer in the growing web of European institutions.

Next in the order of relative effectiveness come the European Economic Community (EEC), NATO, and the Western European Union (WEU)—each of the three having a different degree of influence and relative effectiveness. The EEC has already played an important role in the economic reconstruction of postcommunist Eastern Europe, both through direct economic assistance and by extending to the region the promise of its eventual community membership. Associate membership in the EEC for Czechoslovakia, Hungary, and Poland, which was negotiated in November 1991 and which is currently pending ratification, has been a powerful inducement for the three new democracies to maintain their course of reform.

The EEC is by design, however, poorly suited to address the urgent security issues of postcommunist Eastern Europe, especially the prospect of protracted ethnic violence in the Balkans. This role should be performed by either the restructured NATO alliance or by the WEU. NATO has already made important moves in the direction of reform, which may eventually result in the renegotiation of the 1949 Washington Treaty so as to make the organization capable of responding to regional security crises in Europe, such as the current instability in former Yugoslavia. The decision taken by NATO in May 1991 to establish a British-led mobile force has been an important first step in that direction. The process of reforming NATO and, possibly, merging it with the WEU will likely be accelerated, since NATO is in an ultimately untenable position—that of an alliance whose primary rationale, that is, defending Europe from the Soviet threat, has disappeared and whose bureaucratic structures nevertheless remain intact.

If NATO and the WEU fail to respond to the revolutionary changes in the European balance of power, they will atrophy and eventually become irrelevant to the Continent's security needs. Yet both NATO and the WEU face serious problems that must be resolved before either can assume the mantle of Europe's stabilizer. An issue that NATO will have to resolve soon is what to do with the former Soviet bloc as well as with Russia itself. While the countries of east central Europe may well have a legitimate right to demand membership in that body, many in Brussels fear that such a move, if it excludes Russia, would be perceived in Moscow as a step further isolating Russia and that such a move would thus lead Russia to return to a behavior pattern characterized by paranoid xenophobia, causing new instability. Yet if NATO included Russia, the organization would stand to become a huge, unwieldy behemoth, which in the absence of a unifying threat would atrophy and disappear.

Another great unknown in the future of NATO is the role of the United States in Europe. Given the United States' growing economic difficulties, tension with Europe over economic issues, and the overwhelming longing of Germans under the age of forty to see all foreign troops leave German soil, it is quite possible that the United States will end its massive presence in Europe and resort to unilateralism unconstrained by an atrophied alliance. As far as the WEU is concerned, the organization poses a problem for many east central Europeans because it is perceived, as President Vaclav Havel of Czechoslovakia articulated, mainly as a means of cementing the Franco-German axis and of actually excluding the countries between Germany and Russia from the European system— thereby recreating a "gray zone" consisting of the east central European states, which would not be anchored in the European family of nations.

Reform of the existing European structures will take time, and it would be unrealistic for the postcommunist states to expect full citizenship in the new Europe any time soon. The agreed upon two-stage economic integration of Europe targets the EFTA countries as the first group of states to be brought into the EEC; the Triangle of Poland, Czechoslovakia, and Hungary have been slated for inclusion in the second phase. There has been no serious discussion so far about a realistic timetable for incorporating in the EEC the remaining postcommunist states as they proceed with necessary reforms. Security cooperation with the former Warsaw Pact countries has been treated by the West with even greater caution than economic collaboration has been. While the region has been given assurances of Western interest—in effect, an implicit but tenuous security guarantee from NATO—the developed states of Europe and the United States have been reluctant to take any steps that might bring the post-communist successor states into their security system. So far, NATO has limited itself to half measures, one of them being the decision taken during its November 1991 summit in Rome to set up a special council for consultations with the former Warsaw Treaty Organization members on matters pertinent to pan-European security.

The outcome of the postcommunist transformation in the region is by no means certain. Although the Triangle of Poland, Czechoslovakia, and Hungary is the best positioned among the former Soviet satellites to complete the transition to democracy and the free market, it has been struggling with domestic policy issues. The constitutional deadlock in Poland today and the tense Czech-Slovak relations within the Czechoslovak federation, which threaten to end the federation's existence, are symptomatic of the complexity of the task at hand. The prospects for a successful return to Europe are even more questionable in the Balkans, where the breakdown of Yugoslavia and the legacy of authoritarian politics have so far stymied the reform process.

In the final analysis, an answer to the question whether—and if so, when—the postcommunist states will rejoin Europe will be found first and foremost in the emerging democracies' ability to make the necessary internal changes to claim European citizenship. Most of all, this means finding a formula to accommodate the region's ethnic mosaic and to overcome the legacy of communist underdevelopment.

For the immediate future the most important issue facing the region as a whole is whether the postcommunist Soviet satellites can redirect their energies, away from the settling of past scores and toward the development of their economic and political system along Western democratic and market principles so that in the future they can be accommodated by a larger pan-European design. Ultimately, the question is whether they can cease being the "transition" successor states, shed the label "postcommunist," and either reestablish or create a European identity.

Index